Jerry meticulously takes us ....cover the
path of Christianity's global s.......... .... so important for
us to understand our own jou........

Shane Waters
Co-host, *The Keepers*, Netflix; Podcast host, Shadowspod.com

Dr. Pattengale did it again! Taking history reading to a new level, this book is informative and easy to follow. If more history books were this well written and engaging, we would have a wave of students majoring in history!

Christopher J. Devers, PhD
Assistant Professor, Johns Hopkins University

Wow! Read this book. Jerry Pattengale has turned the story of the spread of Christianity into a hugely compelling tale. This is not some dusty volume filled with strange sounding names and ancient stories, it's an amazing narrative that every believer should read.

My grandfather always said that the really smart people don't make the rest of us feel really dumb. Jerry is a really smart scholar; he writes in a way that everyone can understand. He makes history come alive and complex issues understandable.

I was inspired by Jerry's latest book—he makes complicated Church history read like a great novel.

Rob Loos
Zing Productions, Hollywood, CA

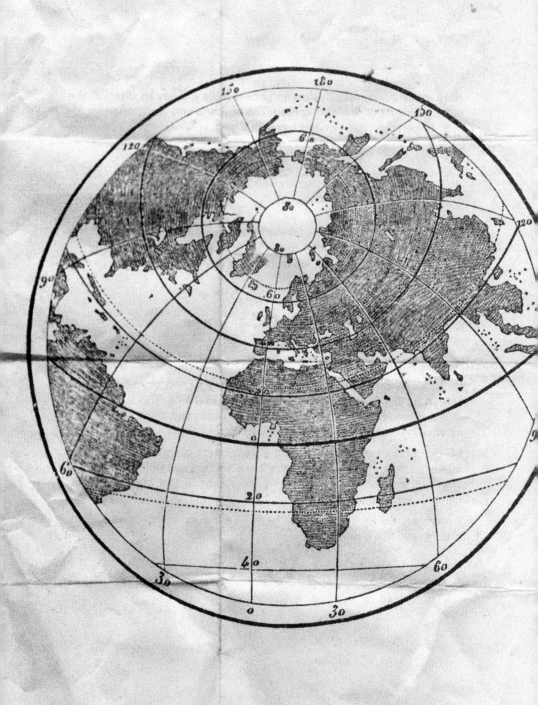

INEXPLICABLE
How Christianity Spread to the Ends of the Earth

Jerry Pattengale

TRILOGY
CHRISTIAN
PUBLISHING

TRILOGY
CHRISTIAN
PUBLISHING

Trilogy Christian Publishers
A Wholly Owned Subsidiary of Trinity Broadcasting Network
2442 Michelle Drive
Tustin, CA 92780

For information about special discounts for bulk purchases, please contact Trilogy Christian Publishing.

Design: Diane Whisner

Manufactured in the United States of America

10 9 8 7 6 5 4 3 2 1

Library of Congress Cataloging-in-Publication Data is available.

ISBN 978-164773-000-0
ISBN 978-164773-027-7 (ebook)

DEDICATION

To Bobby Gruenewald and Bob Hoskins,
two of the humblest leaders and snappiest dressers I know.
Over four hundred million people have already downloaded the
YouVersion Bible app produced by Bobby and Life.Church,
and over a billion people have received the Gospel
through Bob and *OneHope*. They indeed are committed
"to the ends of the earth."

Pattengale's quick pace and winsome relatability effectually, and fairly, convey the dense and often complicated history of Christianity for anyone interested in learning more about the origin and perpetuation of their faith. Be it the pastor, the professor, the Sunday school teacher, the mother, the student, the layperson, or teenager, all can glean something from this book and hopefully be inspired by those who have gone to the ends of earth for the sake of Jesus Christ.

Amy Van Dyke
Lead Curator of Art and Exhibitions, Museum of the Bible (DC)

In this truthful and generous text, Dr. Jerry Pattengale has written an eminently readable, informative, and instructive book about the expansion and growth of the Christian faith in all the world. In his brilliant narrative, he tells a hard and difficult story, where the gospel message triumphs in spite of the monstrous flaws of many of its messengers, and because of the power of God that is in it, and of those who were most faithful in their witness to it even unto death.

Donald L. Cassell, Jr., MDiv, Architect, AIA
Senior Fellow
Director Liberian Initiatives, Sagamore Institute

Jerry Pattengale's books aren't just original, insightful, and scholarly—they're also a joy to read. His latest book, *Inexplicable: How Christianity Spread to the Ends of the Earth,* is a fascinating look at one of the most interesting questions in history: How did Christianity become such a compelling religious movement on every continent? At the hands of a master storyteller, it's a journey well worth taking, and you'll be surprised at where it leads. Get the book. It will give you a remarkable look at why Christianity has made such a powerful impact on the world.

Phil Cooke, PhD
Media consultant, filmmaker, and author of *The Way Back: How Christians Blew Our Credibility and How We Get It Back*

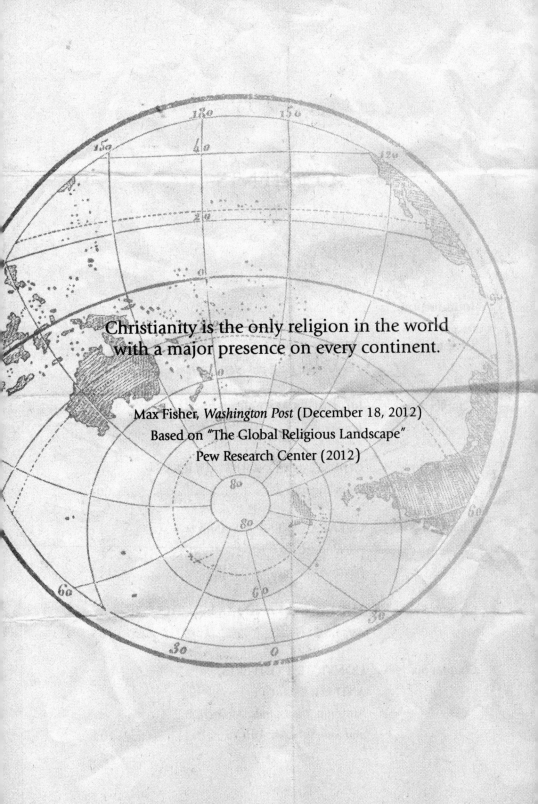

Christianity is the only religion in the world
with a major presence on every continent.

Max Fisher, *Washington Post* (December 18, 2012)
Based on "The Global Religious Landscape"
Pew Research Center (2012)

CONTENTS

�

CONTENTS

INTRODUCTION

The story of Christianity is grand on many fronts as it is "the only religion with a major presence on every continent." We all benefit from ways of organizing the key developments and personalities in this remarkable history, one that is still unfolding. The book you are about to read serves this role. It provides an engaging outline of how Christ's followers carried his message through the centuries and eventually to every continent.

Yes, "to the ends of the earth."

Without overreaching, we follow the storyline of Christian history.[1] For example, we know where some of the disciples traveled and the places of their martyrdoms. For most of them, however, we don't know for sure so we include the leading traditions—and call them such. We also don't talk about the "triumph" of Christianity, as if there were some cosmic competition that was settled. Rather, we see the amazing story of Christianity's humble beginnings and trace how it "turned the world upside down." And, we see how it continues to influence leaders, institutions, and movements today.

From its inception, Christianity was an international movement. Distant magi visited the Christ child. His family fled to Egypt—where eventually Christian communities would claim connections.

Likewise, the prominent Coptic community would persist through the toughest of challenges, especially after the Islamic conquest. Monastic movements would spread from this area to have branches in Europe and worldwide. The unique Christian story among Ethiopians led to its regional persistence. Of course, throughout this expansion the Christians went with the Pentecost promise (Acts 2), the power of the Holy Spirit. Yes, in many ways Christianity's expansion is inexplicable. Faith enters in whenever we try to wrap our minds around supernatural engagement in a natural world—a fundamental Christian claim.

The goal for Christian readers is to finish this book with a more informed faith. For all readers the goal is to find a handy overview of Christianity's spread to the continents. And, to find throughout easily accessible sources and suggested topics for deeper study.

The chapters of this book, like those in Christianity's historic rise, survival, and explosive growth, introduce hundreds of fascinating topics. For example, who wouldn't like to read Perpetua's entire account of her eminent martyrdom in Carthage, from inside the jail? Or, while learning about Rome's collapse who wouldn't want to read the provocative sections of Augustine's *City of God* that have gripped readers for centuries? However, we first need a place to hang these and other stories within the overarching narrative of Christian history.

While hundreds of first-hand accounts inform us about wars, crusades, and movements, a glimpse suffices here to keep our discussion at a manageable length. This book itself is about one-fourth of its original page total. That is, it comes from the historical background text I wrote for producers of the TV series by the same name.[2]

Two thousand years after its founding, Christianity remains not only a living religion with exponential growth in places like Africa and China, but also a popular media topic and shaper of culture. Leading magazines cover aspects of Christianity's narrative like clockwork every Easter and Christmas. The BC-AD dating system (and indirectly the modified BCE-CE version) reflects the importance of the life of Jesus in history. Countless names of schools, holidays, babies, cities, and other touchpoints in societies worldwide reflect Christianity's message and missionaries. An inestimable number of Christian charities tend to the needs of the poor and disenfranchised. This book provides a way to organize the history behind these developments—the spread of Christianity to the continents and the key players and events of these journeys.

The narrative begins in Israel and the early missionary journeys but concentrates on the establishment of Christianity in northern Africa. Throughout its first centuries, whatever was happening with the Roman leaders affected Christians wherever they lived. The same was true of shifts of power from Rome to Constantinople, and then variations of both. The book finishes back in Africa, where Christianity's explosive growth continues. Many scholars have predicted this to be the future center of Christendom. The middle chapters try to follow a logical sequence between the continents. There is no perfect outline to represent Christianity's spread worldwide, but there are tenable ones to help frame the discussion.

Christian history contains the good, the bad, and the ugly. You will find plenty of each in the pages ahead. The contention of this author is that the correct reading and implementation of biblical teachings should lead to good ends—whether in this world or the next. Unfortunately, these same teachings have been misused to cause evil, suffering, and bizarre behavior.[3] At the least, whatever religious or philosophical lens through which you read Christian history, the alignment or misalignment of actions with the Bible is discernible.

The challenge Jesus gave to his disciples has come to fruition: "Go therefore and make disciples of all nations[4]..." The following pages show how this transpired in spite of so many challenges. They also capture the inspiration of Christian heroes through the centuries. Today we are in a trajectory linked with this *community of saints*—"a kind of spiritual kinship with fellow believers from across all ages, sharing aspirations and experiences in common."[5]

Jerry A. Pattengale, PhD
December 16, 2019

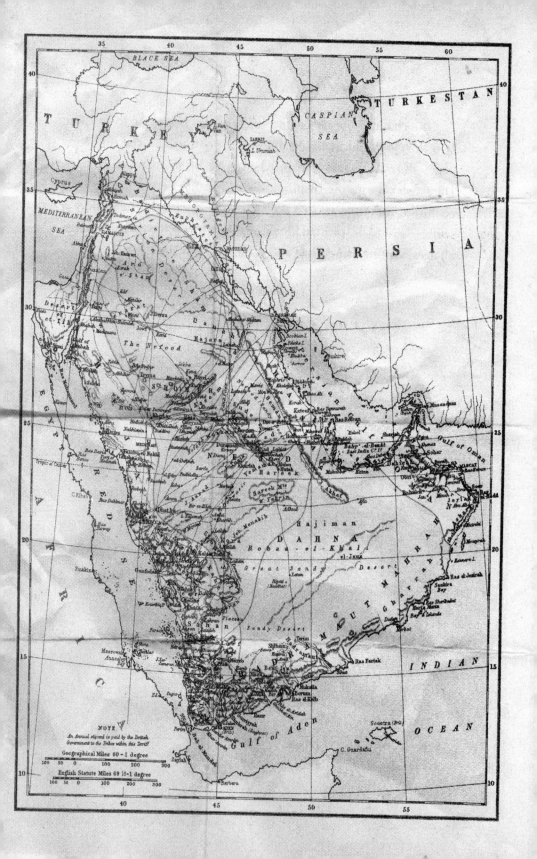

CHAPTER ONE

THE BEGINNINGS

THE MIDDLE EAST AND NORTH AFRICA

They went everywhere gossiping the gospel; they did it naturally,
enthusiastically, and with the conviction of those
who are not paid to say that sort of thing.
Consequently, they were taken seriously,
and the movement spread.

Michael Green, *Evangelism in the Early Church*[6]

We must be global Christians with a global vision
because our God is a global God.

John R. W. Stott

The man hung there limply, flies buzzing about his swollen face, convicted criminals moaning softly to his left and right. His executioners had almost killed him before they even raised his crucified body into the Judean sky. The preliminaries had included a brutal flogging, his captors using him as a human punching bag, and then—for amusement—a mock coronation, mashing a tangle of thorns, a makeshift "crown" onto his weary head.

Stripped, bruised, and covered in blood, the man was nearly unrecognizable. Perhaps this was the practical reason for the inscription over his head: "Jesus the Nazarene, the King of the Jews" (John 19:19). The sign was for identification and an insult—*Does this look like a king to you?* It was further a warning: *This is what happens to those who challenge Rome's absolute power.*

In the shadow of the three crosses, Jerusalem's religious leaders, wearing looks of smug relief, whispered together. Gawkers milled about, occasionally jeering at the dying. Cynical soldiers kept a watchful eye on the restless crowd.

Meanwhile, off in the distance, trying to be unobtrusive, some of the Nazarene's most devoted followers, male and female (Luke 23:49), huddled together in shock and horror, fear and confusion.

What now? What are we supposed to do?

To a person, the followers of Jesus had been utterly convinced he was the long-awaited Messiah...that he had come to restore the kingdom to Israel at last.

No one had ever spoken like this man. No prophet had ever performed the kinds of miracles he had done. Yet in a matter of days, it had all unraveled. The disciple named Judas Iscariot betrayed the teacher to the religious authorities. When those authorities barged into Gethsemane on Thursday night to arrest him, his disciples fled into the darkness. By dawn Friday, Peter, the de facto leader of the group, was vehemently—and repeatedly—denying that he even *knew* the controversial rabbi from Nazareth. A short time later, the same crowds that had hailed Jesus on Sunday were hollering for his execution.

As the group of Galileans watched their dying leader take his final, labored breaths, it seemed obvious that all was lost.

Except that it *wasn't*.

Not by a longshot.

Jesus was only getting started.

The Empty Tomb

The wee hours of Sunday morning brought an earthquake—literally (Matthew 28:2) and figuratively. When some of Christ's female followers went to his borrowed tomb to anoint his body for burial,[7] there was no body in the tomb to anoint. Instead, angels confronted the upset women and informed them that Jesus had risen from the dead, "just as he said" (Matthew 28:6). Before they could process this stunning news, the women met the resurrected Christ himself!

Immediately they rushed away to tell the others. The gospel accounts of these moments are chaotic and hard to piece together, as we might expect—people racing to and fro, confused and overjoyed at once, mourners suddenly morphing into evangelists.

But here's what is clear in these ancient sources: Over the ensuing forty days, the risen Jesus appeared to his followers on multiple occasions. These were not hallucinations. On one occasion five hundred people saw him "at the same time" (1 Corinthians 15:6). And the one they saw was no apparition. Witnesses touched his body, examined the scars on his hands and side, walked and talked with him, ate meals with him. In one sunrise encounter at the Sea of Galilee, the resurrected Jesus reprised the miracle he had performed just before he'd called the group to follow him in the first place (compare Luke 5:1–11 with John 21:1–14). Then he singled out the guilt-ridden Peter and made a special point of restoring and recommissioning him (John 21:15–25).

All these stunning, rapid-fire events could mean only one thing: since Jesus wasn't dead, his movement wasn't either.

The Great Commission

One of Jesus's post-resurrection appearances took place on an unspecified mountain in Galilee. Matthew, one of the original twelve disciples, later recorded Christ's words on that occasion:

> All authority in heaven and on earth has been given to me. Go therefore and make disciples of all nations, baptizing them in the name of the Father and of the Son and of the Holy Spirit, teaching them to observe all that I have commanded you. And behold, I am with you always, to the end of the age (Matthew 28:18–20 ESV)

Christians refer to this command as "the Great Commission" and see it as the Lord's answer to the *What now? What are we supposed to do?* questions. Christ's followers are to take his message of forgiveness and new life to all people everywhere, to show and tell the whole world what it means to follow him.

As job descriptions go, such a mandate was (and, frankly, still is) overwhelming. How in heaven's name can a few ordinary people accomplish such an extraordinary task? The book of Acts, a chronicle of the remarkable birth and growth of the church over its first three decades, explains how. Luke begins his meticulous history with the last words spoken on earth by the resurrected Jesus:

> "Do not leave Jerusalem, but wait for the gift my Father promised, which you have heard me speak about[8].... You will receive power when the Holy Spirit comes on

you; and you will be my witnesses in Jerusalem, and in
all Judea and Samaria, and to the ends of the earth."
After he said this, he was taken up before their very eyes,
and a cloud hid him from their sight" (Acts 1:4, 8–9)[9]

Stunning. Both Christ's supernatural departure...*and* his final
words. Without printing presses or the advantages of modern travel,
without radio or TV, cell phones or the Internet, the good news of
Jesus was about to go viral, first-century style. Once the followers of
Jesus were enabled and empowered by the Spirit of almighty God,
the message of Jesus would begin making its way to "the ends of the
earth." It was both a command...and a promise.

And thus began the wait for the promised Holy Spirit.

They didn't have to wait long.

The Coming of the Spirit

Following Christ's ascension into heaven from the Mount of
Olives (Acts 1:12), Luke says that the eleven apostles "along with
the women and Mary the mother of Jesus, and...his brothers" (Acts
1:14) returned to Jerusalem and retired to a large, upstairs room,
similar to the one they had used some forty-three days earlier for
their "last supper" with Jesus.

St. Jerome, the esteemed Christian writer (d. 420), believed this
actually *was* the same room. In fact, over the centuries, millions of
pilgrims have visited the alleged site. Called the Cenacle (from Latin
for "dining room"), the space is located above the traditional tomb
of King David on Mt. Zion. First-century Christian graffiti and early
plaster bolster this claim.

Whatever one believes about such matters, it *was* in an upstairs room in Jerusalem where this group of 120 diehard devotees to Christ's deity (Acts 1:15) gathered. There they "joined together constantly in prayer" and also appointed a believer named Matthias to replace Judas among the twelve apostles (Acts 1:12–26).

When the day of Pentecost arrived, so did the Holy Spirit. Luke described the history-altering moment:

> And suddenly there came from heaven a sound like a mighty rushing wind, and it filled the entire house where they were sitting. And divided tongues as of fire appeared to them and rested on each one of them. And they were all filled with the Holy Spirit and began to speak in other tongues as the Spirit gave them utterance (Acts 2:2–4 ESV).

Luke records that, because of the festival of Pentecost, Jerusalem was bustling with devout Jews "from every nation under heaven" (Acts 2:5). The supernatural "fireworks" in the Upper Room drew a crowd of astonished onlookers who discovered the Galilean followers of Jesus declaring "the mighty works of God" in their native languages! Luke gives a long list of nations represented: "Parthians and Medes and Elamites and residents of Mesopotamia, Judea and Cappadocia, Pontus and Asia, Phrygia and Pamphylia, Egypt and the parts of Libya belonging to Cyrene, and visitors from Rome, both Jews and proselytes, Cretans and Arabians" (Acts 2:9–11, ESV).

News of this miraculous phenomenon spread through the city faster than a juicy rumor on Twitter. As the crowd in and around the upstairs room swelled in size, some onlookers began offering theories about what they were witnessing.

Peter stepped forward. This was the old Peter, before fear had gotten the better of him. It was also the new Peter, after the truth of Christ's resurrection had forever transformed him. Looking into all those faces, he boldly delivered a message about his Messiah.

He reminded the crowd of ancient biblical prophecies of the Christ given by the prophet Joel and, before him, by King David. For many of his listeners this was the first time they'd heard a clear, concise summary of Jesus's life, death, and resurrection.

After the Spirit-filled Peter connected some important theological dots for his audience, Luke's record says that "they were cut to the heart" (Acts 2:37 ESV). Some began to ask, "Brothers, what shall we do?" (Acts 2:37). Peter replied, "Repent and be baptized every one of you in the name of Jesus Christ for the forgiveness of your sins..." (Acts 2:38 ESV).

Three thousand onlookers responded enthusiastically.

The news of the resurrected Nazarene reverberated through the city. Such talk had infuriated Jerusalem's religious leaders from the beginning—so much so that they had bribed the guards at the tomb of Jesus to spread a rumor that his followers had come during the night and stolen his body (Matthew 28:11–15). Rumors, however, were no match for Spirit-filled witnesses of the risen Christ. This unlikely group of common Galileans—and the other Jews in town from all over—became a holy host of bold witnesses. Beginning at Jerusalem they began to turn the world upside down (Acts 17:6 KJV).

Driving this movement at the center? The life Peter Larson described as "bracketed by two impossibilities: a virgin's womb and an empty tomb"; the one who "entered our world through a door marked 'No Entrance' and left through a door marked 'No Exit.'"[10]

Only a life *that* remarkable could change hearts and alter entire cultures. And so it began at the Upper Room, the increasingly diverse followers of Jesus—Jews and Gentiles, males and females, slaves and free, wealthy and poor—eventually took his message everywhere. With the result that today the Pew Research Center demonstrates, "Christianity is the only religion in the world with a major presence on every continent."[11]

Granted, it would take centuries for the message of Jesus to transform hearts worldwide, but even in utero, even when Christianity consisted of only 120 believers surrounded by a crowd of Jewish pilgrims in the heart of Jerusalem, it had the markings of a global movement.

How easy it is for modern-day Christians (and non-Christians too) to forget that global Christianity began with a *Jewish* fisherman—Peter—proclaiming at the *Jewish* festival of Pentecost in the *Jewish* city of Jerusalem that a *Jewish* carpenter-turned-teacher—Jesus—was the *Jewish* Messiah. Let's not forget either that Peter's message on that occasion was rooted in passages found in the *Jewish* Bible (what Christians call the Old Testament)...and that his audience was thoroughly *Jewish* (which is why he addressed them as "men of Judea" and "men of Israel").

Given these realities, before we trace the remarkable spread of the Christian gospel from Jerusalem to "the ends of the earth," we need to pause and quickly review how the history of the Jewish people forms the backstory of the Christian church.

Christianity's Jewish Backstory

Like every well-told story, the biblical story begins by (a) establishing the *setting*—a perfect world made by God and inhabited by his beloved human creatures (Genesis 1–2)—and (b) introducing an *inciting incident* or dilemma—in this case the rebellion of those human creatures, leading to the ruin of God's creation (Genesis 3). The plot for the rest of the biblical story answers the question "What will God do to rescue his rebellious creatures and restore his ruined world?"

Enter an old man known as Abram, living in ancient Mesopotamia (i.e., modern-day Iraq). In Genesis 12, we read:

The LORD had said to Abram, "Go from your country, your people and your father's household to the land I will show you.

"I will make you into a great nation,

and I will bless you;

I will make your name great,

and you will be a blessing.

I will bless those who bless you,

and whoever curses you I will curse;

and all peoples on earth

will be blessed through you" (Genesis 12:1–3 NIV).

The answer to the age-old question *Why him?* is a deep mystery. In fact, when the God of the Bible first appeared to Abram and made these lavish covenant promises, Abram was a worshiper of other gods (Joshua 24:2).

This is the divine pattern we see throughout the Bible. In his great work of salvation, God graciously calls and mysteriously partners with unlikely people (Deuteronomy 7:7–8). He utilizes unexpected and unexceptional means (1 Corinthians 1:20). God's plan to save the world involved using an elderly man and his infertile wife to create a brand-new nation.

This "wandering Aramean" (Deuteronomy 26:5) became the father of a sprawling—sometimes brawling—family that eventually grew into the nation of Israel. That nation eventually produced Jesus of Nazareth.

Jesus selected Peter and the other disciples, training them to become the leaders of his new faith community. Upon receiving his Spirit at Pentecost they began to spread his message of forgiveness and new life everywhere...but at first it took a little prodding.

The Gospel in Jerusalem

Despite Christ's clear command to make disciples of *all nations* (Matthew 28:18–20), his Jewish followers seemed content to remain in Jerusalem, preaching and teaching the Lord's message. Despite some opposition from the Jewish religious authorities (see Acts 3–5), they enjoyed relative freedom. Consequently, "the word of God continued to increase, and the number of the disciples multiplied greatly in Jerusalem" (Acts 6:7, ESV).

All of this changed with the arrest of a disciple named Stephen. Like the one he followed, Stephen was falsely accused of all sorts of crimes against Judaism (Acts 6:8–7:1). Brought before the Jewish ruling council, the Sanhedrin—the same powerful group that had condemned Jesus—the Spirit-filled Stephen delivered a pointed and passionate sermon (Acts 7:2–53). His listeners became enraged... then outraged. They dragged Stephen outside the city and stoned him. Luke records ominously, "And there arose on that day a great persecution against the church in Jerusalem, and they were all scattered throughout the regions of Judea and Samaria, except the apostles" (Acts 8:1, ESV).

The Onset of Persecution[12]

It's impossible to understand the spread of Christianity apart from the reality of persecution. History is filled with grim examples. For example...

In the mid-second century, the bishop of Smyrna (i.e., Izmir in modern-day Turkey) was an aged man named Polycarp, beloved by early Christians. His popularity was no doubt due to his humility and direct manner—and also because prominent church leaders like Ignatius,[13] bishop of Antioch, and Irenaeus[14] linked him directly to the apostles. (There is credible evidence that Polycarp was a disciple of John, and that John had appointed him bishop.)[15]

When Polycarp was eighty-six, word reached Smyrna that Roman officials were cracking down on all who would not give allegiance to the imperial cult. Concerned Christians urged Polycarp to hide at a nearby farm. He did so, but two captured slave boys reportedly revealed his location—and Polycarp refused to flee any longer. It's even reported that he fed his arresting officers a large meal before leaving with them.

After a candid exchange with an official (appropriately named

Herod), the authorities skipped usual protocol and took Polycarp straight to the stadium. There, according to one chronicler, amidst the mayhem a voice from heaven rang out: "Be strong, Polycarp, play the man." The old saint did just that.

As local crowds filled the stadium, the godly bishop remained firm. Despite pleas for the old man to save himself, Polycarp replied, "For eighty-six years I have been his servant, and he has done me no wrong. How can I blaspheme my King who saved me?"[16] Though many in the crowd called for the beasts, the magistrate determined to burn the bishop alive. When the soldiers tried to nail Polycarp to the stake, he assured them he would die willingly (and wryly added that they were focusing only on temporal flames when they should be concerned about eternal ones).

According to the account, the fires formed a vault around Polycarp and didn't touch him, so the guards killed him with a dagger, after which a fragrant smell filled the arena.[17] The church of Smyrna circulated his testimony, and Polycarp's death inspired churches throughout the empire. His execution is the earliest recorded martyrdom in Christian history outside the New Testament.

Perhaps the best-documented martyr story in the early church was the account of Perpetua. Because she kept a detailed diary, possibly preserved by Tertullian, the news of her persecution spread far and wide. Even the esteemed Augustine of Hippo, North Africa, mentioned her. This diary, one of the earliest surviving texts by a Christian woman, provides a firsthand account of her dungeon and torture experiences. (The details of her death were added by Saturus, one of her contemporaries.)

Perpetua was from a prominent family in Carthage. She was young in years and in the faith. A new mom nursing an infant son, she was taking classes with her servant Felicitas and three young men in preparation for believers' baptism.[18] However, since the emperor

Severus had outlawed, under penalty of death, conversions to either Christianity or Judaism, all five Christians were arrested and charged with violating the imperial edict.

Perpetua's father, his baby grandson in arms, interrupted his daughter's trial, begging her to renounce Christ and make an offering of incense to the emperor. According to the record, she replied, "Father, do you see this vase here? Could it be called by any other name than what it is?"

"No," he replied.

"Well, neither can I be called anything other than what I am, a Christian."[19]

Before turning over the account to Saturus, Perpetua wrote down a vision she had of her upcoming fight against the beasts in the arena. She concludes: "And I awoke; and I understood that I should fight, not with beasts but against the devil; but I knew that mine was the victory."[20] Her last meal—granted as a Roman custom before execution—was an agape feast, communion with her Christian colleagues.

When the end came, Perpetua sang praises to God in an attempt to inspire her fellow martyrs while the gladiators scourged them. According to the record, these believers were then tied like bait to a raised bridge in the arena, and attacked by a leopard, a bear, and a boar.

Surviving these wild animals, Perpetua and Felicitas were then subjected to a crazed bull—which the writer says was made ready by the devil himself for just this occasion. Their executioners initially forced them to strip naked. But even the bloodthirsty crowd was put off by this gross indecency. The women put on robes, after which the raging bull attacked and gored them.

Tertullian cites Perpetua's diary: "She was tossed, and fell on her loins; and when she saw her tunic torn from her side, she drew it over her as a veil for her middle, rather mindful of her modesty than her suffering. Then she...bound up her disheveled hair; for it was not becoming for a martyr to suffer with disheveled hair, lest she should appear to be mourning in her glory."[21] Perpetua also helped Felicitas to her feet to face the bull anew with dignity.

When the bull failed to finish off the women, the gladiators ensured their deaths with the sword. Perpetua's executioner was, apparently, a novice, and his first thrust between her bones wrought pain but not death. She exposed her neck to assist in her final moment in the flesh.

Perpetua died in 203 at age twenty-two. Her story, preserved by her own hand and eyewitnesses, is still being told eighteen centuries later.

Here are two truths about stories like this from church history:

1. They are *not* rare; and

2. They should not surprise anyone. In the Upper Room, Jesus had given his followers this promise, "Remember what I told you: 'A servant is not greater than his master.' If they persecuted me, they will persecute you also" (John 15:20). Similar warnings permeated Christ's teachings (Matthew 5:10–12; 24:9–13). The following day at Golgotha, Jesus's wide-eyed disciples got an awful picture of the kind of persecution the Lord had been referring to (Luke 23:49).

Let's say it again.... The New Testament deaths of John the Baptist, Stephen, and the apostle James[22] were only the first trickle in what would become a veritable flood of blood. Understanding the global reach of the gospel requires knowledge of the numerous regional and empire-wide persecutions Christians faced during those first centuries.

The chart on the following pages gives an overview of the waves of persecution the church experienced until Constantine came to power.

Ten Waves of Persecution in the Early Church

First Persecution **Nero (AD 54–68)**	After a fire burned much of Rome in AD 64, Tacitus wrote that Nero fastened the guilt and inflicted the most exquisite tortures on a class hated for their abominations, called Christians by the populace…. Covered with skins of beasts, they were torn by dogs and perished, or were nailed to crosses, or were doomed to the flames. These served to illuminate the night when daylight failed.[23]
Second Persecution **Domitian** **(AD 81–96)**	Eusebius wrote: "Many were the victims of Domitian's appalling cruelty…. Finally, he showed himself the successor of Nero in enmity and hostility to God. He was, in fact, the second to organize persecution against us."

**Third Persecution
Trajan
(AD 98–117)**

Pliny the Younger wrote of his treatment of believers: "I interrogated them as to whether they were Christians; those who confessed I interrogated a second and a third time, threatening them with punishment; those who persisted I ordered executed. For I had no doubt that, whatever the nature of their creed, stubbornness and inflexible obstinacy surely deserve to be punished."[24]

**Fourth Persecution
Marcus Aurelius
(AD 161–180)**

Marcus Aurelius was sometimes regarded as a noteworthy ruler, but historians allege ruthless treatment of Christians during his reign.[25]

**Fifth Persecution
Severus
(AD 193–211)**

Perhaps the most celebrated and well documented of all martyrdoms—that of Perpetua, Felicitas, and their colleagues in Carthage—took place under Severus.

**Sixth Persecution
Maximinus
(AD 235–238)**

During this persecution, "numberless Christians were slain without trial, and buried indiscriminately in heaps, sometimes fifty or sixty being cast into a pit together, without the least decency."[26]

Seventh Persecution Decius (AD 249–251)

Decius ordered an empire-wide persecution, and made an aggressive and systematic attempt to obliterate Christianity. Anyone who could not produce a receipt (*libellus*) proving he/she had made a sacrifice to the emperor in a civil-religious service was condemned.

Eighth Persecution Valerian (AD 253–260)

Under Valerian thousands were killed, with huge casualties in Carthage and North Africa. In Utica, the proconsul placed three hundred Christians around a boiling limekiln and ordered them to sacrifice to Jupiter or jump in. They all took the leap.

Ninth Persecution Aurelian (AD 270–275)

The persecutions under Aurelian included Britain's most prominent Christian—and perhaps its first—St. Alban (the progenitor of St. Alban's in Hertfordshire, England).

Tenth Persecution Diocletian (AD 284–305)

Diocletian issued at least four edicts, increasingly severe, calling for the destruction of churches and the burning of Scriptures.

Later Persecution under Julian the Apostate (AD 361–363)

When Constantine declared Christianity a lawful religion in 313, many believed that official persecutions were a thing of the past. This was largely true, except when Julian, Constantine's nephew, became emperor.

He passed edicts forbidding Christians from serving in various posts. He also restored the pagan temples. When Julian stripped Christian leaders of their various tax benefits and incomes and made them repay past benefits, many in the pagan community applauded him. Some even turned on Christians, resulting in new persecutions, like the lynching of Bishop George in Alexandria. In some places, Julian's efforts to sow discord sparked riotous fighting between different Christian factions.

Nevertheless, Julian failed to realize two things: (1) Christianity had too firm a root to be dislodged, and as Gregory pointed out (*Oration IV.74*), *to try to do so was nothing less than to destroy the Roman Empire;*[27] and (2) He could not force the masses to love paganism. It was a dying system. Julian lamented *to his high priest*:

> *The Hellenic religion does not yet prosper as I desire....Why do we not observe that it is their [Christians'] benevolence to strangers, their care for the graves of the dead and the pretended holiness of their lives that have done most to increase atheism [Christianity]?*[28]

We have focused much on the violent deaths of prominent Christians. But many of the best-attested martyrdoms were suffered by simple believers. Consider the case of Blandina, a slave girl in Lyon, France, in AD 177. (We know of these events through a letter sent from the church of Lyon to the churches of Asia Minor, and recorded by Eusebius in the early fourth century in his *Ecclesiastical History*.)

The emperor Marcus Aurelius (emperor AD 161–180) was bent on making spectacles of those who offended the Roman gods. Blandina was one of those condemned to die.

She was initially affixed to a pole as food for wild beasts. However, according to tradition, none touched her—to the anger of onlookers.[29] Her presence, appearing with her outstretched arms as if being crucified, inspired the others being tortured in front of her. Some were mangled beyond recognition. Most were scourged. Christians with Roman citizenship avoided such tortures and were simply beheaded.

To attempt to dissuade Blandina from her faith in Christ (after she survived the pole), they brought her into the arena and made her watch the carnage for several days. At last they ushered her into the arena with another young Christian, a fifteen-year old named Ponticus. Blandina encouraged him in his bravery as he was tortured before the deranged crowd.

Having survived the beasts, being whipped, and "the griddle" (a heated iron chair), Blandina "was…thrown to a bull. Time after time the animal tossed her, but she was indifferent now to all that happened to her, because of her hope and sure hold on all that her faith meant, and of her communing with Christ. Then she, too, was sacrificed, while the heathen themselves admitted that never yet had they known a woman suffer so much or so long."[30]

Nevertheless, the jeering crowd exclaimed with the utmost scorn: "Where is their god and what did they get for their religion, which they preferred to their own lives?"[31] After exposing the bodies for six more days the authorities burned them to ashes. Then, in an attempt to prevent a resurrection, they "swept them" into the nearby Rhone River. Ironic to consider the martyrs' ashes flowing from Lyon past Orange, Avignon, Arles, and even beyond the Mediterranean.

Today, visitors to the remains of the expansive Amphithéâtre des Trois-Gaules (the historic arena) can see a pole erected in Blandina's honor.

☧

According to those writers placing faith in the biblical account, an account likely believed by many reading this, how exactly did God use all those terrible waves of persecution to grow his church? Let's look back at the aftermath of Stephen's stoning. One of those scattered was a believer named Philip. Though he promptly changed his location, he didn't change his practice. He "proclaimed the Christ" to receptive audiences in Samaria (Acts 8:4–25) and to a spiritually curious Ethiopian government official on the road to Gaza, before making his way to Caesarea (Acts 8:26–40; 21:8). Little did Philip know how instrumental this seaside city would become in the spread of the gospel of Jesus.

Two World-Changing Visions

Acts 10 introduces us to Cornelius, an Italian centurion stationed in Caesarea. In a vision, he was visited by an angel who told him to send men to fetch a Jewish leader named Peter who was at that time in Joppa, a coastal city some forty miles south.

Shortly before this Gentile entourage arrived, the apostle Peter went up on his rooftop to pray. There he "fell into a trance" (Acts 10:10). Three consecutive times he saw a confusing vision that challenged many of his Jewish presuppositions. Even as he was "perplexed as to what the vision…might mean" (Acts 10:17 ESV), Peter became aware of the visitors from Caesarea outside his door. The next day Peter and some other Jewish followers of Jesus from Joppa headed north with the servants of Cornelius.

When Peter arrived in Caesarea, he went *into* the home of Cornelius—even though it was unlawful for Jews to enter a Gentile residence. Peter was surprised to find a large group of "devout and God-fearing" Gentiles—the centurion's relatives and friends. At once Peter realized the divine meaning behind his strange visions: "God does not show favoritism but accepts from every nation the one who fears him and does what is right" (Acts 10:34–35). The apostle immediately began to summarize the life, death, and resurrection of Christ for the spiritually hungry group of Gentiles in front of him.

"While Peter was still speaking these words, the Holy Spirit came on all who heard the message. The circumcised believers who had come with Peter were astonished that the gift of the Holy Spirit had been poured out even on Gentiles.... So he ordered that they be baptized in the name of Jesus Christ" (Acts 10:44–45, 48).

Thus, in Caesarea Cornelius, his friends, and relatives became the first Gentile (non-Jewish) converts—at least on record. As with the Upper Room, this was a watershed moment for the spread of Christ's message. It confirmed that the gospel was, indeed, for both Jews *and Gentiles*. (A good thing for Christianity's camp, since there are only about 15 million Jews in the world, or roughly 0.2% of the global population.[32])

We don't know much about Peter's ministry efforts after Acts 13 (Luke's narrative shifts its focus to the travels of the apostle Paul). We do know that he spent time in Antioch. Some early church historians claim he was its first bishop, as well as the first bishop of Rome.

It would be another Jew, Paul, who would write to the Christians in Rome, "For I am not ashamed of the gospel, because it is the power of God that brings salvation to everyone who believes: first to the Jew, then to the Gentile" (Romans 1:16). However, Peter was the apostle who enjoyed the remarkable privilege of opening the door of salvation to the non-Jewish world.

The Gospel to Caesarea

Some twenty-five years after the crucifixion and resurrection of Jesus of Nazareth, following the timeline in the multiple recorded biblical accounts, the aforementioned Paul found himself in Caesarea. Unlike Peter who went there to baptize new Gentile converts, Paul went to stand trial.

Luke tells the story. Following his third missionary journey, Paul was arrested in Jerusalem (Acts 21:27–23:22) and sent to Caesarea to appear before Felix, Festus, and Agrippa (Acts 23:23-26:32).

This once insignificant Sidonian coastal village had been transformed into a booming city in 21 BC[33] by King Herod the Great (as a way of honoring Caesar). The city served as the Roman headquarters for all of Judea, Herod's *Judaeae Caput.*[34] The Jewish historian Josephus described Caesar's massive temple here—a few remains are still visible today.[35] The city also boasted an impressive amphitheater and Israel's only deep-water port. Herod had ingeniously re-engineered the once-shallow coastline, and the result was an architectural wonder. Josephus notes that he "triumphed over nature and built a harbor larger than Piraeus" (at Athens).[36] Today, through the most expensive archaeological project in Israel (over $20 million, after $40 million already spent), we are learning more of the details of the Caesarea of Paul's era. Aerial images show the remains of the massive blocks that had effectively created an artificial reef, along with the remains of artificial islands.

In Caesarea Paul was incarcerated for at least two years (Acts 24:27). He was then sent to Rome to appear before Caesar (Acts 26:32). Around AD 57, near the arena at Herod's palace (or *praetorium*),[37] Paul proclaimed to King Agrippa and his sister, Bernice (the grandchildren of Herod the Great), "I am saying nothing beyond what the prophets and Moses said would happen—that the Messiah would suffer and, as the first to rise from the dead, would bring the message of light to his own people and to the Gentiles" (Acts 26:22–23).

How fitting that Paul declared *in Caesarea*—where Peter had baptized the Gentile Cornelius only a few years before—that the "message of light" must be taken to the Gentiles.

How ironic that even as Paul proclaimed the life, death, and resurrection of Christ in Herod's palace, he stood in the shadow of Caesar's temple with its "gigantic statue of Augustus which was no less magnificent than the statue of Zeus in Olympia, on which it was modeled. There was also a statue of Roma, equal in beauty to the statue of Hera in Argos."[38]

Almost two thousand years later, we can still see hundreds of millions of Christians giving devotion to the Messiah Paul preached. And we can safely say that nobody worships Augustus or Roma. In fact, few people even live in Caesarea today.

What happened there—and from there—played out across the world. Even as Paul sailed west out of the shadows of Caesarea, Christians were beginning to shine the "message of light" (Acts 26:23) in more and more dark places.

Before falling into insignificance, Caesarea served as one of the five most influential outposts of the Christian faith, along with Antioch, Alexandria, Rome, and—after AD 330—Constantinople.[39] The spiritual leaders and scholars who lived and ministered and wrote in all these cities helped create the rich legacy of the church of Jesus.

During its heyday, an all-star cast of Christian heroes spent extended time in Caesarea. Origen (d. 253), perhaps the greatest early apologist of the Christian faith, accepted an offer to teach in Caesarea and left Egypt. Once there, Origen wrote his defiant *Exhortation to Martyrdom*[40] and other great works. Perhaps his magnum opus was his *Hexapla*, a six-fold translation of the Hebrew Bible—five columns from Greek manuscripts, and one from a Hebrew scroll he purchased in Jericho. (Like the Dead Sea Scrolls, it was also found in a jar.)

Until his own martyrdom, and except for travels to debate for orthodoxy, Origen taught the rest of his career at the school he founded there. In AD 250, following his own exhortations, Origen refused to recant during the Decian persecutions. In AD 253, he died from injuries received under torture. The detailed account of his suffering is preserved in Eusebius's *Ecclesiastical History*—which was also written in Caesarea.

We could go on and on about the city's influence. Somewhere beneath the city's sands are the stone foundations of the buildings in which St. Basil drafted the Trinitarian theology that the Second Ecumenical Council (AD 382, in Constantinople) would adopt two years after his death.[41] The prominent historian, Adolf Von Harnack, also traces the Nicene Creed's origin back to this very spot, to the place that now looks like a tourist town.[42]

How could Herod Agrippa II have known that his one moment of lasting fame would be his interaction with Paul...or that one day his city would be a primary hub for the life-altering teachings of Jesus the Messiah...or that the apostle named Paul, who utilized his famous port (Acts 18:22; 21:8–16), would be instrumental in establishing Christianity's major presence on every continent. It seems Agrippa failed to realize that what happened in Caesarea *didn't* stay in Caesarea.

In addition to the influential port city of Caesarea, other centers of faith began to emerge to the west of Jerusalem across North

Africa (Alexandria, Cyrene, Hippo, and Carthage), as well as north and west in Antioch, Constantinople, and Rome.

The Gospel to Alexandria and North Africa

Africa is the only country Jesus visited outside of his homeland of Judea (as an infant, with his parents, to escape Herod's jealous clutches; see Matthew 2:13–18). While we know little about that sojourn, we do know that by the end of the New Testament era, Christianity had a strong foothold in North Africa. Who first took the gospel there, however, remains a mystery. The New Testament records the presence of Jewish pilgrims from North Africa at Pentecost (Acts 2:10). It also tells of the conversion of an Ethiopian government official through Philip's efforts (Acts 8:26–39).

In addition to obvious supernatural, spiritual factors that Christians would credit (i.e., the promptings of the Spirit), other factors played into Christianity's expansion into North Africa: prominent trade routes, the attraction of remarkable centers of learning, and natural connections between Jewish communities and Jewish Christians. Alexandria's large, Greek-speaking Hebrew population influenced nearby cities like Cyrene. Cities further west like Carthage were closer to Rome, which explains their theological allegiance and preference for the Latin of Rome rather than the Greek of Alexandria.

Early tradition, including Jerome and Eusebius, claims that the apostle Mark established Christianity in Alexandria in the mid-first century.[43] The late Professor Tom Oden led a large network of scholars of African church history who endorse this Markan thesis,[44] citing the naming of eight early churches named for him and consistent hagiographic mention. Others, like historian Justo Gonzalez, disagree,[45] since "the development of the Christian church is totally obscure until the end of the second century."[46]

Regardless of the historicity of this Markan claim, we know that by the end of the second century, Alexandria was an educational center for Christianity, and also the place where St. Clement introduced the word "clergy."[47]

The great Catechetical School of Alexandria became one of Christianity's two leading educational centers for ministry and theology (the other being the School of Antioch). Prominent voices for the church came from this Alexandrian school. During the late second century, Athenagoras and then Pantaenus led it. Clement of Alexandria instructed the prominent theologian Origen there. Other influential scholars included Gregory Thaumaturgus, Heraclas, Dionysis "the Great," and Didymus the Blind. Ecclesiastical celebrities like Jerome and Basil visited often.[48]

Upon taking root in Alexandria, the gospel gradually spread to all of Egypt, Nubia, and Ethiopia, then west across all of North Africa. Coptic Christianity (derived from the word "Copt" which means *Egypt*) dominated the region. By the end of the fourth century the diocese of Alexandria included all of this territory, including Hippo in modern Algeria where Augustine served as bishop in the late fourth and early fifth centuries.

The church was resilient in North Africa, flourishing despite many outbreaks of persecution. The brutal treatment of Christians eventually wore on some pagans: "It is not surprising that these bloodthirsty sights, which some liked to have on their dining room floors, should have revolted others. Christianity gained adherents. The insult to human dignity was too flagrant."[49] At the time of Tertullian's passing in AD 225, there were more than seventy bishops in Carthage alone. In AD 313, there were some 250.

We would be remiss not to mention how persecutions prompted the spread of the gospel into rural areas. Large groups of Christians fled the cities. The various lists of bishops in ancient letters represent churches far removed from the cities where Christianity first thrived. For example, from the life of Antony of Egypt (251–356) we know that even some small villages in Upper Egypt possessed churches and even convents (*parthenaiai*)."[50]

Although Alexandria became the region's powerful ecclesiastical seat, Cyrenaica (think: modern-day Libya) also had strong Jewish and Christian ties to Judea. The Gospels identify Simon of Cyrene (Cyrenaica's capital city) as the one who carried Jesus's cross (Acts 6:9). In mentioning his sons by name, Alexander and Rufus (Mark 15:21), Mark suggests the disciples' familiarity with this family. The Rufus mentioned by Mark may be the same Rufus Paul mentioned in Romans 16:13. The presence of Christians in Cyrenaica may account for some of the Jewish anger directed at Stephen (see Acts 6:9). Acts 11:18–20 overtly mentions believers from Cyrene.

Another influential Christian center in North Africa was Carthage, a short boat trip across the Mediterranean from Rome to the north. Although we do not know how Christianity reached this area, the account of the martyrs of Scilli (an unidentifiable place in the region) provides the earliest surviving Christian document of North Africa.[51] Carthage was the home of two extremely influential voices in the early church, Tertullian and Cyprian, during the second and third centuries. Tertullian was "the first important Latin spokesperson for Christianity," and Cyprian was "the city's best-known bishop."[52] Through Cyprian's extensive corpus of writings we know something of the daily habits of early Christians. His *On the Unity of the Universal Church* (251) speaks of "the chair of Peter" and stresses the role of the Roman bishopric as the focal point of the unity in the church. His most memorable phrase is, "One cannot have God as a father who does not the church as mother."[53]

Tertullian wrote numerous defenses of the Christian faith and offered considerable insight into the realities of living among rampant paganism.[54] We often hear of "Christian North Africa." From Tertullian's writings, it is clear that this was not the case. The church was growing—as attested by the increasing numbers of bishops across North Africa—but it wasn't until the fifth century that North Africa became *heavily* Christianized.

The Gospel to Antioch

Religious developments in one region had a way of "migrating" to other regions. These early centers of the Christian faith stayed connected through the travels of lay members and ordained leaders. A kind of theological advancement came about via their literary efforts and council involvements. For example, Clement and Origen's fight against Gnosticism in Alexandria benefited church leaders elsewhere. Tertullian's articulation of the doctrine of the Trinity did the same. Eusebius's *History of the Christian Church* cites hundreds of such intersections.

Antioch was also part of this network. We find various references to Antioch among the early believers, including those arriving from Cyrene (Acts 11:20–21). This influential city was where the term "Christian" first surfaced (Acts 11:26).

Antioch was the second or third largest city in the Roman Empire, behind only Rome and Alexandria. By the fourth century at least 500,000 people lived there, with Greek its official language and Syriac in common use. Antioch was hit hard by the great persecutions, especially those of Valerian. However, after the Council of Nicaea, the city was reconfirmed as a key ecclesiastical seat. One of its many churches was its Golden Church where one of the most famous preachers of the first several centuries often preached, John Chrysostom (349–407), nicknamed the Doctor of the Church. Around six hundred of his sermons and two hundred of his letters survive.

Chrysostom was a native of Antioch, and his extreme ascetic life in the nearby mountains damaged his health, prompting a move to the city. In AD 398 soldiers kidnapped him and took him to Constantinople. There they installed him as archbishop. Eventually he died in exile in the mountains.[55]

The Antioch School was second to the Alexandrian School in terms of prominence, and it eventually became identified primarily by its opposition to Alexandria's strong emphasis on allegory. The Antioch School featured such theological "big names" as Nestorius, Chrysostom, and, of course, Ignatius.

In the same way that St. Peter's name is associated with the Vatican, the name of Ignatius is connected to Antioch. We glean considerable knowledge of the early church from his writings. His passion for martyrdom, or as he put it, "to get to God,"[56] was well known. He wrote famous letters to churches in western Asia Minor at Ephesus, Magnesia, Tralles, Smyrna, and Philadelphia, as well as one to Rome and another to bishop Polycarp of Smyrna.

One of Igantius's primary concerns was unity in the church.[57] But his most lasting impact was his work on monepiscopacy, i.e., putting the collective leadership of the elders (*presbyteros*) under one bishop (*episcopos*). Although these two Greek words were used interchangeably in the New Testament and early church, Ignatius introduced a threefold hierarchy to assist with the administrative and spiritual oversight of the flock of God: the bishop was over the deacons and presbyters, who served as a council of advisors.

As new churches developed in a city, these parishes were assigned to the designated bishop and referred to as cathedrals (from the Latin *cathedra*, which is descriptive of a bishop's chair—usually with armrests). This setup is actually similar to the modern-day megachurch arrangement of one church comprised of various satellite "churches." In the early church, presbyters became known increasingly as priests (the ecclesiastical Latin term *presbyter* likely came into Old English as *pr ost* via the Dutch *priester* and German *Priester*). A bishop was thus empowered to ordain priests—though congregations had to ratify the act. The leading bishop in a large province was known as a "metropolitan bishop." The most influential metropolitans were those of Caesarea, Antioch, Alexandria, Rome, and (after 390) Constantinople.[58]

The Gospel to Constantine...and Rome

In AD 312, during the battle of Milvian Bridge for control of the Roman Empire, Constantine had a vision. In the sky he saw the Greek letters chi and rho—the first two letters of Christ's name in Greek. His chroniclers also recounted him seeing a message in Latin, *In hoc signo vinces*, translation: "With this sign, conquer."[59] The histories record that Constantine ordered a chi-rho symbol painted on his soldiers' shields. The next day they went out and won a decisive victory. Constantine thereby became the undisputed ruler of the entire Roman Empire.

Constantine's vision sparked within him a sympathy for the Christian faith—if not an actual conversion. A year after the victory at Milvian Bridge he issued the Edict of Milan, which made tolerance of Christianity the law. Following almost three centuries of intermittent persecution, this decree utterly changed the religious landscape (and profoundly altered the lives of Christians across the empire).

In AD 325, Constantine called the Council of Nicaea to end squabbles among church leaders over the nature of Christ. He wanted answers based firmly on the Bible, not upon traditions or fanciful interpretations (some of which had become full-blown heresies). The result was the council statement commonly referred to as *The Nicene Creed*. (The Council of Chalcedon would officially endorse an expanded form of the creed in 451.)

Constantine established his capital at the eastern end of the empire, in Byzantium on the European side of the Bosporus Straits near Turkey (modern-day Istanbul), renaming it Constantinople, after himself. However, he also cemented Rome's central place in global Christianity by building the ("Old") Basilica of St. Peter (Pope Sylvester I consecrated it in AD 326, but it took decades to complete).

In AD 380, Emperor Theodosius I, though ruling from Constantinople, institutionalized Rome's place in world affairs by passing an edict making Christianity (Roman Catholicism) the religion of the empire.[60] The edict begins: "It is Our will that all the peoples who are ruled by the administration of Our Clemency shall practice that religion which the divine Peter the Apostle transmitted to the Romans, as the religion which he introduced makes clear even unto this day."[61]

It is remarkable to stand in St. Peter's Square today and consider how Christianity has spread and changed over two millennia. Think of it: from a borrowed Upper Room in a house in Jerusalem to the ornate Sistine Chapel with its gorgeous artworks and great literary texts. At the center of the Vatican's plaza stands the repurposed Egyptian obelisk that the Roman emperor Caligula imported from Alexandria in AD 37. History buffs recall that Nero took it and positioned it at his hippodrome (which was just south of today's basilica). That, of course, was the place where countless Christians met their gory martyrdoms—including Peter and Paul, if the early sources are correct.

With the rise of Constantine (and for centuries afterward) Christianity moved from the fringes, always under the shadow of oppressors or foreign governments, to casting its own. The old adage comes to mind, "All roads lead to Rome." Indeed, Roman Catholicism dominates the Christian landscape globally today, 1.3 billion Catholics comprising some 50 percent of the world's Christians—with major growth in Latin America and Africa.[62]

We know the teachings of Jesus were endorsed by believers in Rome by the mid-first century.[63] How did the gospel get there? Luke records that some of those present at the Upper Room during Pentecost were "visitors from Rome, both Jews and proselytes" (Acts 2:10-11 ESV).[64]

The book of Acts also outlines three missionary journeys of Paul, each one taking the gospel message progressively further west. Acts concludes with the great apostle under house arrest in Rome.

From the New Testament texts themselves, and by early church documents along with pagan descriptions, legal conversations, and persecution accounts, we know that the gospel was being embraced all across the empire. By the end of the fourth century, the church had strong centers in both Rome and Constantinople.

The Rise of Monasticism

Pachomius (d. 348) was a non-Christian from a small town in southern Egypt. Forced unhappily into the army as a young man, he met some Christians who treated him kindly. The experience had such an impact on Pachomius, he made a vow to serve others if he were ever able to leave military service.

When he was unexpectedly discharged, Pachomius found a Christian mentor and underwent baptism. Later he moved into the desert to study under an anchorite teacher (i.e., a monk who had withdrawn from society to devote himself to prayer and solitude).

Eventually he built his own shelter in the desert and his brother John joined him in his new ascetic life. It was about this time that Pachomius had his famous vision during which an angel urged him to serve mankind. When Pachomius initially resisted this call, the vision came again, perhaps triggering memories of the vow he had previously made (while in the military) to serve others.

Pachomius built a basic monastery and began recruiting members. After some initial growing pains, the community grew, eventually comprising nine separate monasteries. His sister Mary started comparable communities for women. "In some areas in Egypt there were twice as many women monastics as there were men."[65]

Even as thousands fled to monastic communities in the desert, thousands more flooded into churches for baptism. Suddenly faith was fashionable. For the devout, these developments raised a troubling new set of *What now? What are we supposed to do?* questions. Specifically:

- *Could the church survive when it was no longer fighting for its life?*

- *Would those believers who had stood firm in the face of persecution now succumb to the opposite temptations of social acceptance and an easy life?*

- *How does one live as a true follower of Jesus in a culture that embraces and champions a weak and superficial Christianity?*

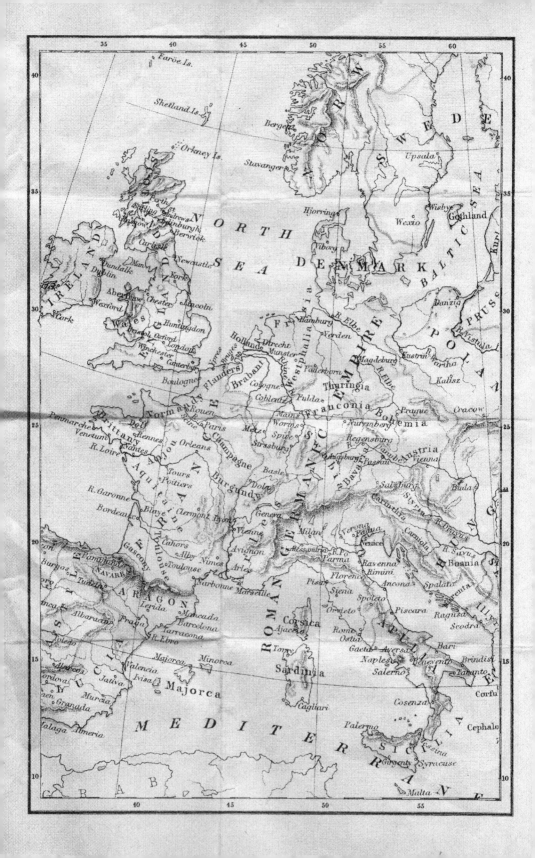

CHAPTER TWO

BIG CRISES AND BIGGER CHANGES

EUROPE

The God who made the world and everything in it....
is not far from any one of us.
"For in him we live and move and have our being"
(Acts 17:24, 27–28).

—*the apostle Paul declaring the gospel of Christ in
Athens, Greece, in the mid-first century*

The Reformers did not see themselves as inventors,
discoverers, or creators.
Instead they saw their efforts as rediscovery.
They weren't making something from scratch
but were reviving what had become dead.

—Stephen J. Nichols,
The Reformation *(Wheaton: Crossway Books, 2007, p. 17)*

It was the 9/11 of ancient Europe.[66] But instead of Twin Towers falling, it was a whole city that collapsed (some would argue an entire empire).

Shocking. Unthinkable. Visigoth hordes under the leadership of Alaric, rampaging through the Salarian Gate on the north side of Rome, then hooting and looting their way through the so-called eternal city—the first successful invasion in eight hundred years.

Terrified Roman citizens fled in every direction, carrying the grim news all over the empire.

Across the Mediterranean, in the coastal city of Hippo, North Africa, "a slim and beardless figure, with a shaven head and sharp features, watched the arrival of...troubled refugees."[67] As the esteemed Bishop of Hippo, Augustine fielded numerous questions from concerned believers: Why would God allow such calamity? Could Christianity survive now that the empire that had protected it since Constantine was no more? Was this the beginning of the end of the world?

Meanwhile, others, far from worrying about the fate of the faithful, actually blamed *Christians* for Rome's fall. (They noted—correctly—that the Goths weren't "barbarians" in the usual sense of the word. In fact, these invaders embraced a non-Trinitarian version of the Christian faith. That would explain why, before departing Rome, they took all the religious artifacts from their plundered treasures and carefully left them in the churches dedicated to the apostles Peter and Paul.)

Sitting down at his desk in Hippo, the brilliant Augustine set about interpreting and explaining these world-altering events. The result was his spiritual classic *City of God*, published in sections between AD 413 and 426. In this landmark work, Augustine argues that humanity is comprised of two distinct groups of people, "one that lives following man, the other that lives according to God, and about which I might call two cities, that is, two societies, of which one is predestined to reign eternally with God and the other to undergo eternal punishment with the devil."[68]

Ironically, even as Augustine wrote, the Vandals—who were Arian Christians like the Visigoths—were amassed at *his* city's gates.

Meanwhile, the shock waves of Rome's collapse were also being felt all the way to the eastern end of the Mediterranean. In his little office inside the Church of the Nativity in Bethlehem, Jerome, the man who had translated the Bible into Latin for the Catholic church, was pacing and wringing his hands. One modern collection of sources captures how distraught he was: "My voice sticks in my throat, and, as I dictate, sobs choke me.... The city which had taken the whole world was itself taken."[69]

☧

Comprehending the astonishing growth of the Christian faith against the dramatic sweep of historical events like this—the endless political zigs, the countless cultural zags—can be confusing. It's a bit like viewing van Gogh's *Irises* at the J. Paul Getty Museum in Los Angeles. Lean in too closely, focus only on the painting's lower right corner, let's say, and all you see are intricate dabs of mostly purple and green oil paint. Take a few steps back, however, and a big, vibrant garden comes into focus.

It's stunning to consider that such beauty was produced in an asylum, a place of immense pain and suffering. For that reason, van Gogh's masterpiece is an apt metaphor for the story of Christianity's spread into and throughout Europe.

Out of chaos, eternal loveliness.

☧

Before we step back from the innumerable details that fill the canvas of Christianity's long, historic spread through Europe and see a bigger picture—seven major developments that caused the church to expand there—let's quickly review how the gospel first made its way from Jerusalem to Europe.

The Gospel's Journey to Greece and Rome

In the New Testament book of Acts, the first-century historian Luke[70] wrote that Peter's famous Pentecost sermon was heard by "visitors from Rome, both Jews and proselytes" (Acts 2:10-11 ESV). It's only logical to assume these new believers in Jesus carried the message of his perfect life, sacrificial death, and mind-boggling resurrection back home. Indeed, ample evidence suggests the teachings of Jesus were being taught and followed by believers in Rome by the mid-first century.

Luke also recorded his eyewitness accounts of the apostle Paul's missionary journeys into Greece (Acts 16:6-10), beginning in the early fifties. Among the significant cities visited were Philippi, Thessalonica, and Berea (Acts 17). In those places, and others, Paul established and nurtured some of Europe's first Christian communities. According to Acts, some of these converts later joined Paul in other Greek cities, like Corinth, to assist in the spread of the gospel (Acts 18 and 20).[71]

Paul's New Testament letters mention that some of the first-century Greek churches provided financial aid to the churches of Judea—indicating the strength of the Christian faith outside of its country of origin.[72] Also in the New Testament, we read of Aquila and Priscilla joining Paul in Corinth from Italy, again demonstrating the spread of Christianity. According to Suetonius—a biographer of the Roman emperors writing around AD 120—Claudius had expelled all Jews believing in *"Chrestus"*[73] (Christ) around AD 49, the year before Priscilla and Aquila met Paul in Corinth (Acts 18).[74] Paul later noted their return to Rome *after* this imperial edict was lifted (Romans 16:3–4).

Luke concludes his Book of Acts with Paul under house arrest in Rome, awaiting his appeal before the emperor. According to the book's final chapter (Acts 28), the apostle was given much freedom to minister to all those who visited him. Evidence suggests both he and the apostle Peter were martyred in Rome in the mid-to-late-sixties.

According to Pliny the Younger, by AD 111–133, Christian converts in Roman territories were disrupting the marketplace by not buying the meats used in pagan rituals. Credible reports of persecution throughout the European territories also attest to Christianity's spread.

In short, by the end of the second century, Christianity was an identifiable movement in Europe. By the end of the third century, it was an established one. By the time of the Edict of Milan in AD 313—which gave legal protections to adherents of Christianity—it is estimated that between five and seven million Europeans were Christians.[75]

With so many people coming to faith, and with influential "Christian hubs" in Jerusalem, Antioch, Alexandria, Constantinople, and Rome, the church of Jesus Christ badly needed some organization.

This became the impetus for the first of seven significant developments in ancient European Christianity....

Establishing Rome as a Spiritual Center

In AD 380, Emperor Theodosius I did something emperors like to do: He issued an edict. This particular decree made Christianity the official religion of the empire.[76] The edict begins:

It is Our will that all the peoples who are ruled by the administration of Our Clemency shall practice that religion which the divine Peter the Apostle transmitted to the Romans, as the religion which he introduced makes clear even unto this day.[77]

Here is one of the most important historical developments in Christian history: Rome's rise to spiritual prominence. The claim of papal authority rests, of course, on the argument that Jesus gave *Peter* the keys to the kingdom (Matthew 16:17–19)—and on the related insistence that each of Peter's successors was, in turn, the undisputed leader of the church.[78]

The church's assertion that Peter was martyred and buried in Rome explains the construction of St. Peter's basilica.[79] In the fourth century, Constantine built a special chamber, the "Memoria," over St. Peter's alleged burial site, designing it so that pilgrims could lower personal items and have them touch the holy relics below.[80]

In truth, this early era of Christian history was not always pretty. In horrific contrast to the gospel of Jesus as practiced by many of the faithful, Pope Damasus (366–84) slaughtered his rivals and took power. He solidified Rome as the faith's governmental and institutional home, and he became something of a marketer. He commissioned the previously mentioned scholar Jerome to translate the Bible into Latin, the common language of the people. (This edition was later termed the Vulgate.) Damasus established Rome as a destination for Christian pilgrimages, hoping to show that, "The faith adopted by Constantine and his successors was no longer an upstart, but could be a religion fit for gentlemen."[81]

And while the bishops in Rome organized, the believers all over Europe evangelized. Edward Gibbon, a rationalist "unsympathetic to Christianity,"[82] famous for writing about the decline and fall of the Roman Empire, noted that while "that great body was invaded by open violence, or undermined by slow decay, a pure and humble religion gently insinuated itself into the minds of men, grew up in silence and obscurity, derived new vigor from opposition, and finally erected the triumphant banner of the Cross on the ruins of the Capitol."[83]

Kenneth LaTourette, former chairperson of Yale University's Department of Religion, wrestled with the mystery of how the Christian faith managed to surpass all the cults and philosophies that competed for supremacy in the Graeco-Roman world. He concluded that Christianity's rise was due to a number of factors, among them the endorsement of Constantine, the disintegration of Roman society, the church's inclusiveness toward all races and classes, Christianity's answers for the Graeco-Roman world's big questions about the connection between matter and spirit, and the moral qualities demonstrated by the faithful.[84]

LaTourette concluded that there was also an enormous *spiritual* factor in Christianity's spread. In short, "Something happened to the men who associated with Jesus."[85] They had front-row seats to his remarkable life and his terrible death. Then the apostles become absolutely convinced that he had risen from the dead, with the result that they became relentless, unstoppable witnesses. Nothing short of martyrdom managed to shut them up. Even then, their faith and courage were contagious. Succeeding generations of converts took up their cause, and took the gospel everywhere.

This is how, despite disintegrating as a political power, Rome became the epicenter of Christianity in the early centuries of the Modern Era. It's why some 1.3 billion people, or about half the world's professed Christians, are Roman Catholic today.

As Rome's religious influence increased, it wasn't long before the papacy and various political powers became intertwined—across much of Europe. The Roman Empire was followed by the *Holy* Roman Empire. Voltaire charged that this marriage of church and state "was in no way holy, nor Roman, nor an empire." Nevertheless, in claiming divine favor and authority in matters both spiritual and temporal, this alliance shaped life for millions, religious and irreligious alike.

This political-spiritual arrangement officially began with the German King Otto I in AD 962—though some point all the way back to the papal coronation of Charlemagne in AD 800. Under it, the Pope was viewed as supreme ruler over spiritual matters on earth, while the reigning emperor had authority over all temporal affairs. It might have seemed a tidy arrangement on paper; however there were always power struggles between emperors and popes. These alliances and allegiances often proved fragile, as in the case of Henry VIII, king of England and Ireland from 1509-1547. When Henry wrote a treatise entitled *Defense of the Seven Sacraments*, protesting the Protestant doctrines of Luther, Pope Leo X gave him the title "Defender of the Faith." Later, when Henry broke with the Catholic Church over his desire to divorce Catherine of Aragon and marry Anne Boleyn, he lost his title and the Holy Roman Empire lost a kingdom—England became Anglican. These sorts of squabbles limited the Empire's ability to expand.

Until 1648, the Holy Roman Empire's territories generally included Austria, Bohemia, Germany and Moravia, parts of northern Italy, modern Belgium, Switzerland, and the Netherlands. In that year the "Peace of Westphalia" effectively ended the dominance of the Holy Roman Empire. Nonetheless, the Empire continued in name and maintained considerable power for over a century. It dissolved in 1806.

The Proliferation of Religious Orders

Around AD 500, Benedict, a young Christian in Nursia, Italy, was inspired by reports from the vibrant monastic communities in Egypt. Consequently, he moved into a cave to begin a new life as a hermit. As word of his spiritual devotion spread, others joined him. In 539, Benedict relocated his growing "order of monks" (eventually known as the Benedictines) to Monte Cassino. In dramatic fashion, he destroyed a pagan altar there and established a new community on that same site.

Benedict is best known for his famous "Rule." This was a kind of written blueprint for how his new community of monks would function. It set forth what was expected from members of the order: a lifelong commitment and unflinching obedience. It also spelled out what adherents could expect: a daily life marked by eight prayer times each day (a figure derived from reading Psalms 119:62 and 119:164), strict—but not harsh—discipline, rigorous labor, and simple fare. Over time, the discipline of study also became part of the Benedictines' regimen.

It's true that throughout the early Christian history of Europe there was frequent interaction between the established monastic communities in Egypt, Syria, Jerusalem, and Rome. But few if any would dispute the fact that it was Benedict's order at Monte Cassino that forever changed the landscape of the Catholic Church…and culture at large. The

Benedictines gained prominence as an order through the patronage of William of Aquitaine (910) at the powerful monastery of Cluny in France. Benedict's "Rule" became the default "standard operating procedure" for monastic life in many orders, and it attracted such notables as Venerable Bede and Boniface (680–754).

Boniface's efforts are worth mentioning briefly. He established numerous Benedictine monasteries in the eighth century, especially in the German territories. His spiritual reputation became legendary after the incident of the Oak of Thor at Geismar.[86] There he allegedly chopped down the pagan, sacred tree, then reminiscent of the Old Testament prophet Elijah's "battle" with the Canaanite god Baal (1 Kings 18), and dared the god Thor to strike him down. Afterward he allegedly built a church from the timber of the fallen tree. One version of the story alleges that this took place on Christmas Eve. After stopping the pagans from sacrificing a child, he chopped down the great oak, pointed at a small fir tree nearby, and likened it to the Christ child. That, according to this particular legend, is how Christmas trees became part of the annual Christmas celebration.

In addition to the Benedictines, a number of other orders began to spring up in Europe:

The Military Orders brought a unique dynamic to the history of Europe and the spread of Christianity.

The Knights Hospitallers (also known as the Knights of the White Cross and the Knights of Jerusalem) were established in 1113 to assist Christian pilgrims. They were easily distinguished by their black robes, which featured a white cross.

When Saladin (1138–1193) and his Muslim successors captured Jerusalem, the Knights Hospitallers were forced to relocate. They became the Knights of Rhodes (1309–1522) and later the Knights of Malta (1530–1798), eventually morphing into a naval force that protected against Muslim piracy. Reestablished in 1834, they continue today as the Order of Malta.

The Knights Templar, recognized in 1128, also protected pilgrims. Linked to Bernard of Clairvaux, Templars assumed the Benedictine monastic life off the battlefield and were easily identified by a red cross on their white habits. The order included four ranks: the heavily armored *knights*, the *serjeants*, or light cavalry, the *farmers*, who oversaw temporal matters, and the *chaplains*, who ministered to the order's spiritual needs. The Templars' great financial gains also led to their persecution and eventual demise in 1312.

Germanic merchants funded the establishment of **the Teutonic Knights** in 1190 during the siege of Acre during the Third Crusade. The order received papal confirmation in 1199. Their white cloak emblazoned with a black cross easily distinguished them from other orders. Like many of the branches of knights, the order received a new rule in 1929 and now works alongside medical or caring institutions.

The Augustinians are not technically a religious order since they splintered into many separate houses or groups. Rather, this is the name given to those who follow the Augustinian Rule. Prominent Augustinians included Thomas à Kempis, author of the classic *The Imitation of Christ*—a text still used in many Christian universities and seminaries—and Martin Luther, the dominant voice of the Protestant Reformation.[87]

The Carthusians were an independent order, comprised of radical ascetics who practiced self-flagellation. They blended the hermitic lifestyle of the desert saints with monastic life by living in individual cells, taking vows of silence, spending long hours in prayer, wearing shirts made from hair (usually goat hair woven into a rough fabric—think "sackcloth," which signifies mourning), and forego-ing meat. The numbers of adherents, never great, grew and then de-clined in the thirteenth century.

The Carmelites of Mt. Carmel in Palestine originally claimed heritage in Elijah. Like Anthony and the desert fathers, this remote group influenced religious life in Europe, and much of the world. They founded an order of Carmelite nuns in 1452, and Teresa of Ávila led a major revival and expansion of the order's convents in the sixteenth century. John of the Cross, later the author of the clas-sic *The Dark Night of the Soul*, was among those drawn to the Car-melite contemplative life. Enamored with the "shoeless spirituality" of St. Francis of Assisi, he and Theresa founded the Discalced (from Latin *dis*, "without," and *calceus*, "shoe") Carmelites (as opposed to the more relaxed Calced rule).

The Cistercians are actually a Benedictine Order. Among its key members were Benedict XII, Eugene II, and his mentor, Bernard of Clairvaux, who advocated the veneration of Mary. The Cistercians advocated a simple life, though not quite as austere as their contem-poraries at the Carthusian monasteries.

Mendicants (from the Latin *mendicare*, which means "to beg") were ascetics who supported themselves through begging. As the church grew wealthy, mendicants took vows of poverty and kept no personal or corporate possessions. The prominent mendicant orders are the Dominicans, Franciscans, Augustinian Hermits, and after 1245, the Carmelites (discussed above). The Jesuits are often seen as mendicants, even though they are officially listed as clerics not friars.

The Dominicans were founded by St. Dominic in Spain in 1216. Because they are also called "The Order of Preachers," their mem-bers have O.P. after their names. Their primary purpose was and is to teach and defend the gospel. The order figured prominently during the Inquisition and helped to lead the Scholastic movement. Prominent members included Thomas Aquinas and St. Catherine.

Franciscans follow the rule of St. Francis of Assisi. They were established under Innocent III (1202) into three orders: the Friars minor, the Poor Ladies (Clares), and the Brothers and Sisters of Penance. Notable members of this order include Bonaventure, Duns Scotus, William of Ockham, Roger Bacon, and Nicholas of Lyra.

The **Augustinian Hermits**, known today as the Augustinian Friars, are a mendicant order and not to be mistaken for the Augustinians mentioned above. Today they number nearly three thousand worldwide and are notable for maintaining a representative in the United Nations as a nongovernmental organization (NGO).

The Jesuits were founded in 1540 by Ignatius Loyola (d. 1556) and are a product of the Catholic Reformation of the sixteenth century. Officially known as the Society of Jesus, the Jesuit order was established to (1) Reform the church through education; (2) preach the gospel to unbelievers; and (3) Fight the Protestant heresy. While this order took traditional vows of poverty, chastity, and obedience, the primary emphasis was on obedience. As the church's spiritual "Green Berets," they achieved phenomenal success for the papacy and the reformed church. Furthermore, as confessors and spiritual directors to kings, Jesuits exerted great political influence.

Amazing to think all these religious orders can be traced back to Peter's sermon in Jerusalem, and his martyrdom in Rome!

If you ever get the chance to cruise the eastern Mediterranean, do your best to see the ruins of Arsuf Castle and Châteaux Pèlerin on the coast of Israel, and Kyrenia Castle and Kolossi Castle on the island of Cyprus. And if you're not the cruising type, here's a spoiler: the reason for these intriguing remains—that date back to the late twelfth and early thirteenth centuries—is found in the mind-boggling, messy story of…

The Battle of Tours, Followed by the Christian Crusades

Here's a good lesson from European history: if you're being invaded by a fierce enemy, it helps to have a military leader on your side with the nickname "the Hammer."

This is what happened at the Battle of Tours in AD 732. No other battle during the Middle Ages had a bigger impact on the history of Europe, and perhaps the world. This victory certainly influenced the spread of Christianity. Here's how:

Following the death of Muhammad in 632, vast territories began coming under Islamic control via military conquest. The Berbers swept through northern Africa, conquering Carthage in 698. Spain fell under Muslim control in 711. Next, Islamic forces, under the leadership of Abdul al-Rahman, crossed the Pyrenees and into the heart of Europe. Charles Martel (a name that means "the Hammer"), a duke and prince in the Merovingian dynasty, led his army of Frankish foot soldiers against the invaders, defeating them in 732. This victory effectively prevented the Muslim conquest of Western Europe.

It did not, however, end religious and military tensions between Islam and Christianity.

Attacks on Christian pilgrims visiting parts of the Holy Land under Muslim control were becoming commonplace. In 1009, the Church of the Holy Sepulchre—thought by many to be built over the very sites where Jesus was crucified and (temporarily) buried in Jerusalem—was destroyed by al-Hakim bi-Amr Allah, the Fatimid caliph of Cairo. Other holy sites in Palestine were also wrecked. Though Christians would later be permitted to rebuild these shrines and resume their pilgrimages, these desecrations, plus other stories of (alleged) Muslim atrocities, were widely reported. Such events stoked a desire to bring all "sacred real estate" back under the church's control.

Other factors were at work.

There were desperate appeals for help from Christians under siege. For example, the Byzantine Emperor Alexius I Comnenus appealed to the Pope for help in repelling Muslim attacks. Hearing such reports were large numbers of Christianized but restless warrior-types—like the Vikings and Magyars. Suddenly these career soldiers found themselves with the opportunity to do the one thing they had been trained to do—fight.

In addition, there was a powerful spiritual component to this "perfect storm"—the Roman Catholic teaching that one could atone for sin by doing acts of "penance" (i.e., performing good works). This doctrine led to the granting of indulgences. These were essentially promises of forgiveness and eternal life, given in exchange for monetary contributions and/or dying for the cause of Christ. In AD 1063, Pope Alexander II gave a special blessing to the Iberian Christians, and granted an indulgence to any person fatally wounded while fighting the Muslims. In 1075 this policy become the official position of the Roman Catholic Church. As we might imagine, such doctrines helped in recruiting Crusaders to fight against Islam on behalf of the Christian faith.

The stage was thus set for a major show of piety and patriotism.

And thus began the grim period of the Christian Crusades (1095–1291). The Battle of Tours may have been a Christian defense against a Muslim invasion of Europe, but the Crusades were overt forays into Muslim-controlled territories. And they included the building of "crusader fortresses."

At least nine crusades ensued…

The **First Crusade.** Following Alexius's request for assistance fighting the Seljuk Turks, Pope Urban II stood at the Council of Clermont (1095) and challenged all Christians to join a war against the Turks. "Christ commands it," he urged, before promising, "Remission of sins will be granted.... I, being vested with that gift from God, grant this to those who go."[88]

One of those inspired was Peter the Hermit, an ascetic hermit from Amiens, north of Paris. He recruited some twenty thousand women, men, and poor knights. Then, while he was fetching supplies in Constantinople, his ragtag group of "peasants and idealists" were slaughtered at Civetot (Civitot).[89]

The "real" crusaders—i.e., trained and experienced knights from central and southern France, Normandy, and Norman Sicily[90]—fared much better. And yet, despite the fact that European Jews had helped finance many of the participants, the crusaders attacked Jewish communities all along the way. Arriving in Jerusalem in 1099, they massacred many Jews—contributing to mistrust between many Christians and Jews that lingers to this day.

In addition to reclaiming the holy sites, the conquerors established small crusader states at Edessa, Tripoli, Antioch, and Jerusalem. However, these enclaves of zealous Christians had little lasting effect and eventually fell to aggressive and angry Muslims after the crusades ended.[91]

The **Second Crusade** is associated with Bernard of Clairvaux (d. 1153). In 1144, reacting to the Muslim conquest of Edessa, he called for a new crusade, saying, "The knight of Christ, I say, is safe in slaying, safer if he is slain. He is accountable to himself when he is slain, to Christ when he slays."[92] This particular "holy war" proved impotent.

When Saladin, sultan of Egypt, recaptured Jerusalem in 1187, Pope Gregory VIII called for the **Third Crusade.** During this disastrous endeavor, the Holy Roman Emperor Frederick I drowned in Cilicia, and a Saracen "whistleblower" named Beha-ed-Din claimed that at the siege of Acre, Christians murdered three thousand bound Muslim prisoners "in cold blood," as retaliation for Muslim mistreatment of Christians.[93] Both religions had bloodied their hands, jointly casting an unpleasant hue on any responsible historical canvas.

In 1202, Innocent II, the most powerful medieval pope, decided to free Jerusalem from Muslim control by going through Egypt. However, the Venetians providing maritime transport for Innocent's crusaders coerced them first into sacking the cities of Zara and Constantinople. As a result, this **Fourth Crusade** featured a horrific massacre (1204) of Eastern Christians at Constantinople by Western Christians! This event permanently split Eastern and Western Christendom.[94] In 2004, Pope John Paul II apologized for this atrocity, saying, "How can we not share, at a distance of eight centuries, the pain and disgust."[95]

The spoils from this crusade included everything from gold and precious gems to the most prized possessions of all—holy relics. Two of the most popular items were the alleged crown of thorns from Christ's crucifixion and "doubting" Thomas's finger (supposedly the one used to touch the wound in the side of the resurrected Christ [John 20:24–28]).

The **Albigensian-Waldenses Crusade** (1209) was launched against heresy, not Islam. A group in southern France known as the *Cathari* (the "pure" ones), or the *Albigensians* (because many lived in the French town of Albi), was attacked because they embraced Manichean dualism: the belief in a god of light (Truth, of the New Testament), and a god of dark (Error, of the Old Testament).

This crusade also targeted the Waldensians—another unorthodox group that followed the radical ascetic teachings of Peter Waldo, a merchant in Lyon, France. The sect survived these attacks only because some Waldensians fled to the Alps of Savoy and Piedmont, and others managed to make their way to central Europe.

The **Children's Crusades** (1208 and 1212) consisted of large groups of children and teens marching east toward Jerusalem. Many died along the way; others were sold into slavery.

The **Fifth Crusade** (1217–1221) focused on Egypt and accomplished nothing of lasting consequence.

The **Sixth Crusade** (1228–1229) resulted in Frederick II, via diplomacy, gaining temporary control of Jerusalem, Nazareth, and Bethlehem. In 1244, however, Jerusalem fell to the Asian Turks and would remain in Muslim hands until 1917.

Louis IX of France, famous for building the Sainte-Chapelle (Holy Chapel) in Paris to house religious relics like the aforementioned crown of thorns, was an unsuccessful crusader. He was captured (and ransomed) during the **Seventh Crusade** against Egypt (1248); he died of dysentery in Tunis during the **Eighth Crusade** (1270).

King Edward I of England led the **Ninth Crusade** (1271). His efforts in Syria were of little consequence, and they ended after a truce the following year. The fall of the remaining Crusader States—Antioch in 1268, Tripoli in 1289, and Acre in 1291—effectively ended the large-scale Crusades. As noted, these military campaigns did little good and much harm.

The importance of Islam's rise for the history of Christianity cannot be overemphasized. The Muslim attacks not only weakened the Byzantine Empire but also paved the way for the creation of the Carolingian Empire in Europe. The Islamic capture of the ancient Christian centers of Jerusalem, Antioch, Alexandria, and Carthage left only Constantinople and Rome to contend for preeminence in the Christian world. It was this situation that enabled the development of a separate medieval Christendom in the West under Charlemagne and his successors.[96]

The Carolingian[97] Renaissance

If you could time travel back to the early ninth century and have lunch at the royal palace in Aachen, you'd enjoy a multi-course meal (no doubt featuring some kind of roasted meat brought in on spits) with dinner guests from a host of nations. While you ate, you might be serenaded or hear a reading—perhaps a history of the great deeds of men of old,[98] or possibly a selection from *The City of God* by Saint Augustine.[99] Presiding over this daily cultural extravaganza? Charles I.

Numerous rulers played crucial roles in the spread of Christianity during the Middle Ages—but none bigger than Charles. In fact, Pope Leo III's unexpected crowning of Charles I as "Emperor of the Romans" on Christmas Day, AD 800, proved to be a hinge point of history.

Like all leaders, Charles was a complicated man. And he wasn't called Charlemagne (or Charles the Great) for nothing. He possessed great ability. He was driven by a great appetite for learning and a great desire to see the church flourish. He was also marked by great contradictions.

Charles—his given name was Carolus—became king of the Franks in 768, and king of the Lombards in 774. Following the prolonged Saxon Wars, 772–803, Charlemagne subdued the Saxons and forced them to confess Christianity.

Evangelism by coercion is unthinkable to most Christians today, but it was an integral part of Charlemagne's reign. At Verden (southern Germany) in 782, Charlemagne had some 4,500 Saxons executed in a single day for refusing to convert. Perhaps, Italian historian Alessandro Barbero argues, he was merely trying to follow the path of biblical kings.[100] Whatever his reason, this much is sure: Charlemagne's letters overflow with religious sentiments, suggesting he possessed either deep—though misguided—commitment to Christ and his church…or a rare gift for holy hyperbole.

Various contemporary accounts of Charles's coronation by Leo exist.[101] Some speculate that the event was an attempt to give him legitimacy in the eyes of the conquered Saxons.[102] It certainly proved monumental in precipitating a series of maneuvers between the East and the West, and between the papacy and the French kings. "It… symbolized a new ordering of the Western world. Charlemagne's empire did not survive as a political unit, but it retained a certain cultural coherence. Thenceforth there would be a distinctively European civilization, different in character from the Byzantine culture to the East and the Moslem culture to the South."[103]

Deeply influenced by Augustine's *City of God*, the powerful Charlemagne became a patron for Christian scholarship. He recruited the Anglo-Saxon scholar Alcuin of York, who implemented the trivium (the teaching of logic, grammar, and rhetoric) and quadrivium (the teaching of arithmetic, geometry, astronomy, and music) in the palace school, a practice that ultimately influenced education throughout Europe.

Charlemagne also had a remarkable influence on European literature, commissioning Alcuin to oversee the preservation of ancient documents, the revision of handwriting styles, and the reworking of the Latin Bible. He further ordered that every parish should have a school (and he funded such church-school construction throughout Europe). He improved the education of clergy, and he revised standard liturgies.

In addition to Alcuin, Charlemagne surrounded himself with learned advisors from other cultures. "He liked foreigners, and was at great pains to take them under his protection."[104] Likewise, he went to extraordinary efforts to have great relationships with foreign leaders "that he might get help and relief to the Christians living under their rule."[105]

From Aachen—on the western border of Germany—the central headquarters of his massive territory, Charlemagne "cherished the Church of St. Peter the Apostle at Rome above all other holy and sacred places, and heaped its treasury with a vast wealth of gold, silver, and precious stones."[106]

Perhaps to a greater degree than any other sovereign in history, Charlemagne was head over all things in his day. He was a warrior of great gifts, a patron of learning, the kindly master of the church, and the preserver of order. When he died, he ruled all of modern France, Belgium, Holland, nearly half of modern Germany and Austria-Hungary, and more than half of Italy and northeastern Spain. He expanded his kingdom as conqueror, but stabilized it as benefactor and educator.[107]

Charlemagne's Carolingian Renaissance is viewed by some scholars as the "most pioneering" of the renaissances. It manifested "fresh and invigorating elements of Greek, Semitic, and early Christian culture" within the "virtually unbroken continuity with Rome."[108]

However, before we leave our discussion of the man credited with shaping "European" culture for Christ, let's not forget the ugly realities of his misguided religious passion. Against the backdrop of all those new schools and a better-educated clergy are the ghastly beheadings of unwilling converts.

The Protestant Reformation

People like to say that lightning never strikes twice in the same place. No one ever points out that one strike is usually enough to do the trick.

This was certainly the case in the life of Martin Luther (b. 1483). A law student from a middle-class German family, Luther found himself trapped in a fierce thunderstorm in 1505. When he was nearly struck by a lightning bolt, he cried out to St. Anne, the patron saint of travelers. Trembling fearfully, he swore he'd become a monk if only the Almighty would spare him. He believed God did precisely that, so months later, true to his word, Luther joined the Order of Hermits of St. Augustine.

Despite earning a doctorate in theology and engaging in a life of rigorous religious discipline, Luther wallowed in guilt. Devoid of any sense of peace with God, he was spiritually and emotionally miserable until he began to read and study what the New Testament teaches about salvation.

Almost immediately he began noting inconsistencies between biblical passages (in Galatians and Romans, especially) and official church doctrine. When he learned that some church officials were extracting money from fearful, uninformed church members through the selling of *indulgences* (i.e., the church's written promise of forgiveness in exchange for the payment of a sum of money), Luther became furious. He fired off a detailed list of reasons why such beliefs and practices were wrong, and nailed them to the church door in Wittenberg. These "Ninety-Five Theses" were a bolt of spiritual and cultural lightning. Long before the Internet, Luther's post went viral (when local printers began circulating copies throughout Germany).

Luther was ordered to take back his statement. He refused, prompting Pope Leo X (r. 1513–1521) to order him to stand trial for heresy before a civil court. At the famous "Diet of Worms," Luther was again given the opportunity to renounce his sharp attack against the church. He boldly refused, stating, "I cannot, I will not recant. Here I stand. I can do no other, so help me God. Amen!"

The Diet declared Luther a heretic and an outlaw of the Empire. Fearful that the Holy Roman Emperor Charles V might harm Luther, Frederick, the Duke of Saxony, had some of his own men dress up as royal soldiers and "kidnap" Luther. While the rest of Europe assumed that the emperor had killed Luther, the duke placed him in secret, protective custody at Wartburg Castle.

For about a year, Luther disguised himself as a local farmer and spent his time translating the Bible into the German vernacular so that everyone might have direct access to God's truth. Luther's Bible not only aided the education of the laity, it also helped the development of a national language and spurred German patriotism. Although Luther never meant to leave the church or incur the disfavor of the Pope, that's exactly where his words and deeds led him.

☧

Luther might have been the most *famous* protester against questionable church beliefs and practices; he surely wasn't the only one. Many were outraged by the moral and ethical lapses of assorted church leaders during the Middle Ages. Modern historians note: "Most of the other ninth and tenth century pontiffs were worldly figures. Several were assassinated, and abuses like simony (purchase and sale of church offices) and clerical marriage were commonplace....this was the low point in the history of the papacy."[109]

In addition to robust theological debates and less-than-pious leaders, the faithful of the Middle Ages were also forced to wrestle with two historic splits, or schisms within the institutional church. The first occurred in 1054 when medieval Christianity essentially divided into western and eastern branches—the Latin Roman church (headquartered at Rome) and the Greek Orthodox (centered at Constantinople), respectively. Fueled by political and religious tensions, this split resulted in differences in theology, practice, ritual, calendar, structure, and culture.[110]

Unlike the Latin church, the Eastern church never embraced some of the "lightning rod" doctrines and practices that ultimately fueled the Protestant Reformation in the West: the concept of purgatory, and the infallibility and supreme power of the Pope. For these, as well as geographic reasons, the Reformation left the Eastern Church essentially untouched.

Another split, the Great Schism of 1378, came about due to papal decrees that "outside of her [the Catholic Church] there is neither salvation nor the remission of sins," and that "...it is absolutely necessary for salvation that every human creature be subject to the Roman Pontiff."[111] The result was rival popes, and a spike in calls for church reform—which would ultimately culminate in Luther's protest.

Religious infighting aside, there were also powerful socio-economic factors coming to a head in the sixteenth century. These involved the laboring poor (who were more likely to be disenchanted with the religious status quo), the middle class (those with more autonomy in business affairs and desires for that same kind of freedom in their religious lives) and royalty (those ruling families who recognized the institutional Church as a threat to their wealth and power).

Luther's teachings influenced society at large, not just the "church world." Emboldened by Luther's statements against wicked leaders, the uneducated peasant class rose up.

In June 1524 a massive revolt broke out near the Swiss frontier. Urban and agricultural laborers demanded the complete abolition of serfdom, the end of oppressive taxes and tithes, clergy reform, the confiscation of church property, and basic privileges such as the right to cut wood in forests owned by the landed aristocracy.

The poor who expected Luther's support were soon bitterly disappointed. He wrote a tract entitled *Against the Murderous, Thieving Hordes of the Peasants*, in which he called upon the nobility to put down the unlawful revolt. The German authorities did, crushing it with ferocity. Historians have estimated that as many as 100,000 peasants were slaughtered.

At the same time, Luther endeared himself to the upper classes. In 1520 he wrote his *Appeal to the Christian Nobility of the German Nation*. He argued that unless the princes destroyed papal power in Germany, reform would never come about. These words fell on welcome ears. Many princes otherwise confused by or indifferent to the complexities of the religious issues were swayed by patriotism. One can therefore argue cogently that Lutheranism played a role in the development of German nationalism.

In the end, Holy Roman Emperor Charles V lacked the resources to oppose Protestantism effectively within Germany. So in 1555, he agreed to the Peace of Augsburg, officially recognizing it. Each German prince was given authority to determine the religion of his territory. Dissidents, whether Lutheran or Catholic, had to convert or leave.

Lutheranism spread very quickly into Scandinavia, Flanders, and Switzerland (thanks largely to Ulrich Zwingli). In some of these new areas, its ideas were challenged and changed. Soon it became clear that the reform movement begun by Martin Luther would lead, not to one separate church, but to multiple Protestant sects.

The Anabaptists were just one of the groups who sought to take the Reformation even further. They renounced infant baptism, and called for all who joined their number to be re-baptized (hence the name *Anabaptists*). Largely from the lower classes in urban areas, the Anabaptists called for a complete separation of church and state. As we'd expect, they consequently suffered terrible persecution at the hands of both Catholics and other Protestants.

In Geneva, John Calvin (1509–1564) played a key role in tweaking Luther's theology and popularizing it. He was a brilliant young man, entering the University of Paris at the age of fourteen and receiving a master of arts degree at the age of eighteen. From Paris he went to the University of Orleans to study law. There he came under the influence of the disciples of Martin Luther and converted to Protestantism.

In 1541, he established a theocracy in Geneva, which according to contemporary theory meant divine rule through reformed ministers and civil magistrates. Very quickly Geneva became the model of Christian community for sixteenth-century Protestant reformers. While Luther subordinated the church to the state, Calvin made the state subordinate to the church. He also succeeded in arousing Genevans to a high standard of public and private behavior. Austere living, religious instruction for all, public fasting, and evening curfew became the order of the day. Dancing, card playing, fashionable clothes, and heavy drinking were strictly prohibited.

The social and economic applications of Calvin's theology—which stressed the depravity of humanity and the sovereignty of God—made Calvinism the most dynamic force in sixteenth- and seventeenth-century Protestantism.

The Catholic Reformation and Counter Reformation

If, in the words of Pope Leo X, the great Reformer Martin Luther was a "wild boar" creating havoc in the Lord's vineyard, then numerous other "piglets" were also rooting around inside the church grunting loudly for change. The question on everyone's minds was: Would the Catholic Church reform itself and stem the tide of Protestantism?

Yes it would. The Catholic Reformation is the movement that began prior to 1517 and sought renewal through stimulating new spiritual fervor. The Counter Reformation was an effort in the 1530s to slow (or halt) the spread of Protestantism. These movements were not mutually exclusive, and after about 1540 they progressed simultaneously.

From these concerted efforts came five important developments:

1. The Spanish Inquisition

2. The establishment of new religious orders

3. Missionary activity

4. A renewed emphasis on education

5. The Council of Trent

The Spanish Inquisition. In 1469, Ferdinand of Aragon and Isabella of Castile married and made the kingdom of Spain a fiercely Catholic state. (Some would argue that "fiercely" is putting it mildly, for beginning in 1478 and lasting three centuries in some form, the Spanish Inquisition persecuted between 100,000 and 200,000 alleged heretics, executing as many as 5,000.)

In 1492—a date typically associated with the voyage of Columbus

—the monarchs captured Muslim Grenada and launched a persecution of non-Catholics. Conversion or banishment was the grim choice offered to both Muslims and Jews. (Even as Columbus set sail from Castile, throngs of non-Catholics were being deported from the same port city.) Even in new territories like Mexico, "apostolic inquisitors" carried out heresy trials. The sad irony is that within twenty-five years of Hernán Cortés's landing in "New Spain" (i.e., Mexico) in 1519, 131 people were condemned for heresy—many of them natives who were likely new Christians.[112]

New Religious Orders. A central component of the Catholic Reformation was the creation of new religious orders. For example, in the fourteenth century, the Brethren of the Common Life began in the Netherlands. Rather than rail against weaknesses in the Church, this order of lay leaders advocated for living out the faith simply and practically. Instead of focusing on the kind of scholastic—and humanistic—thinking that they felt dominated the Church, the Brethren practiced the *devotio moderna* (or new faith) that said, "The essence of Christianity is a spiritual communion with God through Christ." Instead of academic logic, "Scripture reading and an internal spirituality were essential."[113] The group promoted devotional reading, and produced fine manuscripts.

In 1514 (three years *before* Luther posted his "Ninety-Five Theses") a new order called the Oratory of Divine Love began in Genoa with the blessing of Pope Leo X. The term *oratory* in this context denotes speaking, reflecting, praying, and confession.[114] Members sought to live out what one *devotio moderna* member wrote—*The Imitation of Christ.*[115]

Because of their work among the poor, the sick, the orphaned, and widowed, this and similar orders—like the Capuchins who took vows of poverty—won favor among the people. Ironically, Bernardino

Ochino, the superior of the Capuchins and one of the most famous preachers of his time, converted to Protestantism, and fled Italy in 1542 for Calvin's Geneva! Even so, "the order survived...and so did the movement."[116]

Missionary activity. The famed explorer/conquistador Hernán Cortés (d. 1547) was commissioned to discover new lands and acquire new riches for Spain. In so doing, he was also expected to export the Catholic faith. Deeming the Church's regular clergy as aloof and impassive, he wanted simple friars who would work closely with the people and preach in a highly emotional vein.[117] On his expedition to Mexico, Cortés took two mendicant friars with him, and he asked for more.

> His argument was that the friars would live in poverty, and would be able to set a good example for the natives, whereas the secular priests and prelates would live in scandalous luxury and would not be actively interested in the conversion of the Indians. In response to this request, twelve Franciscans went to Mexico. On their arrival, Cortez knelt and kissed their hands. But their task was not easy, for there was great resentment against the Spanish and their religion among the Indians. On the other hand, it seemed clear to the Indians that the Christian God had defeated their own gods, and therefore many Indians, while not forgetting the violence being done against them, rushed to request baptism, thus hoping to gain the support of the powerful Christian God.[118]

In nearly every territory missionary priests had to counter the atrocities done at the hands of the conquistadors. Father Juan de Estrada Ravago, the renegade Franciscan, gave of his own means to help the natives and settlers in Costa Rica. In Colombia the Dominican Luis Beltran exhausted himself advocating for justice, and Pedro Claver became an early version of Mother Teresa, ministering to slaves, people in squalor, and even establishing a leprosarium. The result?

"By the end of the sixteenth century, most of the original inhabitants of Central America called themselves Christian."[119]

An emphasis on education. Accompanying this missionary zeal to claim new territories—like Mexico (New Spain) for the Catholic Church—was a renewed interest in education, for both priests and laity. Franciscan Juan de Zumarraga "had a printing press taken to Mexico—the first in the Western hemisphere—and with it printed many books for the instruction of the Indians."[120] He later helped start the University of Mexico.

The Society of Jesus (i.e., the Jesuits), meanwhile, focused on the top down, instead of with the parishioners themselves. Founded by Ignatius Loyola in 1540, the order's role in fighting the spread of Protestantism often overshadows its enormous role in spreading Christian education across Europe. The order's philosophy was to "give purpose and direction to basic human passions—harmony with the Catholic doctrine of free will."[121] Its influence was incalculable.

The Council of Trent. Meeting intermittently between 1545 and 1563, this convocation was the Church's official and most formal attempt at reform. It did not satisfy all expectations—chiefly, it was unable to foster reconciliation with the Protestants. However, for four centuries the doctrinal and disciplinary legislation of Trent served as the basis for Roman Catholic faith, organization, and practice.

Among other things, the council established the Scriptures and Tradition as the ultimate sources for religious truth and authority in the church. It also confronted ancient abuses, forbidding the sale of indulgences, forcing clerics to give up their mistresses, and requiring each bishop to visit every church in his diocese at least every two years.

Why did reform take so long? The answer is found in the personalities of the popes themselves, their preoccupation with political affairs in Italy, and the incredible difficulty of reforming a complicated bureaucracy like the Roman Curia. For example, Pope Leo X (1513–1521) opened his pontificate with the words, "Now that God has given us the papacy, let us enjoy it." This typified the attitude of many of the Renaissance popes.

Unfortunately, Leo's successors weren't exactly able to "enjoy" the papacy, thanks to a certain king named Henry VIII…

The English Reformation

Henry's problems with the Church began when he tried to obtain an annulment of his marriage to Catherine of Aragon. By 1527, Henry was convinced that the relationship—which had produced numerous miscarriages and stillbirths, only a single daughter, Mary, and no male heirs—was cursed by God. Perhaps more importantly, Henry had also fallen in love with Anne Boleyn, one of the women of his court.

Normally, securing an annulment on the grounds of a wife's failure to produce a male child would not have been a problem. This had been done many times in the past; however, nothing about Henry's situation was normal.

In truth his marital mess was a royal soap opera set in a minefield of prior papal decrees (considered infallible), tricky family connections, and high-stakes political ramifications. The result, predictably, was inaction. When he got sick of waiting, Henry called an assembly of the English clergy and, through threats, induced them to recognize him as the head of the Catholic Church in England. Henry next pressured Parliament in 1534 to pass the Act of Supremacy. This law declared the English king to be the "Protector and only supreme head of the church and clergy of England."

Henry then appointed Thomas Cranmer, an avowed Protestant, to be the new Archbishop of Canterbury, traditionally the highest Church office in England. The two of them jointly declared Henry's marriage to Catherine to be null and void. And the next thing anyone knew, Anne Boleyn was queen.

In creating an Anglican Church, Henry wasn't attempting to bring Protestantism to England. He was far too conservative theologically (i.e., still too Catholic) for that. He simply wanted to divorce and remarry, and to do that, he needed to control the Church in England. All that changed initially was a rejection of the Pope's authority to decide matters of faith on British soil.

It was Henry's *third* wife, Jane Seymour, who finally gave him a son. Upon Henry's death in 1547, this male heir, Edward, assumed the throne (as a child). By the time Edward died in 1553 at the tender age of sixteen, Protestant beliefs were slowly gaining popularity in England.

Enter Mary Tudor, the only child of Henry and Catherine of Aragon. Mary had been raised by her staunchly Catholic mother. Consequently, as queen she determined to return England to the arms of the Holy Mother Church. In so doing, she earned the nickname "Bloody Mary"...in large part by burning some five hundred Protestant "heretics"—including Thomas Cranmer—at the stake. (Her nickname proves a bit harsh in the light of the masses Protestant leaders killed, often other Protestants.)

When Mary died in 1558, Elizabeth Tudor, the daughter of Henry and Anne Boleyn, ascended the throne. Though raised as a Protestant, Elizabeth's primary concern was re-establishing a national sense of order and stability. A true politician, she decided on a policy of moderation, refusing to ally herself with either the extreme Catholics or fanatical Protestants.

A significant aspect of the English Reformation was the progress that took place in the field of Bible translation. In 1382, John Wycliffe, desiring common people to have access to God's Word, translated the Bible from Latin into English. Authorities burned every copy of his Bible they could seize and banned the rest. In the early sixteenth century, William Tyndale began utilizing Gutenberg's remarkable invention—the printing press—to publish English Bibles in Germany, which he then smuggled into England. For these acts he was strangled, burned at the stake, and declared the "Father of the English Bible" (since the King James Bible scholars relied heavily on Tyndale's translation).

Other influential English Bibles followed—the Coverdale Bible (1535) and the Great Bible (1539), famous for having been chained to pulpits in churches across England. In 1560, English exiles fleeing to the European continent to escape Queen Mary's persecutions revised the Great Bible, and included notes from Protestant scholars like John Calvin and John Knox. The result was the Geneva Bible (1560)—which was later brought to America in the early seventeenth century by some of the Puritans.

In 1568, Elizabeth commissioned the Bishops' Bible as a kind of moderate response to the heavily Protestant Geneva Bible. And of course in the early seventeenth century, King James I assembled an all-star team of scholars to produce what would become known as the "Authorized Version" or King James Bible.

✼

"You will be my witnesses" and "I will build my church," Jesus had promised his disciples.

Perhaps no region on earth, according to the faithful, demonstrates the incomparable power of Christ to make good on his word more than the continent of Europe.

Indeed, the story of Christianity's spread to and throughout European cultures is a complicated narrative...a head-spinning mix of heroes and horrors, hubris and humility, holy things and heavenly places.

No matter where you go on European soil, you see reminders of the gospel and proof of Augustine's belief in "two cities"...the iconic Roman Colosseum; the exquisite Winchester Bible at Winchester Cathedral; the abbey at Monte Cassino, Italy, established by St. Benedict, then used by the Nazis and bombed by the allies in World War II; the three heretics' cages hanging from the church steeple in Munster, Germany; the severed head[122] of Oliver Plunkett, a seventeenth-century Irish martyr, on display at St. Peter's Catholic Church in Drogheda, Ireland; the magnificent Rose windows of Notre Dame Cathedral in Paris, dating to the thirteenth century, which have survived wars, revolutions, and in early 2019, a devastating fire.

Up close it's an indecipherable mess of seemingly random events. When we step back and look, though, we see it...out of all the chaos and pain, a strange, coherent beauty.

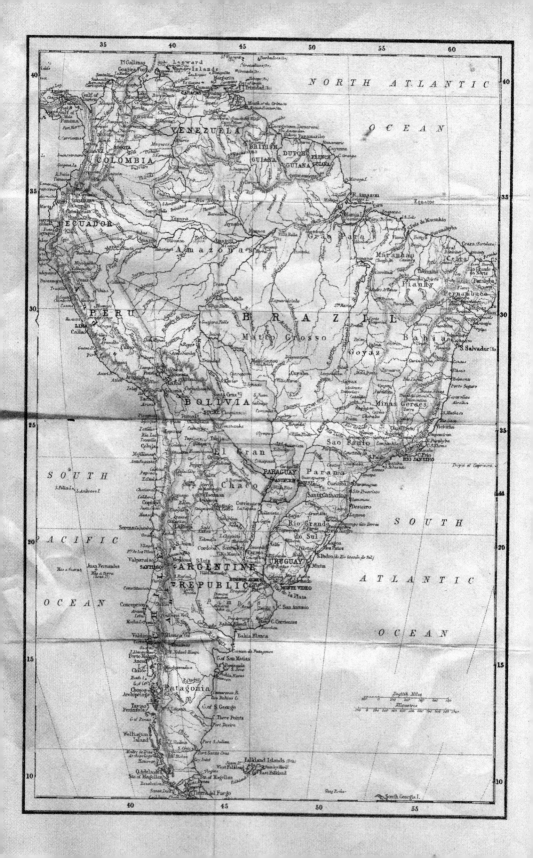

CHAPTER THREE

CHRISTIAN CONQUISTADORES

LATIN AMERICA

We came here to serve God and also to get rich.

Bernal Díaz del Castillo (d. 1584)
Reflecting on his explorations
in Latin America with Cortés

A few years before Martin Luther ever thought of nailing anything to the church door at Wittenberg, Germany, an obscure believer five thousand miles across the Atlantic Ocean was already hammering on the church. Hammering *hard*.

Why was Antonio de Montesinos—who lived on an island paradise in the Caribbean—so worked up?[123] Because for almost two decades—beginning with Christopher Columbus's discovery of the "New World" in 1492—"Christian conquistadores" (how's that for an oxymoron?) had been flooding into Latin America in order to evangelize and/or exploit (depending on your perspective) the indigenous peoples there.

Like Luther's "Ninety-Five Theses" (which would send shockwaves through the church when posted in 1517), the riveting sermon of de Montesinos in 1511 stunned audiences in both Latin America and Europe. It began with a verbal thunderclap, "I have climbed to this pulpit to let you know of your sins, for I am the voice of Christ crying in the desert of this island, and therefore, you must not listen to me indifferently, but with all your heart and all your senses...."[124] Following that bruising introduction, the message was a mash-up of the Hebrew prophets Elijah and Amos, with a little Jonathan Edwards' "Sinners in the Hands of an Angry God" mixed in to lighten the mood.

This little-known event from history prompts numerous questions: How did the message of Christ get from Jerusalem to a small island in the Caribbean? How did Columbus—who once was the toast of Spain (and popular enough to have a holiday named after him)—come to be seen a pariah? What factors account for the astonishing spread of Christianity in the Americas?

(In truth, to speak of "the astonishing spread of Christianity in the Americas" is sort of like mentioning "the exciting voyage of the *Titanic*." One short, breezy phrase doesn't begin to capture the event. We must be global Christians with a global vision because our God is a global God to tell the full, complicated, often regrettable story.)

You likely learned the poem in elementary school:

In fourteen hundred and ninety-two,

Columbus sailed the ocean blue.

He had three ships. He left from Spain.

He sailed through sunshine, wind and rain.

The poem goes on in warm couplets like this, speaking about how brave Columbus was, and how nice the natives were. It mentions snoring sailors, the search for India, and multiple transatlantic crossings.

But it glosses over—or completely leaves out—key details of the story. It very easily (and very honestly) could have included stanzas along the lines of:

> Those Spaniards sailed and they were bold.
> (And in their hearts most dreamed of gold.)
>
> Carried west by ocean breezes,
> They also brought some strange diseases.
>
> Once on shore, they raised their voices,
> Gave their hosts some brutal choices...
>
> "Repent and let the Spirit fill you.
> Get baptized now, or we will kill you.
>
> "And if you trust that Jesus saves,
> You'll get to come and be our slaves!"

You get the idea. The arrival of European "Christians" in the Americas (and their impact over the ensuing decades and centuries) was not an Instagram moment for the people of God. The eminent historian Justo Gonzales has summarized that era grimly but accurately, "In the name of Christ, thousands were slaughtered, millions enslaved, entire civilizations wiped out."[125]

The whole sad, sorry episode brings to mind the observation—often attributed to Dorothy Sayers—that God has endured three great humiliations in carrying out his plan to rescue our sin-scarred world: (1) the *incarnation*—the infinite Creator entering his own creation as the human infant Jesus; (2) the *cross*—the Holy One willingly sacrificing his life for sinners; and (3) the *church*—God staking his mission and reputation on a motley group of not-always-so-Christ-like Christians.

What can we say? Big chunks of the history of the church are *not* for the squeamish. And yet, looking at the church in Central and South America in 2019—perhaps as vibrant and strong as anywhere else on earth—the faithful simultaneously claim that the power of God can turn messes into miracles

It would be nice to think that the voyage of Columbus came about this way: One morning in 1492 during a devotional time (or royal chapel service), the Spanish monarchs Isabella and Ferdinand read (or heard) the Lord's words in Matthew 28:18–20 and were pierced to the heart. Filled with a holy desire to see all people everywhere find new life in Christ, they immediately leveraged their imperial power. They summoned an adventurous explorer named Christopher Columbus to the palace and commissioned him to sail "the ocean blue" in search of hidden peoples who had never heard the good news.

What a wonderful thought! (And also naïve and wrong…)

The actual backstory is as follows…

Columbus and the Conquistadores

Because Columbus was Italian—and a devoted Catholic—he benefited from papal connections. Because of his nautical expertise and bravado, he was able to gain the trust and secure the backing and blessing of the Crown of Castille (i.e., Queen Isabella and King Ferdinand in what is modern-day Spain). Promised the title "Admiral of the Ocean Sea," the governorship of any new territories he discovered, and 10 percent of whatever treasures he could get his hands on, Columbus and company set sail in 1492 aboard three ships: the *Santa Maria* (the expedition's flagship), and two smaller vessels, the *Niña* and the *Pinta*.

On October 11, the weary sailors spotted land, and when Columbus stepped ashore, he named this new territory San Salvador ("Holy Savior") and claimed it for the Spanish crown. However, this was neither Asia nor India—the desired destination of Columbus's mission—but only a small island, one in a chain of islands (i.e., the present-day Bahamas).[126]

The explorers continued west, reaching and making landfall in Cuba, but finding no real riches. (They did, however, pick up a new habit from the locals: smoking tobacco leaves.) Heading east from Cuba, the expedition came to another large island, which Columbus named Hispaniola ("little Spain")—and which we know today as Haiti and the Dominican Republic.

On Christmas Day, the *Santa Maria* hit a sandbar (or coral reef) offshore and was irreparably damaged. After negotiating with a local Taíno chieftain, Columbus ordered his men to dismantle the ship and use its timbers to build a fort nearby. This encampment, named La Natívida, was to be the temporary home to thirty-nine stranded sailors. Their instructions were to search for gold and wait for Columbus to return with reinforcements and more supplies.

Prior to arriving back in Spain, Columbus managed to send one of history's earliest press releases to his royal benefactors. Thanks to Gutenberg's newfangled printing press, portions of the explorer's "trip summary" were published and disseminated. Suddenly Columbus was a celebrity, a national hero. (Had there been paparazzi in the sixteenth century, they'd have been camped out at the port of Palos to capture his arrival. Even without paparazzi, there was much fanfare.)

In the letter, Columbus praised "his highnesses" (Ferdinand and Isabella) and wrote of his discovery and naming of San Salvador. He described meeting "Indians" (so-called because he mistakenly believed he had reached India), and he played up their response to his arrival:

> They all believe that power and good are in the heavens, and they are very firmly convinced that I, with these ships and men, came from the heavens, and in this belief they everywhere received me, after they had overcome their fear.

Columbus mentioned that he had taken seven of the "Indians" as slaves and would be bringing them back home. (Indeed, they were paraded through the streets for onlookers to gawk at.) The explorer further told his royal supporters that he would gladly return and take as many slaves "as they ordered to be shipped." At the same time, Columbus expressed his belief, in glowing terms, that these people—whom he labeled "idolaters"—would become Christians.

> Our Redeemer has given this victory to our most illustrious king and queen, and to their renowned kingdoms,

in so great a matter, for this all Christendom ought to feel delight and make great feasts and give solemn thanks to the Holy Trinity with many solemn prayers for the great exaltation which they shall have, in the turning of so many people to our holy faith, and afterwards for temporal benefits, for not only Spain but all Christians will have hence refreshment and gain.[127]

"Gain" was code for *gold*. Throughout Columbus's letter, mixed in with all the flowery religious sentiments, are tantalizing mentions of riches. Though he grossly exaggerated the presence of gold in the Bahamas—as well as spices and other valuable goods—Columbus possessed a keen understanding of the two things it would take to secure royal funding for future expeditions: lots of *reminders* of the heavenly streets of gold awaiting new converts, and *samples* (or at least believable *assurances*) of gold from the lands he was exploring.

Christ had told his followers in no uncertain terms: "No one can serve two masters; for either he will hate the one and love the other, or he will be devoted to one and despise the other. You cannot serve God and wealth" (Matthew 6:24 NASB). Nevertheless, this uneasy tug-of-war between gold and the gospel would accompany the spread of the Christian faith throughout Latin America.

Columbus's letter proved to be a smash hit. Within the year it had been translated into multiple languages and the Latin version ultimately went through nine editions—some with woodcut illustrations.

The tone of this letter suggests that Columbus was concerned with these people as humans and genuinely interested in helping them achieve salvation through conversion. It is equally clear, however, that Columbus believed it to be his and Catholic Spain's right and duty to subjugate and exploit these same people. Here we see a tension that continued throughout the Spanish colonial experience in the Americas.[128]

Because Columbus touched on every key theme—riches and righteousness, or "God, glory, and gold"—he got his funding. (This, despite the fact that he *hadn't* found a passageway to Asia, *hadn't* discovered any riches, and returned with only a few natives—and one less ship than he'd begun with!) Isabella and Ferdinand opened the royal treasury!

Therefore it was that in October of 1493 Columbus set out again with *seventeen* ships, more than a *thousand* men, plus a number of domesticated farm animals. In less than a month he and his party were back in Hispaniola (after briefly exploring other islands to the southeast).

What they found was horrifying. La Natividad[129] had been burned to the ground, and all its inhabitants were dead. Columbus learned that some of his men had mistreated the locals, even enslaving some of them and committing atrocities like rape. When the Taíno got fed up, they rose up.[130]

This proved to be a short-lived victory for the indigenous Taíno people of Haiti. Soon, all five of their kingdoms on Hispaniola fell to the Spanish invaders. Columbus moved his base seventy miles east and established Spain's first settlement in the Americas at St. Isabela, before moving again to Santo Domingo in 1496.[131]

The Genocide Studies Program at Yale estimates that when Columbus first arrived in Hispaniola there were several hundred thousand Taíno—possibly as many as one million. Twenty-two years later, due to brutal subjugation, massacres, and disease, only 32,000 Taíno survived.[132]

Columbus died himself in 1506, when he was only fifty-four. But before he sailed off into the great beyond, the famous explorer left an indelible mark on this world. His voyages irrevocably changed Western society—and not necessarily for the better. This is why Latin American history uses the arrival of Columbus in 1492 as a hinge point. Scholars speak of events as being either pre-Columbian or post-Columbian.

This is also why Columbus (even though he still has a national holiday named after him) isn't the most popular of historical figures. The same goes for all the other European explorers who followed in his wake to find gold and glory in the Americas.

☧

Some argue that the age of exploration—and specifically the conquest of Latin America—was merely "a continuation of the Crusades." They note that Spain and Portugal planted their flags not only in foreign soil, but also through the hearts of indigenous cultures that would never recover.

In 1513, Vasco Núñez de Balboa stood on the shore of the Pacific Ocean in Panama, claiming a remarkable "discovery" for the Europeans. Because it was the feast day of Michael the archangel, Balboa named this spot the Bay of San Miguel. In one hand he held his sword; in the other hand, a standard engraved with the Virgin Mary. After these pious religious expressions, Balboa proceeded to conquer the area's peoples and take their gold and pearls.

In 1521, Hernán Cortés (d. 1547) defeated Montezuma, and

plundered massive amounts of gold and riches from the Aztecs. The lavish wealth generated from Cortés's conquests was used to fund future efforts to spread Catholic Christianity throughout Central and South America. But that's not all. It also helped pay for the Spanish church's efforts to fight heresy back home via the Inquisition, expel Jews and Muslims who would not convert, and counter the growing popularity of Protestant theology.

For the longest time, Cortés, with help from writers like Cervantes, was regarded as a noble leader, akin to Julius Caesar. The general consensus was that Providence guided Cortés in wiping out the violent Aztecs (who were said to commit human sacrifice about as often as we moderns check our smartphones).

It turns out the reported numbers of human sacrifices (as high as fifty thousand according to Cortés's confessor) were grossly inflated. Alvaro Enrigue, writing in *The New York Review of Books* (2018), notes that such figures are preposterous, that they would mean "more than 137 sacrifices a day, five an hour, one every twelve minutes, twenty-four hours a day."

Matthew Restall, Director of Latin American Studies at Pennsylvania State University, notes how the perception of Cortés has changed over time:

> Any military occupation that directly or indirectly caused the deaths, in less than a century, of 90 percent of the population is hardly one to celebrate. It is true that Aztec civilization continues to be seen as a particularly bloodthirsty one, but the general assessment of it has also become more sophisticated. If Cervantes—a knowledgeable dissident in his time—lived today, he would recognize Cortés as a genocidal killer.[133]

It's for all these reasons that the name Cortés is reviled to this day by many Latin Americans. "Cortés" is a byword for the brutal military tactics that defined early Spanish presence in this region. Also, the explorer and his troops are blamed for the spread of smallpox in Latin America, which decimated the native population.

☧

Between 1533 and 1535, it was Francisco Pizarro's turn (d. 1541). He is famous for crushing the Incas of Peru. In some ways he's become a symbol for the confusing amalgamation of national interests in the New World and the twisted ideas about "aggressive" faith that emerged from the Crusades. Pizarro is described by historians as merciless and conniving, "the perpetrator of untold inhumanities." And yet, to the end of his life, he viewed himself as an upstanding Christian leader. In fact, as he lay dying from battle wounds he made, from his own blood, the sign of the cross on the floor so that it would be the last thing upon which he gazed in this world.[134]

Other explorers and conquistadores fanned out through Mexico, Central America, and South America to establish Spanish rule. With the settlement of Buenos Aires in 1580 the continental stage of Spanish expansion ended, and the newcomers concentrated on the occupation of the vast areas staked out earlier.[135]

When the smoke cleared, what was visible wasn't pretty.

> The civilizations of the Aztecs, the Incas, and the late Missippian cultures of North America were destroyed. While Europe had been foundering in the Dark Ages, the peoples of the Americas had established cultures with highly developed astronomy, mathematics, literature, and cosmology. Their books, their science, their cit-

ies and temples—all were destroyed in the effort to extirpate all forms of idolatry, as well as to subdue resistance by eliminating symbols of national pride and culture.[136]

One of those who worked to "purge" these native cultures of every vestige of their former religions was Juan de Zumárraga (d. 1548), the first bishop of Mexico. Under his leadership, priceless ancient texts and temples were destroyed to make way for Christianity.

We cringe at the loss of such artifacts, and yet...Zumárraga is also the one who introduced the first printing press into the New World. He also "laid the groundwork for the University of Mexico."[137] He is also credited with popularizing chocolate among Europeans. This would not be much consolation to the Mexicans who suffered under Spanish oppression.[138] Think of him next time you eat a Snickers bar.

It's jarring to consider Jesus at the Mount of Olives, just before his return to heaven, telling his disciples he would give them the power to be his witnesses "to the ends of the earth" (Acts 1:8)...and then to read a chapter like this one, describing the brutish "power" of so many unholy "witnesses" who came to the New World with a lust for territory, free labor, and gold. In short, the spread of Christianity in the New World included, sadly,

> ...a militant, violent confrontation of Western Christians with people holding vastly different views. The expansion of Christianity had a transforming, but not always positive, impact on the faith itself.... Alongside the material motivations for overseas enterprises was a clearly expressed obligation to spread Christianity. Conversion was an aspect of conquest.[139]

Thanks to Columbus and the other explorers mentioned, a huge, previously unknown land mass larger than Europe—and with no evidence of the gospel's prior presence—had to be taken into account. Although some Christians—devout European priests like Peter Claver and Bartolomé de las Casas—had a genuine desire to share the love of Christ with all these unreached civilizations, not all the pertinent parties (as we've seen) had altruistic intentions.

Motives—especially royal motives—were mixed. Suppose this New World discovered by Columbus *did* contain a shortcut to India that could bypass Muslim-controlled lands? What might happen to a nation's economy if its traders *were* able quickly to fetch the Asian silk and Indian spices so desired by the populace? Imagine if places like Haiti and Florida actually *did* contain rivers of gold and fountains of youth.

Given such questions, more and more transatlantic expeditions were commissioned. Meanwhile, as explorers continued searching for that elusive "express shipping lane" across the Americas to the Pacific, Spanish and Portuguese ships continued to dock and unload all sorts of marketable goods—everything from North American furs and Brazilian lumber to slaves and sugar cane. What's more, by the end of the sixteenth century all this aggressive exploration and colonizing had practically doubled the size of "Christian territories"!

While European Protestants had focused on *theology* (and attacking traditional Catholic views and practices), European Catholics had turned their full attention to *geography*. Spain and Portugal quickly realized that explorers (like Columbus) could expand their territories and fill their national coffers.

England was late to the colonization party. Although Henry VII had commissioned the explorer John Cabot in 1497—and Cabot had investigated some around Maine—Henry VIII was far too distracted. The thing he was most interested in exploring was the question, "How can I get a divorce so I can marry my mistress?" His marital drama (and the religious tension it generated) meant, in part, England simply did not engage in serious colonizing/missionary efforts in the sixteenth century. The one exception was the short-lived Roanoke colony in 1584 under Queen Elizabeth I.

Neither was France a major player in the sixteenth century rush to the New World. The French tried futilely to establish a few settlements before finally experiencing some lasting success in and around Quebec in the early seventeenth century. Of course, by 1750 the French controlled the massive territory from the mouth of the Mississippi River at New Orleans northward to Nova Scotia. By this time Latin America and large areas of North America were firmly in Spanish and Portuguese control.[140]

The Columbian Exchange

Change the names of the monarchs, the explorers (or conquistadores), and the lands being colonized, and the "Columbus story" was replayed repeatedly in Latin America. According to novelist James Michener—who lived for extended periods in Mexico—the European conquerors "discovered, occupied, developed and ruined" every place in which they set foot.[141]

The *Columbian Exchange* is the title often given the important historical back-and-forth between Europe and the New World at the time of Columbus. We're using and broadening the phrase here to frame the *ongoing interaction* between European Christianity and Latin American Christianity. Traditional historians have looked at a host of factors: agricultural, cultural, biological, economic, etc. Here we're focusing quickly on the birth, growth, and life of the Latin American church as an institution. What were the key events in the five-hundred-plus years since greedy European explorers and well-intentioned priests first came to the Americas in search of gold and souls, respectively?

We could say that Columbus triggered eight *exchanges* through which we can profile the spread of Christianity in Latin America. The region's history begins with the arrival of the "church militant" on American shores in the time of Columbus. It continues today with the "full-circle" arrival of the first Latin American pope in church history—Pope Francis I in 2013—in Vatican City to lead the same church! The first three exchanges explain the historical roots of Latin Christianity. The final five show the fruit of those events.

Spanish Christianity in the New World

For Spanish Christianity, 1492 was a banner year—and not solely because of the voyage of Columbus. In early January, the Castilian forces of Isabella and Ferdinand finally defeated the one remaining Muslim outpost in Granada, effectively reclaiming all of Spain for the Church. (This was the only place in Europe where the Crusades were truly successful.)

This hard-won victory emboldened the monarchy. Dissent was crushed. Loyalty to the Spanish crown was demanded—even over loyalty to Rome. In late March, the Alhambra Decree (or "Edict of Expulsion") was issued, giving all Jews living in Spain the ultimatum to convert to Christianity or leave. In August Columbus departed on his great adventure. Meanwhile, the Spanish Inquisition—begun in the late 1470s—was ramping up.

The year 1492 demonstrates how centuries of (a) fighting Muslim infidels (a campaign called the *Reconquista*) and (b) rooting out heretics had combined to produce an aggressive Spanish Christianity. It was this kind of combative faith that set sail for the New World. Royal objectives were clear: conquering peoples, colonizing lands, collecting gold and other wealth, and converting souls. Therefore "evangelism" by clergy and conquistadores was viewed through a militaristic lens. In many (if not most) cases, it was motivated by human power rather than divine love. Even so...

> It is important to realize that these men—soldiers as well as clerics—were not hypocrites. They truly believed that they were serving God. They became incensed when the inhabitants of the land could not perceive the superiority of Christianity. They had masses constantly said for salvation of their souls.... Hernando Cortes, the conqueror of Mexico, kissed the hem of the robes of the first Franciscan missionaries arriving at the newly conquered land. Obviously, to say that they were sincere does not mean that they were good—and even less that what they did was good. It does mean that they were convinced that in their deeds they were serving...God.[142]

The ones being conquered were not so convinced. History tells of the "Indian" leader named Hatuey who was appalled by the Europeans' insatiable, brutal quest for gold. He once used a basket of gold and jewelry to warn his people that the invaders are "innately cruel and evil." Pointing to the basket, he said, "Here is the God of the Christians."[143]

Hatuey eventually fled from Hispaniola to Cuba. When he was captured and offered baptism as a means of escaping hell, Hatuey reportedly asked, "Do Christians go to heaven?" When told that the good ones do, Hatuey replied that if that were the case, he'd just as soon go to hell.

Of this event (and many like it) the Dominican reformer Bartolomé de las Casas could only say that *this* was "the reputation and honor that our Lord and Christian faith have earned as a result of the actions of those 'Christians' who have sailed to the Americas."[144]

Spanish Practices in the New World

The Iberian (i.e., Spanish and Portuguese) explorers of the sixteenth century brought not only a "muscular" version of Christianity to American shores. They also brought three practices that greatly shaped the ensuing culture of Latin America: the *patronato real*, the *encomiendas*, and the *reducciones*.[145]

Patronato real ("royal patronage"). This authority, giving "the crown the right to make nominations for all American ecclesiastical posts, from priest to bishop,"[146] was granted in 1508 by Pope Julius II. Such a decentralization of power had enormous implications in the creation and ongoing life of the Church in the New World for two reasons: (1) it allowed for "an unparalleled union between crown and cross"[147] and (2) it essentially gave the Spanish monarch(s), rather than the Vatican, absolute jurisdiction over church structure in the Indies. In the words of Diarmaid MacCulloch, this amounted to a "papal abdication."[148]

Pope Julius II's successors found, to their immense regret, they were unable to "undo" this concession. It quickly led to "naked greed and brutality,"[149] and its effects were enduring. Long after the Americas had been "conquered" and millions of converts claimed (at least through token baptisms), the monarch continued to wield this sweeping authority. Thus the indigenous peoples and European settlers in the Americas were subject to royal prerogatives in every aspect of life.

Encomienda. This authority, bestowed by the Spanish crown, gave colonists the right to force natives to render service and pay tribute, essentially creating a feudal system. Though the holder of an *encomienda*—called an *encomendero*—was charged with treating his workers well, protecting and Christianizing them, "in reality, the encomienda was slavery."[150] To add to this indigenous labor force, the Spanish and Portuguese also imported African slaves.[151]

The system worked like this: new Spanish settlers in the Americas were required to read a document—in Spanish—called the *Requerimiento* to the non-Spanish-speaking people they were subjugating. This unintelligible (to the native peoples) communiqué set forth the absolute rights of the Spaniards in the New World and the expectation that the "Indians" would peacefully become passive subjects of the Spanish crown. The conquerors made clear that should the natives refuse to acquiesce to their authority, they would then, "with the help of God," wage war against them, and they would be within their rights to enslave men, women, and children.[152]

The encomienda, as much as any other factor, caused the destruction of indigenous civilizations in the Caribbean.[153] Those trapped in this brutal system found themselves at the very bottom of society. It is estimated that as much as 95 percent of some local populations were starved or worked to death by Spanish settlers.[154]

The irony in this detestable practice is that, centuries before, following the decline of the Roman Empire, Christians had led the charge *against* slavery. It was the church that helped bring about its eventual disappearance in all but the fringes of Christian Europe.[155]

Reducciones. The word reduction derives from the Latin word meaning "to lead back" or "to reduce." In Latin American history, it refers specifically to communal farms, and more broadly to a movement started by the Jesuits. The members of this religious order were convinced, for example, that the Guarani people of Paraguay had once known the true faith, but had been led astray by Satan. This idea derived from observed surface similarities between Guarani and Christian symbols and practices. The Jesuits' mission therefore became to "lead back" or "reduce" the Guarani to Christianity.[156]

To this end, the Jesuits established model communities in the wilderness regions of Paraguay, Brazil, and Colombia. On these remote farms, they offered hundreds of thousands of indigenous peoples protection from Spanish slavers. And in these *reducciones*— which were marked by intense organization and self-discipline (some critics would argue this strictly regimented life looked a lot like slavery)—the Jesuits sought to win converts.

In similar fashion Martín de Valencia (d. 1534) presented a different idea of what "conquest" in the New World could look like. He led a group of Franciscan friars into native lands and cultures in what historians have called a "spiritual conquest".[157] His group was known as the "Twelve Apostles of Mexico," and they engaged natives respectfully and taught and worked among them.

Spanish Saints in the New World

So far the story of "the spread of Christianity in Latin America" has been thoroughly bleak. Power-hungry monarchs. Greedy and violent conquistadores. Horrible people doing hellish things in the holy name of Christ.

While the conquistadores's ships brought Bibles and Christian priests to Latin America, most interactions with the people of the region were contrary to Christianity itself. (The old phrase comes to mind, "What you *are* screams so loudly, I cannot hear what you are *saying*.") It's estimated that because of the Spanish invaders, Central America alone may have lost as many as 24 million of its 25 million inhabitants!

Though the record is both appalling and embarrassing, it shouldn't be surprising. From start to finish the Bible makes clear that our fallen world is marked by evil and darkness and populated by sinners. The New Testament further shows that among those who claim the name "Christian," we will always find immature believers, worldly believers, and, yes, even "make-believers." Not the best advertisements for the gospel! But always, in every generation, we also find a remnant that possesses extraordinary faith—men and women who really do live—and love—like Jesus.

From a human standpoint it is only because of these faithful saints that the Latin American church managed to survive those first centuries—and eventually thrive.

Why, given all those terrible first impressions of Christianity, did millions of Latin Americans come to believe in the Christ of the Gospels? To answer this question we need to look at some of those heroes of the faith: missionaries who were voices in the wilderness, sometimes literally...renegade priests who tended to the humanitarian needs of the indigenous Indians and imported slaves.

Let's look briefly at several individuals who were advocates for the natives and/or slaves: Francisco de Vitoria, Bartolomé de las Casas, and Pedro Claver. We also need to remember the modern martyr Archbishop Oscar Romero from El Salvador, due to his place in the contemporary Latin American landscape.

Francisco de Vitoria (d. 1546)

An eminent thinker, writer, and debater in the early 1500s, Francisco de Vitoria was the chair of theology at the University of Salamanca, the premier educational institution in Spain. Through a network of connected colleagues he kept abreast of all "the news and information that was arriving from the Americas."[158] Because so many of the reports were so awful, Vitoria decided to use his "intellectual horsepower" to advocate for the oppressed people of Latin America.

His rejection of the authority of the *Requerimiento* document[159] was an absolute bombshell. Specifically, he argued that the Pope had no temporal power over Indian aborigines (or any other unbelievers). He further stated that a refusal on the part of native peoples to recognize papal authority was insufficient reason for making war on them or seizing their possessions.

In Vitoria's mind, the lands being infiltrated by Iberian conquistadores were foreign lands with autonomous, local governments—however primitive they may have been. He insisted that the "Indian" peoples were not sub-human (despite reports of cannibalism and human sacrifice) and that any enslavement or subjugation of such peoples was indefensible. He urged forceful intervention in the New World only in cases where human rights were already being violated—the most obvious example being human sacrifice.[160]

Vitoria's vigorous legal advocacy for vulnerable foreign populations earned him a distinguished place in the pre-history of modern international law.

Bartolomé de las Casas (d. 1566)

The name Las Casas is as familiar in Latin American culture as the names Lincoln or Kennedy are in North America. In fact, in lists of great Spaniards the name Las Casas is often not simply listed, but adorned with glowing descriptions. For example, in this history of the fall of Santiago, Las Casas alone is singled out for praise:

> This city for more than three centuries had been the Spaniards' own; round it were centered some of the proudest memories of the race. In its history were great dates, mighty names—Balboa, Cortez, Columbus, *Las Casas the humane, the almost saintly* [emphasis added]. From this harbor sailed on their memorable expeditions, Cordova, Grijalva, Cortez; at this port had touched De Leon, Pizarro, De Soto, and Christopher Estevan, in those old days when the New World was new.[161]

Why such reverence? Because Las Casas was a tireless advocate for native peoples. Even today his name is synonymous with humanitarianism.

It wasn't always this way. As a young man, Las Casas was a colonist, a dreaded *encomendero*, both in Hispaniola *and* Cuba.

Then, in 1514, at the age of forty, something happened to Las Casas that changed his life (and the lives of millions) forever. Stumbling upon this verse from the (apocryphal) Book of Sirach: "If one sacrifices from what has been wrongfully obtained, the offering is blemished; the gifts of the lawless are not acceptable" (34:18 RSV).

The following Sunday, the chastened Las Casas informed his stunned congregation he was divesting himself of the natives under his authority. Going forward, he would only serve and defend those he had previously subjugated.[162]

He joined a Dominican order and began fighting relentlessly for the Indians. He became the bishop in Chiapas, Mexico, where he tangled constantly with encomenderos in his congregation. He traveled back and forth to Spain to complain of abuses. He wrote extensively about native abuse at the hands of the Spanish. His most famous work? *A Short Account of the Destruction of the Indies*, a highly emotional document filled with jarring descriptions that evoke the kind of outrage seen in the biblical prophets:

> [The Spanish] snatcht young Babes from the Mothers Breasts, and then dasht out the brains of those innocents against the Rocks; others they cast into Rivers scoffing and jeering them....
>
> The Lords and Persons of Noble Extract were usually expos'd to this kind of Death; they order'd Gridirons to be placed and supported with wooden Forks, and putting a small Fire under them, these miserable Wretches by degrees and with loud Shreiks and exquisite Torments, at last Expir'd.[163]

Some of the numbers Las Casas recorded in his assorted works for native victimization were probably exaggerated, but the inhumane descriptions of Christian depravity in the New World are beyond dispute. Ultimately his work was instrumental in the enacting of *The New Laws*—an official (though largely ineffective) attempt to stop abuse of the Indians.[164]

In 1550 at Valladolid, Spain, at the behest of King Charles V, the elderly Las Casas engaged in a spirited, closely watched, days-long debate with Juan Gines Sepulveda, a renowned philosopher. The topic? The rights and treatment of Native American Indians in the New World. Las Casas' powerful arguments prevailed, and official policies were altered. "They did not, however, have an impact on the experience of Amerindians."[165]

Like all human leaders, Las Casas was flawed. Regrettably, in his impassioned opposition to the enslavement of Latin peoples, he recommended using African slaves instead. What can we say about this huge moral blind spot? Perhaps the better question to ask is what do we say about the logs in our own eyes (Matthew 7:5)?

Not all advocates for the indigenous peoples of Latin America were lawyers and/or high-ranking officials. Some were simple priests, like...

Pedro Claver (d. 1654)

In 1610 a young Jesuit named Pedro (aka "Peter") Claver felt a call to serve God in the New World. Leaving his native Spain he sailed to Cartagena in the Caribbean and became an ordained priest. Claver is worth mentioning because he was, in a real sense, the "Mother Teresa" of seventeenth-century Colombia.

Cartagena was a key city in the lucrative slave trade that had been flourishing in the Americas for about a century. With grim regularity slave vessels came and went, containing in their foul-smelling holds hundreds of kidnapped Africans. Some of these captives—often up to one-third—were already dead by the time the ships arrived. The rest—at best exhausted and emaciated, at worst diseased—often wished they were dead.

Fortunately, the first face seen by most of these terrified Africans was the kindly face of Father Claver. As soon as a ship docked, he (together with his interpreters and helpers) would board, go down into the hold, and begin ministering to the souls in chains. As the slavers unloaded their "human cargo," Claver and company would distribute water, clothing, fruit, and food. They bound wounds, offered brandy, administered medicine, and showed basic dignity. Only after such tangible expressions of love did Claver dare talk of God's love. He believed, "We must speak to them with our hands by giving, before we speak to them with our lips."

Early in this sacrificial ministry, Claver declared himself "the slave of the slaves forever."[166] By all accounts, it's a vow he kept to the end of his life. Because of such humble, tireless service, Claver reportedly baptized around 300,000 Africans during his forty years of ministry—and this during the time when the abuses of the encomiendas were rampant![167]

In caring for the arriving slaves in this way, some might argue that Claver was only preserving them for a bitter life of mistreatment and hard labor—with a vague assurance of heaven tacked on at the end. The slaves didn't seem to feel this way. Many—after their brutal experiences—fell at his feet in thankfulness for his kindnesses. They "called him their master, their protector, their father; never thinking they did enough to express their gratitude."[168]

Like other saints who appeared during the Latin American conquests—and there were more than we think—Claver's story is remarkable. Between slave ship arrivals, he prepared meals for those housed at the local leprosarium, or he tended to Africans who were caged on the docks. Such devotion brought him into conflict with white elites. Nevertheless, he remained a shining example of true Christianity in dark times.

Ironically, Claver spent his last days in the care of an uncaring slave! He often was left unclean, and in horrid conditions. But at the end, his room filled with pilgrims from all socio-economic classes, including both free and enslaved Africans.

The Roman church canonized him in 1888. That same year African slavery was abolished in Latin America.[169]

Archbishop Óscar Romero (d. 1980)

In the audio[170] a soft-spoken man celebrates Mass in Spanish. Suddenly, we hear a loud bang, a moment of stunned silence, then the sounds of hysteria and confusion.

The shocking 1980 assassination of Archbishop Óscar Romero at a hospital chapel in El Salvador is a fitting final stop in our quick (and woefully incomplete) tour of Central and South American "saints." The day before his death, during a radio broadcast, the popular Romero had appealed directly to the soldiers of the military civilian junta that ruled El Salvador through violence and fear:

> In the name of God, in the name of this suffering people whose cries rise to Heaven more loudly each day, I implore you, I beg you, I order you in the name of God: Stop the repression![171]

For this, the long-time crusader for human rights, the courageous champion of the poor, was gunned down by a sniper's bullet. Six days later, on Palm Sunday, some 250,000 Salvadorans attended Romero's funeral. This service too was shattered by gunfire (and explosions), leaving dozens dead and more than two hundred injured. These violent events triggered the nation's twelve-year civil war, which claimed the lives of more than 75,000 El Salvadorans.

Romero, often called the "voice for the voiceless," was far from the only priest murdered in this region and era. Before his death, in a pastoral letter he stated, "In less than three years, more than fifty priests have been attacked, threatened, calumniated. Six are already martyrs—they were murdered. Some have been tortured and others expelled [from the country]. Nuns have also been persecuted."[172]

In his death, Romero became a symbol of the best of incarnational Christian theology and self-sacrifice. Beloved by oppressed masses everywhere, it was only a matter of time (2015, to be precise) before the Roman Catholic Church declared Romero a martyr and beatified him. Three years later, the first Pope ever from Latin America—Pope Francis—wore Romero's bloodstained sash from 1980 in the ceremony that canonized the El Salvadoran as a saint.

Oninda and Justo Gonzalez speak of "the two faces of the Church in Latin America." One was the "dominant face" that "justified what was being done in the name of evangelism." The other was the face protesting injustice, "particularly against injustice in the name of Christianity," and "voices of prophetic protest that were seldom matched in the British colonies."[173]

It was this second face—the brave souls who criticized the Europeans' cruel treatment of indigenous peoples, and decried their love for gold and goods over God and the gospel—who are the real story of Christianity's staying power and growth in Latin America.

Let's turn our attention now to five long-term results from all those ships bringing Spanish conquistadores, Spanish practices, and Spanish saints to the New World...

Liberation Theology

In 1968, Pope Paul VI visited Latin America—the first-ever papal visit to the tumultuous region. He arrived, not surprisingly, by military helicopter. What prompted the pontiff to gather the Roman bishops of Latin America for a special meeting in Bogotá, Colombia? A new grassroots movement with big theological implications.

In the 1960s, something called *liberation theology* was sweeping through Latin America. This novel way of contextualizing the gospel in poor and oppressed cultures grew out of the same systemic poverty and injustice that Archbishop Romero would later decry. (Though Romero was more famous for protesting human rights abuses, and liberation theologians largely concentrated on the socio-political theories of Karl Marx.) In 1971, the Dominican friar Gustavo Gutierrez published A *Theology of Liberation*, the seminal text in this new tradition.

Liberation theology rejected Marx's atheist assumptions; however, it was very receptive to his analysis of social inequality and class struggle. According to this theological paradigm, Marx's secular presuppositions were problematic, but his analysis of the issues was regarded as an insightful critique on capitalist exploitation and power structures.

Some proponents of liberation theology were quick to point out its undeniably prophetic tenor. To hear them tell it, the Jewish prophets were preaching against the same exploitation and injustice that are the focus of Marx's analysis. Opponents were quick to note the absence of obvious social activism or political/economic agendas in Jesus's life or in the New Testament church. They warned against a Christianity that is so earthly minded, it's no heavenly good.

Protestantism

From the fifteenth through the eighteenth centuries, Latin American Christianity was exclusively Roman Catholic. The church held almost complete sway in governmental and cultural affairs.

In the early 1800s this began to change. European independence movements like the French Revolution and the American Revolution in the English colonies to the north sparked Latin American interest in similar freedoms—including religious autonomy. Increasingly, the new leaders of Latin American republics—liberal emperors like Pedro II of Brazil, for example—were open to new ideas, both political and religious.

This made Protestantism intriguing. Originating as something of an independence movement, it had "liberated" itself from an overly autocratic and "foreign" leadership—and it was *new*. Given the proliferation of denominations and movements within it, Protestantism seemed more adaptable, more open to dissent and debate. To some, the Roman church still possessed a controlling, medieval mindset. Rome, for example, had the "Index," an official list of prohibited books. Also, the church was too monolithic when considering controversial issues.

Given all that, in the early nineteenth century Bible societies began to appear in Latin America. As the region opened slowly to

Protestant influence, its spiritually progressive nature and its theme of "spiritual liberation" resonated and gained traction.

The Rise of Pentecostalism

Pentecost, by way of quick review, is the annual Jewish spring festival that celebrates both the early harvest and God's giving of the law to Moses at Sinai. For the Jews who believed that Jesus was the promised Messiah, this ancient feast took on new meaning shortly after his death, resurrection, and ascension into heaven.

While Jews from all over the world were gathered in Jerusalem to observe Pentecost, the Lord made good on his promise to "clothe" his followers "with power from on high" (Luke 24:49); he sent the Holy Spirit (John 16:7–15).

Due to the Spirit's miraculous enablement, those first followers of Jesus suddenly found themselves hearing a rushing wind, experiencing fire from heaven, and proclaiming the good news of Christ *in languages they'd never learned* (Acts 2). This supernatural event resulted in the conversion of three thousand Jews and is seen by most as the official birth of the Christian church. The book of Acts goes on to record other, similar miraculous works of the Spirit done through that first generation of believers—divine healings, dreams and visions, prophetic utterances and more instances of "speaking in tongues."

Fast forward to the early twentieth century. A small congregation of Christians in Los Angeles began reporting similar works of the Spirit. When the famous San Francisco earthquake of 1906 occurred, people began to flock to this group's meeting place on Azusa Street. A great revival broke out. Around the same time, similar experiences of the Spirit were being reported by Methodists in Korea, former Hindus in India, and elsewhere.

All these events together (and other outpourings of the Spirit) are regarded as the beginning of modern Pentecostalism, a form of Protestantism that also emerged in Latin America in the early 1900s.

Among those who helped popularize Pentecostalism south of the United States border was a Methodist Episcopal missionary named Willis Collins Hoover (d. 1936). He merged Pentecostal theology with Methodist ideas about church structure in Chile. (For this he was forced out of the Methodist Episcopal Church.)[174]

Gabriel Garcia was instrumental in the Mexican Pentecostal movement in the early twentieth century,[175] as was Ruben C. Ortega, who helped found the Apostolic Church of Faith in Jesus Christ, which now numbers more than a million members. Ortega became increasingly extreme in his views, leading one historian to describe him at the end of his life as being "clearly insane."[176]

In 1926, Eusebio Joaquín González helped found The Light of the World Church in Mexico. Members of this large, controversial church view themselves as "restorationists, believing that God has called them to restore primitive Christianity."[177] The church is now exporting its beliefs to the United States and elsewhere.

Bottom line, Latin American Pentecostalism, wildly popular now in its various stripes, has both ardent devotees and harsh critics. Among the latter, some note the celebrity (even near-messianic) status of some prominent Pentecostal pastors. Others express concern about the propensity of some in the movement to preach a prosperity gospel that all but ignores eternal issues of the soul and focuses instead on temporal health and wealth.

Latin American Evangelicalism

Luis Palau from Argentina is, arguably, the most prominent example of twentieth-century Latin American evangelicalism. Palau is a textbook evangelical, in that he focuses on preaching the gospel of Christ and trusting that it will gradually transform entire cultures as it first transforms individual hearts. Thus, instead of emphasizing economic, political, cultural programs designed to bring wide-scale liberation, Palau's evangelical model focuses on liberating people spiritually—one life at a time.

To reach the most people most efficiently, the standard evangelical ministry model has long been to organize a series of religious meetings (formerly called "crusades") in larger towns or cities. These gatherings involve hundreds or even thousands of people gathering (usually nightly) in a big tent (or arena or stadium) to hear gospel-centered songs and sermons. The goal of these meetings is to urge people to convert, to believe the gospel, and become followers of Christ.

Palau, who was educated at Multnomah Bible College in Eugene, Oregon, and became a US citizen in his late twenties, embraced this approach. Not surprisingly, the Argentinian evangelist is often referred to as the "Latin American Billy Graham," since he patterned his ministry after Graham's and even preached alongside him at times. Like Graham, Palau travels and preaches internationally—not just in Latin America.

In truth, Palau represents both aspects of our "Columbian Exchange." He's from South America, yet was educated in North America—where he embraced a very American style of evangelism.

Pope Francis

In March of 2013, Jorge Mario Bergoglio was elected to the papacy. Talk about historic! He was the first Pope to take the name *Francis* (after Francis of Assisi), the first Pope from South America, the first-ever Jesuit Pope, and the first Pope to announce his election to the world via Twitter.

Bergoglio was born in 1936 in Buenos Aires, Argentina, to Italian immigrants—and devout Catholics. As a kid he cultivated a cheerful spirit and a love for soccer and basketball. After earning a degree in chemistry, he worked briefly as a technician before deciding to enter the priesthood. He became a Jesuit, earned a degree in philosophy, and taught high school psychology and literature.

Following his ordination in 1969, he completed his training in Madrid, Spain, then returned to Argentina in 1972. For the next decade—during a time of grave political unrest—Father Bergoglio supervised other priests, traveled extensively, visited the poor, heard confessions, celebrated Mass, and taught catechism classes.

In 1982, he was ordained bishop of Buenos Aires—although he adamantly refused the pomp that usually came with the office. He insisted on walking or taking the subway, rather than being chauffeured. He asked people to refer to him simply as Padre Jorge.

Soon he became archbishop, and in 2001, Pope John Paul II designated him a cardinal. When John Paul died four years later, Bergoglio almost became the new Pope. However, the cardinals chose Joseph Ratzinger (aka Pope Benedict XVI) instead. Friends reported that Bergoglio seemed relieved not to have been elected—gladly returning to his regular duties.

In late 2011, just before his seventy-fifth birthday, Cardinal Bergoglio applied for retirement (a process that can sometimes take a couple of years). He began to dispose of his books and personal effects and was making plans to move into a retirement home in his hometown of Flores.

Before Bergoglio's resignation was accepted, however, Pope Benedict abruptly stepped down, citing health reasons—the first papal abdication in almost six hundred years. The following month, after two days of voting by the cardinals, the seventy-six-year-old Bergoglio was elected! The Pope's official Twitter account announced "HABEMUS PAPAM FRANCISCUM." The translation of this Latin phrase? "We have Pope Francis."

And thus we come full circle. The continent that eventually embraced the gospel of Jesus, in spite of all the terrible things that the Spanish Catholics brought with it, ended up supplying the world's 1.3 billion Catholics with a new leader.

Next we turn our attention to the continent to the north. In the sixteenth century the Spanish boldly sent out conquistadores to claim the New World in the name of the Catholic Church. In the seventeenth century, Protestant Puritans began traveling to the New World to *escape* the church, particularly the Church of England.

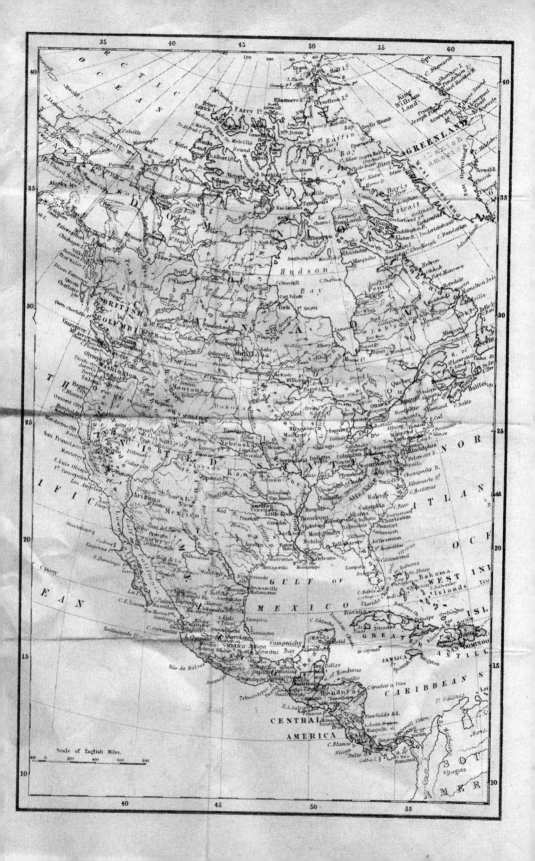

CHAPTER FOUR

GREAT AWAKENINGS AND
NEW VOICES

NORTH AMERICA

... for the Glory of God, and Advancement of the
Christian Faith, and the Honour of our King and Country,
a Voyage to plant the first Colony in the northern
Parts of *Virginia*...

The Mayflower Compact, November 11, 1620

From ancient times, Christians have used a *fish* to symbolize their faith.[178] They might have chosen a *boat*.

The great story of God is dotted with marine craft: Noah's massive ark...the fishing boats that ferried Christ and his disciples about the Sea of Galilee...the large merchant vessels that the apostle Paul used to traverse the Mediterranean in the first century...and those that countless Spanish friars boarded in the sixteenth century to cross the Atlantic to Latin America.

In the last chapter we saw Father Peter Claver eagerly boarding each new slave ship that sailed into the South American harbor of Cartagena, Colombia. At the same time—November of 1620—some 2,200 miles north, in the area we know today as Massachusetts, members of the Wampanoag tribe were warily watching a three-masted ship anchored off Cape Cod. For several weeks, the natives observed men from the ship coming ashore daily to erect some kind of crude settlement.

During this frenetic construction project—hurried due to the fast approach of winter—these seafaring newcomers encountered a member of the Pawtuxet tribe. To their astonishment, the man, named Tisquantum, spoke English (a skill he'd obtained from time spent in England, they learned). The settlers took to calling him Squanto, and he proved to be a godsend. He served as their teacher and tour guide. He offered practical farming advice as well as tips on where to hunt and how best to fish the area's waters. He further served as an interpreter and mediator during the group's interactions with other tribes.

Even with the invaluable assistance of the kindly Squanto, only about half of the approximately one hundred settlers survived Cape Cod's brutal winter. Those that did managed to build a viable colony. The following fall, to commemorate one year in the New World, they held a harvest celebration with members of the Pokanoket tribe. There's no evidence the attendees ate turkey and dressing, no chance that they watched football and took naps after their big feast. Nevertheless, this event is considered the genesis of our modern Thanksgiving holiday.

These newcomers were, of course, "the Pilgrims," their ship was the *Mayflower*, and these events were the beginning of the Massachusetts Bay Colony at Plymouth. This is the *best-known* settlement in what we know today as North America. It was not, however, the *first*.

For at least a century prior to the English Pilgrims settling at Plymouth, the Spanish had been trying, without success, to establish a foothold in North America. Juan Ponce de León explored Florida in the early sixteenth century. Tradition says he was hoping to find the mythical fountain of youth. History tells us that what he got instead was an arrow in the chest. Rushed back to Cuba—by ship, of course—the famed explorer died.

In 1526, Lucas Vázquez de Ayllón attempted to found a Spanish settlement near the South Carolina/Georgia border. It failed to get off the ground. Hernando de Soto came ashore at Tampa Bay in 1539, made a big exploratory loop north and west through what today is the southeastern United States. In 1542, a fever struck him down. In 1559, Don Tristán de Luna y Arellano tried to establish a colony in Pensacola, Florida. It unraveled. Repeated setbacks like these eventually prompted Spain's Catholic King Philip II to give up trying to conquer and settle Florida....

Until the monarch learned that some French Protestants (known as the Huguenots) had built a coastal fort—Fort Caroline—in what would one day be Jacksonville, Florida. Philip summoned Pedro Menéndez de Avilés, a conquistador noted for his brutality, and instructed him to handle the situation.

Menéndez and his Spanish troops loaded up their ships and set sail, establishing a Catholic settlement at St. Augustine. From there, they marched north and overwhelmed the Huguenot forces commanded by Jean Ribault. They also dispatched most of the French settlers at Fort Caroline—even those who freely surrendered. Altogether some 350 Huguenots were executed—which explains the grim name given the site of this massacre: *Matanzas*, Spanish for "slaughters."

This tragedy effectively halted French efforts to colonize this part of the New World. And even though the establishment of St. Augustine gave the Spanish the honor of having founded "the oldest permanent European settlement in North America," it would be those later British settlements farther north in New England and Virginia that would establish the historic foundation of the future United States.

As the Spanish discovered, colonizing North America wasn't easy. Before the arrival of the *Mayflower* at Plymouth in 1620, another group of English settlers began building a colony in August of 1587 on the island of Roanoke (off the coast of North Carolina). After assessing their needs, John White, the group's leader, got back on his ship and returned to England for supplies. His timing was terrible...or unlucky...or terribly unlucky. He sailed straight into a naval war between England and Spain, which prevented his prompt return. When he was finally able to cross the Atlantic again—in August of 1590—he found his fellow settlers gone and the Roanoke colony effectively "lost." All that remained was a wooden post with the cryptic word "Croatoan" carved into it.

In 1607—still more than a decade prior to the founding of Plymouth—another group docked at Jamestown in Virginia. King James described the mission in purely spiritual terms: the "propagating of Christian religion to such People, as yet live in Darkness and miserable Ignorance of the true Knowledge and Worship of God."[179] Most historians see a different, less-altruistic motive in England's belated entry into the colonization competition: an attempt to counter the political dominance of Spain—and the religious influence of Catholicism—in the New World.

And the settlers? They had their own reasons for sailing west.

What prompted 102 souls[180] to uproot their lives and board the *Mayflower* with all their worldly goods? Some were opportunistic traders, merchants, and craftsmen hoping to discover lucrative new business opportunities in the New World.

Others were fiercely religious—and deeply frustrated. In England they'd come to be known as Puritans. That is, they were Protestants who wanted to purify the Church of England from every vestige of Catholic faith and practice. "As petitioners to King James I (1603–1625) put it in 1603, the true church ought not to be 'governed by Popish Canons, Courts, Classes, Customs, or any human invention, but by the laws and rules which Christ hath appointed in his Testament.'"[181]

When some of the English Protestants lost hope that the state church would ever change to their satisfaction, and when they grew tired of its control over their lives, they took literally the command of 2 Corinthians 6:17—"Wherefore come out from among them, and separate yourselves." They became Separatists—actually fleeing England for places like Amsterdam and Leiden in the Netherlands.

So when King James I issued a charter to the Virginia Company, a trading company, to establish a colony in the New World, it's not surprising that some Separatists had life-altering, world-changing epiphanies: *We could be an ocean away from the prying eyes and meddling hands of the Church of England! In the New World, we could be free to form independent congregations and strictly follow our own interpretation of the Bible! At last we could live out the true faith, and establish a pure and biblical church!*

They jumped at this opportunity, signing a contract with the Virginia Company to settle on the Hudson River (in what today is New York City). However, due to bad weather and crude navigational equipment, they ended up 220 miles to the northeast in Massachusetts.

This travel snafu precipitated a crisis. Some of the business-minded settlers aboard the *Mayflower* argued that since the group hadn't landed at the Hudson River, the contract they'd signed with the Virginia Company was invalid—they simply didn't have royal permission to settle in New England. The debate became heated. Just when it looked as though this colonial experiment might fall apart before it ever got going, the group agreed to draw up a new charter.

This concise agreement, known today as the Mayflower Compact, stipulated that the group would endeavor to create a unified society that remained loyal to King James; that it would create (and abide by) whatever laws, ordinances, and offices necessary for the good of the colony; and that all these things would be done "for the Glory of God, and Advancement of the Christian Faith." Of the fifty adult male passengers of the *Mayflower*, forty-one signed the document, including two indentured servants.

Signing the charter was the easy part. As previously mentioned, the group's first year in Plymouth was brutal. Only half the population survived. But conditions improved and the settlers began getting the hang of life in a New World. By 1627 the situation had stabilized; there were 160 Pilgrims. Over the next century, waves of radical, separatist Puritans settled the northeast coast of America.[182]

In the first wave was the ship *Arbella*, arriving in 1630. An English attorney named John Winthrop was one of the devout Puritans aboard. He rallied his fellow Puritan colonists with "one of the most destiny-laden sermons ever preached in America," often referred to as "The City on a Hill" sermon.[183] Borrowing heavily from the Old Testament book of Deuteronomy, Winthrop suggested that the same promises given to the ancient Israelites by God could be enjoyed by the Puritans in the New World.

Wee shall finde that the God of Israell is among us, when ten of us shall be able to resist a thousand of our enemies; when hee shall make us a prayse and glory that men shall say of succeeding plantations, 'the Lord make it likely that of New England.' For wee must consider that wee shall be as a citty upon a hill. The eies of all people are uppon us.[184]

In 1633, when William Laud (a leader with little tolerance for dissenters from the Church of England) became Archbishop of Canterbury, more Puritans packed their bags and boarded ships. The Great Migration was on. During the 1630s, some nine thousand Puritans made the transatlantic journey. By 1691, the two colonies at Plymouth and Massachusetts Bay formed the Province of Massachusetts Bay in 1691, eventually evolving into the Commonwealth of Massachusetts and one of the thirteen original states. And so a persecuted, radical minority in the Old World became, through transatlantic migration, a dominant force in the New World.[185]

We can't overlook the fact that religious dissent played a *major* role in America's founding. Many would argue that this hunger for "spiritual independence" is actually part of the nation's DNA. Maybe, maybe not. But one truth is undeniable: any society built on a desire for religious autonomy produces and/or attracts citizens who want religious autonomy.

It wasn't long before Puritan communities and congregations in the colonies began to be surrounded and infiltrated by those with other religious ideas and divergent approaches to spirituality. Sadly, the same people who had been persecuted in England for challenging the religious powers-that-be immediately resorted to persecuting those in the New World who didn't conform to their way of thinking and believing! Alexis de Tocqueville highlighted this inconsistency in *Democracy in America*, noting that the Puritans forgot "completely the great principles of religious liberty."[186] Their eagerness to impose their own doctrinal ideas on the public at large made it apparent that what they had clamored for in England wasn't so much religious freedom as religious power and authority.

America's Christian Beginnings?

Given the huge Puritan migration in the early 1600s, the question is often asked—and fiercely debated—*Was America founded as a Christian nation?*

Rabbi Daniel Lapin, an Orthodox rabbi, has noted:

> There is no need to guess what was in the mind of the Pilgrims as they landed in the New World. They bequeathed us a written document, the Mayflower Compact, signed just prior to disembarking their ships on November 11, 1620. It is difficult to interpret that document as anything other than a Christian statement of purpose.[187]

Other facts are also beyond dispute:

- The vast majority of adult males aboard the *Mayflower* (forty-one out of fifty) signed this contract.

- The Pilgrims chose as a symbol for Plymouth the overtly Christian symbol of four figures, divided symmetrically by St. George's cross, each holding John Calvin's burning heart.

- Subsequent waves of British colonists were overwhelmingly Christian and Protestant.

While the early British colonies may not have been founded for aggressive "evangelistic" purposes (as was the case with many Spanish Catholics in Latin America), they were clearly communities bound together, in large part for religious self-expression.[188] The presence of devout Christians and pious Christian leaders among the first European immigrants is clear. John Witherspoon, a Presbyterian clergyman, was among the founding fathers. Many of the fifty-five signers of the Constitution were members of orthodox Christian churches and were candid about the Christian underpinnings of their decisions.

At the same time, other founders like Thomas Jefferson and James Monroe were Unitarian Deists. Thomas Paine and Ethan Allen were non-Christian Deists.

The continual arrival of new colonists meant the arrival of other religious groups and competing spiritual ideas. The charter issued by King James in 1624 stipulated that Virginia would be a royal colony in which Anglicanism would be the official state religion. Residents were legally required to belong to the Anglican Church and to support it financially. Dissenters in Virginia were not granted freedom of worship.

In 1628, immigrants came on ships from Holland to settle in New Netherlands (i.e., modern New York City). There they established the Dutch Reformed Church.

In the early 1630s, while Jesuit missionaries were attempting to convert Native Americans in the northeastern United States, King Charles I issued a charter to Lord Baltimore, a wealthy Catholic, to establish a colony in America. His son led this effort, creating in 1634 a refuge for persecuted Catholics in what today we know as the state of Maryland.

In 1636, Roger Williams, who had clashed fiercely and frequently with his Puritan neighbors in the Massachusetts Bay Colony, and who had famously claimed that "forced worship stinks in God's nostrils,"[189] founded a colony for dissidents he called "Providence." Established in the area we call Rhode Island, this was intended to be a place where people could be free to live according to their consciences.

Further south were Presbyterian, Quaker, and Baptist populations. "Dr. James Hutson of the Library of Congress...estimates that at the time of the Revolutionary War, some 70–80 percent of the population attended church on a regular basis."[190]

Given these facts, it's easy to see why some argue that America was, at least once upon a time, a Christian nation.

David Barton (via his think tank WallBuilders and multiple books) is one of the more active voices arguing that America had a Christian founding. He appeals largely to religious statements made by America's founders in public documents and private correspondence. There indeed are volumes from which to choose. He has amassed a considerable following, and is prolific in various mediums. On the surface, it seems a bit mystifying in light of the support for this general topic that there is even a need to make the argument—which is his point.

Scholars Barry Hankins and Thomas Kidd of Baylor University are in agreement that the Bible was frequently quoted, cited, and alluded to in America's early history. However, they have pushed back against some of Barton's assertions, noting that Barton doesn't always distinguish between statements that merely show benign support for the basic moral teachings of Christianity and those that signal wholesale acceptance of the fundamental tenets of the Christian faith.[191]

Hankins has also pointed out that Barton never really defines what he means by the phrase a "Christian nation." Does he mean that America was—and perhaps still is

- *demographically Christian* (a notion that is hardly controversial);

- *legally Christian* (a notion that is difficult to support, given that no founding document explicitly declares the nation such); or

- *actually redeemed by the blood of Jesus Christ* (a notion that evangelical theologians would find repugnant)?[192]

Though the two camps approach sources differently at times, they both find religious moorings for the United States important. Kidd notes Patrick Henry's famous "Give Me Liberty or Give Me Death" speech as a prime example. Delivered in 1775, the message is chock-full of Bible references.[193] Of course, even skeptics like Thomas Paine utilized Scripture liberally in their writings, probably because they grasped the Good Book's popularity among the growing populace.[194]

And speaking of the Good Book, we can't responsibly ignore the gigantic role it played in the spread of Christianity throughout North America, and in other social developments.

The Bible and Other Religious Writings

At the Pilgrim Hall Museum in Plymouth, Massachusetts, you can see some of the actual artifacts brought to America by those first British settlers more than four hundred years ago. A sword, a wooden chest, a cradle used by Oceanus Hopkins, who was born *during* the *Mayflower's* voyage. Other items in the museum's collection are a Bible owned by William Bradford, the first governor of the Plymouth Colony, and another Bible that belonged to colonist John Alden.

Bradford's Bible was a Geneva Bible[195], a version of the Holy Scriptures immensely popular among the Puritans.[196] The Geneva Bible was produced—where else?—in Geneva, Switzerland, by Protestant Reformers Miles Coverdale and John Knox (who were "disciples" of John Calvin). They released the New Testament in 1557 while the Catholic monarch Mary was still on the English throne. The Old Testament followed in 1560. The Geneva Bible would not be published in England until 1576.[197]

The Geneva Bible was more compact than other English Bibles[198] and more understandable because it included clearer language, explanatory notes (from a Puritan perspective), and short book introductions. What's more, it was the first English Bible to utilize chapter divisions and verse numbers, *and* it was affordable. No wonder so many loved it.[199]

The other Bible that is a must-see at the Pilgrim Hall Museum is the one formerly owned by colonist John Alden. We don't know for sure if it came with him on the *Mayflower* (or whether it was shipped at a later date)—only that it was printed in London in 1620, and it is a King James Bible, prompting the question *How and why did England's new king get a Bible translation named after him?*

It was no secret to anyone that the newly crowned King James disliked the Geneva Bible. Because of its many anti-royalist marginal notes, he called it "untrue, seditious, and [full of] dangerous and traitorous conceits." Therefore when a Puritan leader at a royal conference in early 1604 asked the king about funding a committee to create a new Bible translation, his royal highness was immediately favorable and his royal checkbook sprang open.[200] Fifty-four scholars were summoned to work on six different translation teams. After seven years of rigorous research and translation, the new King James Bible was rolling off the presses.

This royally "authorized" version of the Bible quickly caught on. In his celebrated book on the five hundredth anniversary of the King James Bible (KJV), Gordon Campbell writes:

> [T]he colonists...soon settled on the KJV, which was from the mid-seventeenth century the only available English-language Bible. The Middle Colonies (now Delaware, New Jersey, New York, and Pennsylvania) welcomed migrants of many Protestant persuasions (Baptists, Congregationalists, Dutch Reformed, Presbyterians, Quakers, and so on), and, as English emerged as the dominant language, so the KJV became the Bible of the colonists.[201]

As more and more people of faith (and no faith) settled in the New World, missionaries and clergy saw a glaring need, and entrepreneurs saw a great opportunity. America was desperate for Bibles and ripe for religious literature.

Case in point: In the mid-1600s, a Puritan missionary named John Eliot wanted to share the message of Christ with native peoples living around Massachusetts Bay. In 1649, he received funding for a new translation of Holy Scripture when Parliament passed *An Act for the Promoting and Propagating the Gospel of Jesus Christ in New England*. He set about translating the Bible into an Algonquian dialect, and in 1663, printed the first complete Bible in British North America in the dialect of these Native Americans.

This sort of outreach by mission-minded Christians would continue. In 1804, the British and Foreign Bible Society under William Oglethorpe published the Mohawk Gospel, a translation of the Gospel of John drafted and published by "a printer, soldier, interpreter, trader, and Mohawk chief born probably in Scotland of a Scottish father and a Cherokee mother."[202] In 1818, the American Bible Society released its printing of this Gospel with some corrections,[203] and leaders debated whether the language should be in English ("to civilize" these Indians of the Six Nations of the Iroquois Confederacy, mainly on east coast and northern territories through Michigan, and settling in Canada). Or, provided in the Mohawk language—to help preserve their culture.[204]

Before that, the Aitken Bible, or the "Bible of Revolution," met the need for new Bibles for English colonists during the Revolutionary War. John Aitken, a Philadelphia printer originally from Scotland, was commissioned by Congress in 1782 to print thirty thousand copies.[205] At four by six inches, his Bible was designed to fit in a soldier's coat pocket. This was the first printing of an English Bible in America.

In 1807, a group called The Society for the Conversion of Negro Slaves produced what became known as The Slave Bible. Today, only three copies are known to exist. In 2018, Fisk University loaned its copy to the Museum of the Bible in Washington, DC and it quickly became the museum's most visited exhibit. The Slave Bible is not without controversy. It was used to teach enslaved Africans how to read, and to introduce them to the Christian faith.

> Unlike other missionary Bibles, however, the Slave Bible contained only "select parts" of the biblical text. Its publishers deliberately removed portions of the biblical text, such as the exodus story, that could inspire hope for liberation. Instead, the publishers emphasized portions that justified and fortified the system of slavery that was so vital to the British Empire.[206]

By 1800, there were nearly one hundred different Bible translations. In 1816 the American Bible Society (ABS) was founded. Its mission was nothing less than to place a Bible in every household in America.

The group had a series of famous presidents including John Jay, John Quincy Adams, Francis Scott Key, Rutherford B. Hayes, and Benjamin Harrison. Well-funded, and well-run, ABS gave out millions of free copies of the Scriptures in the nineteenth century. It (and other Bible distribution groups) were yet another decisive factor in Christianity's growth in North America.

It wasn't just Bibles that Christians in North America used to practice and propagate their faith. Printers churned out other religious literature by the wagonload.

In 1640, 1,700 copies of *The Bay Psalm Book* (a collection of biblical psalms) came off the press of Stephen Day, a printer in Cambridge, Massachusetts. This was the first book published in British North America—only 20 years after the landing of the *Mayflower*.[207]

A more widely disseminated work was *The New England Primer* (ca. 1690), from the press of the fiery anti-Catholic journalist Benjamin Harris. For almost half a century, this was the only elementary textbook in the colonies. Cheap and containing an overt Christian message, *The New England Primer* "promoted literacy...and solidified a Calvinist ethic in colonial America.... Themes of sin, death, punishment, salvation, and respect for authority were displayed through alphabetic rhymed couplets, poems, prayers, and scriptures."[208] Some versions contained the Westminster Shorter Catechism (a list of concise theological questions and answers). Other versions also included John Cotton's *SPIRITUAL MILK FOR American BABES, Drawn out of the Breasts of both Testaments for their Souls Nourishment.*

By 1830, *The New England Primer* had sold between six and eight million copies,[209] making it an important resource in the spread of the Christian faith in the American colonies. Noah Webster summed up its impact this way: "It has taught millions to read and not one to sin."

Another influential, Christian-themed publication was *McGuffey's Reader*. This set of books was the brainchild of William Holmes McGuffey, a professor at Miami University in Oxford, Ohio. Upon the recommendation of his longtime friend Harriet Beecher Stowe, McGuffey began producing this series in 1836.

In the foreword of the original reader McGuffey wrote, "The Christian religion is the religion of our country. From it are derived our prevalent notions of the character of God, the great moral governor of the universe...."

Ultimately the series included readers for students in grades one through six, and its selections, like the *New England Primer*, contained a regular offering of biblical narratives and principles.[210]

"Between 1836 and 1890, McGuffey's publisher printed and sold more than one hundred million copies of *McGuffey's Reader*. Practically every American who attended public schools during the second half of the nineteenth century learned moral and ethical lessons from *McGuffey's Reader*."[211] The series remains popular today—especially among homeschool families.

Christian Colleges

Primers and readers helped millions of American *children* learn the basics of the Christian faith. Older students—at least those with the intellectual ability and financial means—received even more training in the Bible through a college education. Prior to the Revolutionary War, American colonists had already established nine colleges—and all but the University of Pennsylvania had religious links.[212] The nine schools include the current Ivy League colleges (except for Cornell University, which wasn't founded until 1865). The other two of the original nine American colleges were Rutgers and the College of William and Mary.[213]

Harvard was the first, established in 1636 with an endowment from the Reverend John Harvard, for the purpose of providing educated ministers for churches. Today, Harvard's ornate Johnston gate, which leads to Old Harvard Yard, includes a stone engraving taken from *England's First Fruits* (1643). It reads:

> After God had carried us safe to New England, and wee had builded our houses, provided necessaries for our lively hood, reard convenient places for Gods worship, and setled the Civill Government: One of the next things we longed for, and looked after was to advance Learning and perpetuate it to Posterity; dreading to leave an illiterate Ministery to the Churches, when our present Ministers shall lie in the Dust.[214]

By 1701, some Puritans, fearing that Harvard had become theologically liberal, started Yale for the same purpose. In 1746 Princeton was founded after some felt that Yale was becoming too secular! (Not many people likely know that Nassau Hall, on the Princeton campus, was the site of Continental Congress meetings during a four-month period in 1783, effectively making Princeton the nation's temporary capital.[215])

This desire to see both colonists and Native Americans hear and understand and live by the truth of God only grew. In 1769, Reverend Eleazar Wheelock, a Congregationalist pastor from Connecticut, founded Dartmouth College in New Hampshire "as an institution to educate Native Americans."[216] The school's motto, "a voice crying out in the wilderness," is taken from Isaiah 40:3 and pictures the school's original mission of being a frontier outpost for reaching Native Americans.

American ingenuity kept coming up with new ways to propagate the gospel.

The Sunday School Movement

In 1860, Abraham Lincoln visited a Chicago slum known as "Little Hell." He was curious about the stories he'd heard of a young, energetic ex-shoe salesman named Dwight Lyman Moody who supposedly was gathering scores of poor, uneducated, inner-city street kids in an abandoned saloon each Sunday for a kind of makeshift school. The curriculum? The Bible.

Lincoln was impressed with Moody's "Sunday school," and reports say that Honest Abe addressed the children that day, telling them: "I was once as poor as any boy in this school, but I am now President of the United States, and if you attend to what is taught you here, some of you may yet be President of the United States."[217]

President-elect Lincoln was on his way to the White House. Mr. Moody was on his way to becoming one of the world's most famous evangelists.[218] Everybody knows the big things Moody did: establishing the large Illinois Street Church in Chicago (known today as Moody Bible Church), founding three influential schools (two in Northfield, Massachusetts, and one in Chicago—now called the Moody Bible Institute, f. 1886).

God alone knows how many young lives Moody impacted through his "Sunday school."

The Sunday School Movement was another significant factor in the spread of Christianity in North America.

Some credit Hannah Ball in Buckinghamshire, England (1769)

as being the pioneer of this phenomenon, and Robert Raikes (d. 1811), publisher of the *Gloucester Journal*, its most prominent advocate. Insisting that, "The world marches forth on the feet of small children," Raikes used his wealth to start schools for poor children from the inner city. Since many of these kids worked in factories Monday through Saturday, Raikes held his classes on Sunday. Using the Bible as a textbook, lay volunteers as his faculty, and his newspaper to spread the word, Raikes and his team got busy. Twenty years after his death, more than a *million* British children were receiving some sort of religious training each Sunday.

As the Moody story shows, America also saw a surge in Sunday school education. According to Edwin Wilbur Rice, president of the American Sunday School Union, there were 180,000 such schools in the United States by 1825. And as far as the claim that the movement originated in England, Rice had this to say:

> It is generally conceded by American students of first-hand documents that such schools of a character like to those founded by Raikes, with all their essential features, were to be found in America long before his day. These schools had many of the features as well as the form common to the modern Sunday-school, which entitled them to be counted forerunners of the modern movement.[219]

By the time of Lincoln's inauguration, Sunday schools had spread throughout the States.[220] Historian Timothy Larsen at Wheaton College Illinois summarizes well the rise and fall of this movement:

> It is important to realize that Sunday schools were originally literally schools: they were places where poor children could learn to read…. Within decades, the movement had become extremely popular. By the mid-19th

147

century, Sunday school attendance was a near universal aspect of childhood.... In both Britain and America, universal, compulsory state education was established by the 1870s. After that, reading and writing were learned on weekdays at school and the Sunday school curriculum was limited to religious education.[221]

American Revivalism

If Moody was effective as a teacher of young street toughs (and he was), he was even more influential as a preacher and evangelist. And he was only one of many powerful heralds of the gospel in the New World. To be sure, no discussion of North American Christianity would be complete without noting the enormous impact of American revivalism.

The social and political landscape of the colonies spawned a free-market approach to almost everything, including religion. Early on, there were no established churches; and particularly as settlers migrated westward, no state churches. Such a spiritual vacuum created a kind of religious free-for-all. Every community was up for grabs. The only question? Who could make the most compelling case for their version of the Christian faith?

It didn't take long for one truth to come to light: Whenever the gospel is faithfully proclaimed by gifted and/or charismatic communicators, hearts are pierced and—sometimes—entire communities are changed. And so it was that open-air, evangelistic preaching became a common sight. Suddenly Methodist circuit riders were crisscrossing the frontier on horseback, preaching up a storm, winning souls for Christ by the droves, and starting churches every place they stopped.

Henry Alline was an itinerant preacher in Nova Scotia who founded several Baptist and Congregational Churches there after 1775.

The faithful in the Old World were led by (often stuffy) high-ranking bishops. In the New World the populace was mesmerized by celebrity preachers and evangelists—men like George Whitefield, Jonathan Edwards, and John Wesley. Often these revivalists were roundly criticized for peddling the gospel like slick salesmen and vulgar entertainers. Later evangelists—Charles Grandison Finney in the nineteenth century, Billy Sunday in the late 1800s/early 1900s, and Billy Graham in the second half of the twentieth century—were also critiqued for theatrics and playing on peoples' emotion.

To be fair, American revivalism did sometimes resemble a traveling circus, right down to the big, portable tents. In frontier areas that lacked any semblance of "culture," revivals were elaborate, entertaining, high-octane affairs. People came from miles around to witness the spectacle. Often new converts would be overcome with emotion, weeping over their sins and/or rolling on the ground in spiritual ecstasy. Regardless of their method or mystery, emotional or stoic moments, the new converts proved through the ensuing decades to be anything but fake news.

The most notable occasions in America's unique revival history are called the Great Awakenings. Historians often refer to a series of revivals between 1725 and 1760 as "The First Great Awakening." This period of spiritual fervor was highlighted by the itinerant preaching of the Anglican evangelist George Whitefield.[222] When he preached in the church of the famed Jonathan Edwards in Northampton in 1745, the normally stoic Edwards wept.[223] Dr. John Hannah, long-time professor of church history at Dallas Theological Seminary, once claimed, perhaps partially in jest, that Whitefield was such a gifted communicator he could bring an audience to tears merely by saying the word "Mesopotamia."

A "Second Great Awakening" occurred between 1780 and 1830, ushering in what some historians call "the Protestant Century." While the Methodists (influenced by John Wesley) advanced strong Arminian doctrines, the graduates of Yale College (influenced by the theology of Jonathan Edwards) preached Calvinism.

Near the end of this period, Charles Finney earned the title "the Father of American Revivalism" for his key role in a series of revivals in upstate New York (1825–35). These meetings may have resulted in as many as a half million converts. An ardent abolitionist, Finney served the last decades of his life as president of Oberlin College, the first American educational institution to accept both African Americans and women.[224]

It was in 1831, just after this Awakening, that de Tocqueville visited America. He surveyed the social and spiritual landscape and concluded, "…there is no country in the world where the Christian religion retains a greater influence over the souls of men than in America."[225]

Beyond these first two Awakenings, there is considerable debate over how to categorize the significant religious activity that took place between 1850–1930 and 1960–1980. In the nineteenth century, the abolitionist movement was steered, in large part, by Christian leaders and groups. The Social Gospel and millenarianism fueled new initiatives and denominations, such as the Holiness movement. Important African-American voices like that of Martin Luther King, Jr. emerged in both the church and public discourse.

These revivals and awakenings altered the soul of American Christianity in at least two prominent ways. With their heavy emphasis on personal conversion, they made the Christian faith more democratic, encouraging laypeople to take responsibility for their own spiritual condition. They also continually demonstrated to the faithful how many people needed to be reached with the gospel message.

Slavery and Christianity

Here is one of those ugly historical facts that make modern-day people of faith cringe, blush, and look for the nearest exit:

Jonathan Edwards, the revered Christian theologian and preacher, and George Whitefield, the esteemed Christian revivalist, were slave owners.

Edwards "accepted slavery as a normal part of life, an institution ordained by God in Scripture."[226] Consequently he and his wife, Sarah Pierpont Edwards, acquired slaves to help with chores. Though he spoke out against overseas slave trading and called for improved conditions for slaves, he chose not to emancipate his own.

Whitefield also called for the humane treatment of slaves and expressed concerns for their spiritual well-being. And yet this same man who established the Bethesda orphanage in Georgia called for the legalization of slavery in the state. Historian Mark Galli concludes: "As an evangelist, Whitefield was unconventional and remarkable. Lamentably, his views on slavery were conventional and unremarkable."[227]

Therein lies the hypocrisy—some would say the insanity—of it all: Christians committing the morally indefensible act of enslaving other people against their will, then arguing that such people should be treated humanely so that they might want to become Christians![228] It's no different than the sad scene that played out all across Latin America at the hands of Spanish conquistadores.

Mark A. Noll, professor emeritus in history at Notre Dame, identifies three categories of American Christians in the whole slavery debate: theological conservatives, radicals, and those in between. Conservatives were those who found sanction for slavery in Scripture. Radicals were abolitionists who resented a holy text that at times condones (and even commands) slavery. The in-betweeners were those who saw the evils of slavery and sought (in vain) for a solution that would placate both sides. In effect, American Christians faced the unique challenge of reading and interpreting Scripture in the context of republican political thought and commonsense moral reasoning, or what Noll terms commonsense republicanism.[229]

And yet, while slaves suffered, and slave owners and abolitionists argued, something else was taking place: The emotional gospel preaching of the revivalists was resonating with enslaved Africans, so much so that by 1800, one-fifth of all American Methodists were black. The awakenings were fostering an African-American Christian culture that expressed itself in the fervency of extroverted Evangelical Protestantism rather than in the cooler tones of Anglicanism.[230] What made the appeal of the revivalists so appealing?

> Central to the answer must be the Evangelical demand for a personal choice that gave dignity to people who had never been offered a choice in their lives....Related was Methodism's insistence on complete personal transformation or regeneration, an attractive theme in lives which offered little other hope of dramatic change. Moravians brought song. And uninhibited celebration of God's blood and wounds to people who knew much of both. Moravians also insisted that God was pleased by cheerfulness, a congenial thought in a culture which remembered better than Europeans how to celebrate. And at the centre was the library of books which was the Bible, in which readers could suddenly find themselves walking into a particular book and recognizing their own life.... Protestant American enslaved people had texts which gave them stories and song. They sang

about the biblical stories which made them laugh and cry, in some of the most compelling vocal music ever created by Christians, "Negro Spiritual": a fusion of the Evangelical hymn tradition of the Awakenings with celebratory rhythms and repetitions remembered from days of African freedom.[231]

In spite of inhumane treatment both by institutions and individuals, large numbers of enslaved peoples and their descendants became Christians. Many of these individuals became leaders in the anti-slavery movement, and in post-war initiatives for social justice. Who were some of the key figures leading the oppressed in their hope for change?

Christianity's Spread through African Voices

When Dutch slavers pushed the first twenty African slaves off their ship at the British colony of Jamestown in 1619, it was far more than a transaction between countries and people groups. It was a nightmare, a gross injustice of the highest order.

As mentioned, many of those slaves found hope in the Christian gospel. Others, while enslaved, or later as freedmen, became ministers and preachers of that good news.[232]

John Stewart (ca.#1786–1823) became the first black missionary to Native Americans—the Wyandots, a branch of the Huron tribe that had resettled by Upper Sandusky, Ohio. His journey through the woods and, by canoe, down rivers, often alone, just to reach this settlement is amazing. His exploits made him America's first Methodist home missionary.

Stewart had the assistance of a black interpreter, Jonathan Pointer (whom the Wyandots had kidnapped as a boy). When rival missionaries learned he was preaching without a license, they complained to church leaders. However, the Methodist Episcopal Church ordained him *at the request of the Indians*—who had gone from taunting to loving him. His work prompted the formation of the Methodist Missionary Society in 1820.[233] One of the key chiefs who converted, "Between-the-logs," gives the following account:

> [T]he Black Man, Stewart...came to us and told us he was sent by the Great Spirit to tell us the true and good way. But we thought he was like all the rest—that he too wanted to cheat us and get our money and land from us. He told us of our sins and that drinking was ruining us and that the Great Spirit was angry with us. He said that we must leave off these things. But we treated him ill and gave him little to eat, and trampled on him and were jealous of him for a whole year. Then we attended his meeting in the council house. We could find no fault with him. The Great Spirit came upon us so that all cried aloud. Some clapped their hands, some ran away, and some were angry. We held our meetings all night, sometimes singing, sometimes praying. By now we were convinced that God had sent him to us. Stewart is a good man.[234]

In the 1760s, the Wheatley family in Boston purchased a precocious slave girl from Gambia, West Africa. They named her Phillis and gave her their last name. The Wheatleys educated her, took her regularly to church, and eventually freed her. Though Phillis wrote exquisite poetry, American publishers would not publish her for racial reasons. An English aristocrat, Selina Hastings, Countess of Huntingdon, helped her find a British publisher, and in 1773,

Wheatley became the first African American to publish a book of poetry, *Poems on Various Subjects Religious and Moral*. One line is worth quoting here: "Remember, Christians, Negroes, black as Cain, /May be refin'd and join th' angelic train."

Lemuel Haynes (1753–1833) was another prominent black voice, becoming the first African-American pastor of an all-white congregation. Biracial and abandoned by his parents, Haynes became an indentured servant in Granville, Massachusetts. After fulfilling his commitment to the Rose family, he served as both a minuteman (1774) and in the Continental army (1776). He married a white woman and had ten children.[235] Witty, brilliant, and a gifted preacher, Haynes was beloved by his community. And yet, after thirty years of service, when his congregation discovered he was black, they voted him out of office.

Another African-American woman of note was Jarena Lee (1783–ca.#1850–57), regarded as "the first significant black female preacher in America."[236] Her pastor in New Jersey, Richard Allen, the founder of the AME Church, told her she couldn't preach—because the Methodists didn't allow female preachers. Lee wondered famously, "And why should it be thought impossible, heterodox, or improper for a woman to preach? Seeing the Saviour died for the woman as well as the man. If the man may preach, because the Saviour died for him, why not the woman? Seeing he died for her also. Is he not whole Saviour, instead of half one?"

Eight years later, when her church's scheduled speaker was unable to deliver his message, Lee spontaneously rose from her seat and exhorted the congregation. Impressed by her gifting, Bishop Allen commissioned Lee to be an evangelist.[237]

Traveling nearly three thousand miles on foot in the Northeastern United States and Canada, Lee preached nearly seven hundred sermons. She documented her story in a published autobiography, *The Life and Religious Experiences of Jarena Lee* (1849).

In 1784, at the age of thirty-eight, Absalom Jones bought his way out of slavery (he had first purchased his wife's freedom).[238] He began attending St. George's Methodist Church in Philadelphia, where blacks were welcomed...until too many slaves and ex-slaves started coming. One day Jones was physically removed to the "slave gallery." This incident prompted him and other black members to leave the church. With Richard Allen, Jones cofounded the Free African Society (the first organization of its kind for assisting freed slaves). In 1802, he helped establish the first black Episcopal Church—the African Episcopal Church of St. Thomas—which would become one of the largest congregations in Philadelphia. Jones was the first black man to be ordained a priest in the denomination.

There was a similar exodus of blacks from white churches in other urban areas. Disgruntled black Christians in New York formed Zion Church after rejection from attending St. John's Methodist Church. By 1868, Zion Church claimed 164,000 members.

Over the decades, this church body produced an all-star lineup of leading Christian voices: Frederick Douglass, Harriett Tubman, and Sojourner Truth. All three were escaped slaves who had survived brutal conditions. Each of these leaders played a unique role in the spread of Christianity, especially in its attractive appeal for social justice. Douglass was "the foremost African-American leader of the early nineteenth century." Sojourner Truth was an abolitionist and leading voice for women's rights. Tubman, also known as Moses, was a key leader of the Underground Railroad. Douglass and Sojourner were also preachers and gave some of the most memorable speeches of their time. The July 4, 1852, speech of Douglass, given in Rochester, New York, is typical:

I take this law (legalized slavery) to be one of the grossest infringements of Christian Liberty, and, if the churches and ministers of our country were not stupidly blind, or most wickedly indifferent, they, too, would so regard it.[239]

He repudiated preachers who "have shamelessly given the sanction of religion and the Bible to the whole slave system" and called them out, saying, "The existence of slavery in this country brands your republicanism as a sham, your humanity as a base pretense, and your Christianity as a lie."

Sojourner Truth is fondly remembered for, among other things, her "Ain't I a Woman?" speech at a Women's Convention in Akron, Ohio, 1851. At just 356 words, the speech became legendary. In it, she alludes to the story of Adam and Eve in Genesis 3: "If the first woman God ever made was strong enough to turn the world upside down all alone, these women together ought to be able to turn it back, and get it right side up again! And now they is asking to do it, the men better let them."[240]

Frances Dana Barker Gage, the moderator of the convention, later said:

Amid roars of applause, she returned to her corner leaving more than one of us with streaming eyes, and hearts beating with gratitude. She had taken us up in her strong arms and...turned the sneers and jeers of an excited crowd into notes of respect and admiration. Hundreds rushed up to shake hands with her.

Other North American Heroes of the Faith

As is the case on every continent, the regrettable examples of "Christian" faith in North America's history are easy to see. The heroic figures, though numerous, are not always so visible. We pause here, however, to highlight **Roger Williams** and **Anne Hutchinson**, who represent some of the nobler multitudes. Both of these individuals walked an arduous path, and both demonstrated remarkable faith and resilience in fighting for religious freedom.

Because of differences with other Puritan leaders, Williams was charged and convicted of sedition and heresy in 1635. As a result, he was expelled from the Massachusetts Bay Colony. Leaving behind a pregnant wife and two year-old daughter, Williams departed during a blizzard in the dead of winter. Had he not known the language of the Narragansett Indians, he likely would have starved during his days of wandering. This experience did, however, allow him to negotiate with the Indians for the purchase of land for his new colony at Providence.

Three years later, Hutchinson and her husband were banished from Massachusetts, largely because of her belief that God's grace—not one's moral lifestyle—gave a person assurance of salvation.

Hutchinson wanted to take orthodoxy farther than it was willing to go. Salvation was by faith, not works, all agreed. But orthodoxy declared that after salvation, good works gave evidence of that salvation. Hutchinson challenged that assumption.

In doing so, Puritan leaders felt she broke the essential bond between morality and religion, thereby threatening to undermine the very foundation of Puritan society. She was branded an "antinomian," literally one who is against the law.[241]

The Hutchinsons left behind a house, land, and farm animals. A few years later in Rhode Island, Anne buried her husband, prompting her to move again into the area we know today as the Bronx, in New York City. There, in 1643, Hutchinson and six of her children were killed by members of the Siwanoy Indian tribe. According to one account, the natives involved in the massacre deceived her, feigning friendship, and then, seeing that the group had no protection, returning later with violent intent.

Catholic Christianity in North America

Because they had banned French Huguenots from immigrating to the New World, French Catholics dominated the Canadian territories (or "New France," as they referred to the land mass). Even so, Catholic missionaries had to deal with warring factions of Indians, especially the Mohawks and the Huron. Because the Mohawks (part of the Iroquois Confederacy) were armed with muskets from Dutch traders, they generally dominated the Huron in battle.

Caught in this crossfire was Father Isaac Jogues. Perhaps no missionary to North America ever had a more adventurous or more torturous experience. Jogues—who did a *lot* of traveling by boat (i.e., canoe)—enjoyed ministry success among the Huron Indians north of the Great Lakes. Among their bitter enemies, not so much.

In 1642, while on a trip to fetch supplies, Jogues was captured by the Mohawks near Ft. Orange (i.e., modern-day Albany). To keep him from taking up arms against them in the future, the Iroquois chopped off his thumb (they also ate some of his fingers)! Tortured for months, Jogues managed to escape, but not before becoming conversant in the language of his captors. After receiving kind treatment from the Dutch at New Amsterdam, Jogues returned to France, where he was given a hero's welcome, and where, with papal permission, he was permitted to celebrate mass (another priest had to hold the communion elements for him).

In 1646, dismissing his prior experience, Father Jogues returned— by ship, of course!—to northern North America and resolved to reach out to his former captors. Initially, the Mohawks received him, but when hardships came in the form of crop failure and some sort of viral epidemic, the tribe blamed Jogues and his companions.

The missionaries were apprehended, stripped bare, beaten, and slashed with knives. Finally Jogues was killed with the blow of a tomahawk. When the news of his death reached Quebec, his fellow missionaries celebrated a massive Thanksgiving rather than a Requiem mass for the repose of his soul.[242] The Catholic Church later declared Isaac Jogues and his brothers martyrs and saints.[243]

The story is told that a group of Frenchmen later captured a certain Mohawk, and took him to Three Rivers where he boasted that he had been Jogues' killer. This confession infuriated some members of the Algonquin and Huron tribes there, prompting the Jesuits to take the man into protective custody. After a few weeks in their care, the man asked for Christian baptism, and expressed a desire to take Isaac Jogues' name. The Jesuits complied.

A few days later, some revenge-minded Algonquin tribe members dragged the converted Mohawk away and killed him. One of the Jesuits allegedly said, "God willing, there are now two Isaac Jogueses in heaven."[244]

How Soon People Forget

The story of North American Christianity in one sense is the story of a deep religious tension at the heart of public life. The nation's founding immigrants came to seek "freedom of religious expression," but in many minds, that freedom came with a giant asterisk. The Puritans, for example, advocated personal freedom of conscience and religion, but they also wanted a society built upon and adhering to the *beliefs they held*.

The separation between public and private life that most take for granted today was entirely at odds with the way these early Americans conceived of civil society. Rather than a secular culture marked by complete religious freedom, they wanted an explicitly Christian society where the lines between citizenship and church membership were blurred. Indeed, in colonial America's earliest days, in certain areas one was not allowed to participate in politics, much less vote, without being an official church member.

But the wide-open spaces of the North American continent and the constant emergence of unaffiliated churches in the beckoning frontier worked to prevent state control of religious life. The rich diversity, vitality, creativity, and mobility of the young American population made religious monoculture an impossible, even ridiculous idea. Eventually the religious freedom championed by figures like Roger Williams and Anne Hutchinson began to win the day, especially in the newer states and western territories.

By the time of the Civil War, the spread of Christianity would become inextricably linked to the bloody battle and the long reconciliation of slavery positions. From the splintering of the Wesleyans from mainline Methodism to a mélange of new denominations, social activism would become the new face of hundreds of upstart Protestant denominations that would eventually claim half of Americans. Catholicism, especially via lingering Spanish settlements and Irish immigrants, would become America's largest single denomination at around 21 percent of the US population.[245]

The spread of Christianity to and through North America follows the same pattern we've seen on other continents: the gradual rise of institutions that helped shape culture in good and sometimes not-so-positive ways; the emergence of larger-than-life individuals, usually beset by difficulty and often hampered by flaws and blind spots, who nevertheless made huge contributions to the advance of the gospel, and oftentimes doing all that in a way that required some kind of boat ride.

Here's one final fascinating fact: in 1622, even as those brave, seafaring Puritans were working hard in Plymouth, Massachusetts, to get their new colony up and running, the Roman Catholic church was canonizing perhaps its greatest missionary.

St. Francis Xavier (d. 1552) was a Jesuit priest who spent much of his life traveling by ship to far-flung places—despite his propensity for violent bouts of seasickness. What drove him? Nothing less than an unquenchable desire to take the gospel to yet another continent—Asia.

In the next chapter, we'll see how Xavier and others helped spread Christianity among those in the Far East.

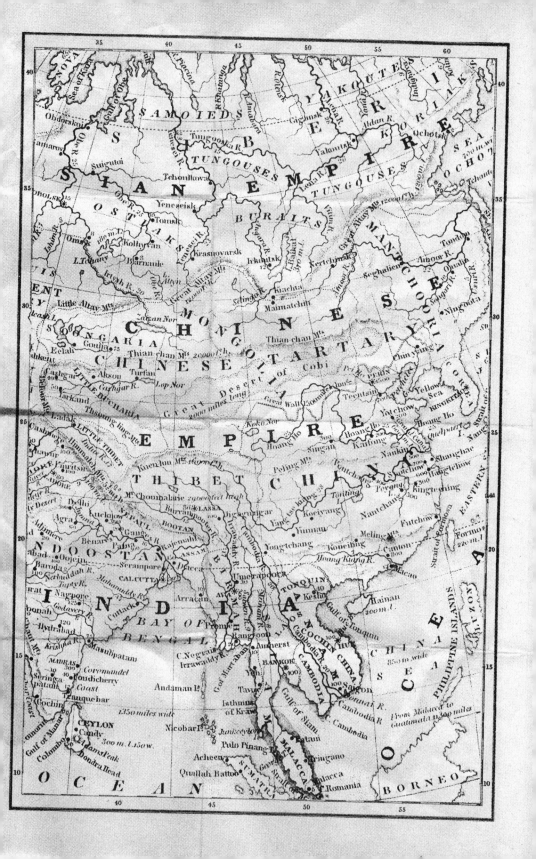

CHAPTER FIVE

THE FAR EAST AND FAR REACHES

ASIA

Tell the students to give up their small ambitions and
come eastward to preach the gospel of Christ.

Francis Xavier, *missionary to India and Japan*

Should I have a thousand lives,
I should not spare one not to give to China.

Hudson Taylor, *missionary to China*

To belong to Jesus is to embrace the nations with him.

William Carey, *missionary to India*

If you think that megachurch a few miles up the highway is massive, you should visit the Yoiddo Full Gospel Church in Seoul, South Korea. Each Sunday, beginning at 7 a.m., the church's fifteen-thousand-seat auditorium fills up *seven* times—the final service beginning at 7 p.m. It's remarkable to think that this congregation—the largest in the world with more than 800,000 members—began in 1958 with five people in a tent.

Seoul is a long way—geographically and culturally—from Jerusalem. So how is it that the message of a first-century Jewish rabbi became so precious to so many Asians in the twenty-first century?

The spread of Christianity to Asia begins with a skeptic named Thomas.

When Christ's first followers breathlessly reported they'd just seen the resurrected Lord, Thomas was incredulous. The apostle John remembers him protesting, "Unless I see the nail marks...and put my hand into his side,[246] I will not believe" (John 20:25).

Thomas's "crisis of faith" didn't last long. A week later, while all eleven apostles were huddled in a locked room, the risen Christ suddenly appeared in their midst.

This was no apparition, no hallucination. In front of the entire group, a very-much-alive Jesus challenged Thomas to "reach out your hand and put it into my side. Stop doubting and believe" (John 20:27).

A few more encounters like this (John 21; Matthew 28:18–20; Acts 1:8) and the disciple initially reluctant to believe in the resurrection became the disciple willing to go *anywhere* to proclaim the resurrection! Tradition tells us that Thomas responded to the Great Commission of Jesus to "make disciples of all nations" by taking the gospel in the mid-first century all the way to *Asia*.

Today in fact, in the Indian city of Chennai, some 3,100 miles southwest of Jerusalem by air—about 4,700 by land—you can visit the cathedral of St. Thomas, and view what the locals insist is Thomas's tomb. The story told is that while he was praying and/or preaching the gospel on an Indian hilltop (now called St. Thomas Mount), someone thrust a spear—not into his side but into his back. Relics at the well-visited shrine there include the spear tip allegedly used to kill Thomas...and, purportedly, one of his toe bones!

Modern-day doubting Thomases can decide which, if any, of

these claims they believe. However, it doesn't require any faith—only a straightforward review of history—to see that the message of Christ did, in fact, make its way to (and throughout) Asia, via the toe bones of a colorful cast of characters.

Though the New Testament mentions "Asia" nineteen times, this is not the Asia of modernity. The Jews said to be from Asia (Acts 2:9) at Pentecost when the church was born were from the western region of what used to be known as "Asia Minor" (i.e., modern-day Turkey). This "Asia" was a relatively small Roman province where the apostle Paul and other believers spent much time preaching and planting local churches (see Acts 13–16, 18–19).

By "Asia," we are referring here to the massive landmass bound on the north by the Arctic Ocean, on the south by the Indian Ocean, on the east by the Pacific Ocean, and on the west by Europe. Encompassing more than 17 *million* square miles, modern-day Asia makes up roughly 30 percent of the earth's total land area! As of June 2019, the continent (which includes both India and China, the world's two most populous countries) was home to some 4.5 billion people!

Estimates are that as many as 375 million[247] Asians identify today as *Christian*. In addition, while Seoul, South Korea, has its fair share of believers, the great majority are spread throughout India, China, Mongolia, and Japan.

The Spread of Christianity in India

The earliest accounts of Christianity's spread claim that the original apostles took the gospel to every continent on earth. Origen of Alexandria (ca. 185–264) is among the first proponents of this storyline.

The discovery of the New World, however, cast serious doubts on this notion. The best-attested apostolic traditions are Peter and Paul preaching Christ in Europe (described in the New Testament narratives), Mark going to Africa, and (as already mentioned) Thomas taking the gospel to India. The claim is that Thomas evangelized in the states of Kerala and Tamil Nadu in South India and the Punjab area in North India.

A rich center of trade in the first century, Kerala is situated at the southern tip of India. The area is "sun-drenched, humid, lush green...and teeming with people." Many of those people are Syrian Christians (who make up the majority of the Christian population there). Because they are convinced that the apostle Thomas is the one who baptized their ancestors, the name *Thomas* is seen everywhere in Kerala, "appearing on everything from baptism registers and the neon signs of jewelry stores and bakeries to the nameplates of dental surgeons and real estate developers' ads." [248]

It should not be surprising that innumerable area churches also bear the apostle's name. Due to their heavy Eastern Orthodox roots and influence, church liturgies here use Syriac, which is similar to Aramaic, which is the Hebrew dialect that Jesus—and Thomas—spoke. [249]

One of those church buildings, the Thiruvithamcode Arapally

(named by an Indian king) is located in Kanyakumari, the most southern district of India. Locals insist the structure was built in AD 57. If true, it's the oldest existing church building in the world.

History is full of references to Christian activity in India from early in the Common Era. In his lifetime, Bardesanes (AD 154–223), a Syrian gnostic and missionary, wrote about Christian groups in North India that attributed their conversion to the apostle Thomas. In the early third century, there were reports of bishops from the Church of the East evangelizing in Northwest India, Afghanistan, and Balochistan (a province of Pakistan).

Eusebius of Caesarea (AD 263–339) told of Pantaenus, a Greek theologian from Alexandria, visiting India during the reign of Emperor Commodus and finding Christians living there and using a version of the Gospel of Matthew.

The *Anglo-Saxon Chronicle* records that King Alfred the Great (AD 849–899) sent gifts to the Christians who were living in Kerala in 883.

In 1292, the explorer Marco Polo mentioned Christians in Southern India. In 1500, Pedro Alvares Cabral, the discoverer of Brazil, was allowed by the king of Cochin in South India to bring priests to evangelize local communities.

These missionaries were followed by the Jesuit Francis Xavier who won converts to Catholicism on the west coast in India. When Xavier died in 1552, his body was preserved in Goa, India. It remains there today, on display—as both a pilgrimage destination and a tourist attraction—at the Cathedral de Bom Jesus.

In 1705, Lutheran missionaries from Germany, Bartholomäus Ziegenbalg and Heinrich Plütschau, began work in the Danish settlement in Tranquebar (on the Bay of Bengal). The fort and church established there still exist. These Lutherans translated the Bible into the first Indian language—Tamil—and then into Hindustani. Their mission eventually spread to Madras and other areas. The Tamil Lutheran Church still exists in south India.

William Carey, arguably the most famous Protestant missionary to India, didn't arrive until the end of the eighteenth century. Carey was a devout English Baptist and a true scholar who, frankly, was appalled by his fellow Protestants' disinterest in foreign missions. He lamented believers who "sit at ease and give themselves no concern about the far greater part of their fellow sinners, who to this day, are lost in ignorance and idolatry."[250]

With the unofficial motto "Expect great things from God; attempt great things for God!" Carey settled his family in Serampore (in eastern India near Calcutta). The Careys' early years there were miserable—full of loneliness, illness, and regret. Carey wrote, "This is indeed the valley of the shadow of death to me," then added, "But I rejoice that I am here notwithstanding; and God is here."[251]

Even as his wife deteriorated mentally, Carey continued his relentless work of translating the Bible into Bengali, Sanskrit, and other languages. He established Serampore College in 1818. Despite the fact that the British East India Company considered missionary work in British territories illegal, Carey led some higher caste Bengalis to Christ.

In his forty-one years on Indian soil (never once taking a furlough, mind you), Carey won some seven hundred converts. Some go-getters might regard this number as meager (after four decades of intense ministry). Yet his tireless efforts inspired other influential missionaries, among them Adoniram Judson (d. 1850), who served in Burma for forty years, Hudson Taylor, whom we shall meet shortly, and David Livingstone (d. 18730, whom we'll read about in our final chapter on the spread of Christianity to Africa.

By the early 1900s, Indian believers were not only *coming to* Christ in faith, but *going for* Christ to spread the gospel. Case in point: Sadhu Sundar Singh (b. 1906), who converted to Christianity from Sikhism after losing his mother and having a divine encounter and vision of Christ. Singh became a powerful missionary to Afghanistan and Tibet. How and where he died, God only knows.

Time and space don't allow us to list even a fraction of the countless other Christians, both foreign and indigenous, who had a gospel impact on the Indian people. The most famous in recent years is surely Mother Teresa (b. 1910), the diminutive, Nobel Peace Prize–winning nun who became known as the "saint of Calcutta," after establishing the order known as the Missionaries of Charity in 1950. She received her missionary call on the Darjeeling train, then returned to Calcutta to care for the destitute and dying, which she did until her own death in 1997.

In recent years, persecution of Christians in India has increased. In 1999, Graham Staines, a missionary from Australia who worked in leper communities in Orissa, was burned to death, along with his two sons, as they slept in a jeep. In 2007, anger over Christian Christmas celebrations resulted in the torching of scores of churches and Christian villages. More recently, the elections of 2014 and 2015 gave a ten-year mandate to militant Hinduism. This turn of events has led to violence directed against Christians, who are perceived by many as being unpatriotic towards India.

The Spread of Christianity in China

When we review the spread of the Christian faith throughout China (and the adjacent regions of Mongolia and Taiwan), the metaphor of walls seems unavoidable. After all, who in the world hasn't heard about the Great Wall of China, "the only man-made structure visible from the moon"?

Actually, this oft-repeated claim isn't true; it's one of those urban legends that refuses to die. The Great Wall *can't* be seen from outer space. No matter. The Great Wall is nevertheless an architectural marvel and the object of intense fascination.

Witold Rodzinski, Poland's former ambassador to China, titled his 1984 book *The Walled Kingdom: A History of China from Antiquity to the Present*. He noted that the Great Wall stretching across Northern China not only helped repel the ancestors of the Huns, it also defined the world's largest culture by demarcating "the Chinese agricultural population from the nomadic way of life."[252]

We could add: The Great Wall also serves as fitting symbol for China's reception of religious outsiders through the centuries.

Individuals and nations erect walls for all sorts of reasons, but here's what's clear from history: The very existence of any sort of barrier implies differences...and usually signals fear. From the Athenian Long Walls of Pericles' lore to the US-Mexico border wall debated today in Washington, DC, wall building reflects a concern to protect life—or at least a way of life.

This is why—against the backdrop of a wall-filled world—it's arresting to read the letter the apostle Paul wrote to some first-century Christians living in Asia (Minor). In it, the great missionary referenced the Lord's intention to be a wall-buster, not a wall-builder: "For he himself is our peace, who has made the two groups one and has destroyed the barrier, the dividing wall of hostility" (Ephesians 2:14).

Clearly, Paul was talking there about spiritual and cultural barriers. He wanted to see the gospel of Christ break down the walls of racial and religious animosity that existed between first-century Jews and Gentiles.

And the missionaries who came to Asia after him...saints like Matteo Ricci, Hudson Taylor, and Lottie Moon? They longed to break through the centuries-old wall surrounding Chinese society that kept it isolated from the world and oblivious to the gospel of Jesus. Given China's anti-Western, anti-Christian xenophobia, they had their work cut out for them.

History shows that over the centuries China's leaders have systematically erected all sorts of barriers—political, cultural, and, yes, even physical—to protect the Chinese way of life. Due to negative experiences, the Chinese have long been suspicious of foreigners sowing the seeds of Christianity.[253] Nowhere is this tension better seen than in Diarmaid MacCulloch's description of nineteenth-century missionaries (mostly Protestants) arriving in Chinese ports aboard the same British ships that were filled with addictive opium that was wreaking havoc in Chinese culture.[254]

Compared to many other countries, China was more advanced culturally...and more isolated. This made evangelism there a very different experience from taking the gospel to a continent like Africa, where by western standards, missionaries found a relatively primitive and accepting culture.

Most people in the West don't realize that for much of human history China wasn't just progressive, it was one of the most sophisticated civilizations in the world. The Chinese invented a basic seismograph early in the *second* century. They had a vaccination for smallpox long before any Western culture. They built suspension bridges, had stirrups enabling horseback combat, and were printing some six hundred years before Gutenberg. They were also highly developed philosophically, and they had complex, organized bureaucracies that far exceeded those in Western nations. Because China was so advanced, encounters with other nations often began with the question, "What do these outsiders have that we would even want?"

Nowhere was this attitude of superiority, self-sufficiency, and isolationism symbolized more vividly than in the country's Great Wall. The story of Christianity's spread in China is a centuries-long mission to breach great barriers, literal and metaphorical, with the gospel of Christ.

Let's look briefly at some of the key players and moments in that effort.

The Arrival of the Nestorians

The earliest Christian influence in China came via a Nestorian missionary named Alopen, who arrived in northern China in 635 with biblical texts, other Christian writings, and a desire to share the gospel. (Some would say "a *false* gospel," due to the Nestorian teaching—condemned at the Synod of Ephesus in AD 431—that Jesus Christ was not one person with two distinct natures, divine and human, but rather two distinct persons, the human one under control of the divine.)

Tang Emperor Taizong, oblivious to the finer points of Christian theology, gave Alopen his blessing and an official endorsement, saying, "This religion benefits all men. Let it be preached freely in Our realm."[255]

It *was* preached freely. Converts were made. We know this because in 1625 a stele (i.e., a stone slab dating to AD 821 and chronicling 150 years of Nestorian Christianity in northern China) was discovered. Around 845, a government crackdown on religious groups essentially eradicated Nestorian Christianity.[256] It did little, however, to halt the spread of Buddhism. These events, in effect, laid the groundwork for a great spiritual wall against the gospel.

In the thirteenth century, Franciscan missionaries arrived. But soon after this, the western Mongols began converting to Islam, effectively boxing out Christianity yet again.

China's spiritual wall got higher.

A Franciscan came to China with the family of Marco Polo and established the first bishopric in Beijing. But a plague effectively doomed this attempt of evangelism. Yet again, Christianity was walled off.

Matteo Ricci and the Jesuits

Following the rise of the Ming dynasty in 1368, two rival approaches to evangelism began to shape Chinese Christianity. The Jesuits, led by the brilliant Matteo Ricci (1552–1610), decided it would be inappropriate to show up in one of the world's most sophisticated cultures with the attitude, "Your worldview is all wrong."

Observing how much Confucian philosophy already permeated

Chinese culture, the Jesuits decided instead to acquiesce wherever possible to local culture and customs. They borrowed Chinese terms and invested cultural forms with Christian meaning, attempting to syncretize the philosophical ideas of Confucius with the teachings of Christ. *How could this hurt,* they reasoned, *since Confucius was only a scholar and philosopher, not a religious figure, much less a deity?* By the mid-seventeenth century, the Jesuits had developed liturgies for worship in Chinese and adopted Chinese dress and culture. Due to Ricci's policies, even ancestor worship came "to be viewed not as a religious ceremony, but as a permissible civil observance."[257]

Priests from the rival Franciscan and Dominican orders looked on in horror. They saw the Jesuits' approach as a watering down, if not an outright alteration of true Christianity.

Ricci was undeterred by such criticism. He pressed on. Equal parts philosopher, moralist, scholar, and inventor, he slowly won favor in the capital. He and the Jesuits, with their tolerant and respectful approach, utilized certain Western scientific advantages—clock making and mapmaking, for example—to gain sway with the upper classes. Some Jesuits even received appointments to the imperial court.

Eventually, Paul Hsu, an imperial prince, was converted to the Christian faith, and the Jesuits were placed in charge of the official astronomical bureau (even correcting the calendar in 1611, the year after Hsu's death).[258] And the result? Whether we call it "syncretism" or a "Confucian-Christian *synthesis,*"[259] Ricci's overall philosophical approach led to a misunderstanding of biblical teachings among the literary elite, and spawned a serious backlash several years after his death in 1610.[260]

The Chinese Rites Controversy

The Jesuits' controversial approach to evangelism sparked the Chinese Rites Controversy. Most Catholics were in agreement with the criticisms of the Franciscans and Dominicans: The Jesuits methods were overly accommodating, if not borderline heretical. In 1704, Pope Clement XI banned their missionary approach.

However, because the Kangxi Emperor admired the intelligence and demeanor of the Jesuits and wanted them to remain, he appealed to Rome. When his pleas fell on deaf ears, the Chinese leader signed an edict forbidding evangelism altogether and expelling all remaining missionaries. Allowing only a few Jesuits to remain as advisors, the Chinese began persecuting Christians.

Just like that, another layer of bricks was added to China's great spiritual wall.

Robert Morrison's Chinese Translation of the Bible

In January of 1807, as the Scottish Presbyterian minister Robert Morrison (1782–1834) was en route to China to engage in mission work, he struck up a conversation with the ship's owner. Hearing his passenger's plans, the man said skeptically,

"And so Mr. Morrison, you really expect to make an impression on the idolatry of the great Chinese Empire?"

"No, sir," the young missionary replied, "I expect God will."[261]

God did...but not in the way that anyone expected.

To his great disappointment Morrison was not allowed to enter Mainland China upon his arrival. He was stuck outside the wall![262] A crisis? Perhaps, but then again the Chinese word for *crisis* literally means "dangerous opportunity." Morrison took advantage of this less-than-desirable situation. Hunkering down on Macau Island offshore, he spent more than a decade studying the Chinese language and translating the Bible into Chinese. He completed the New Testament in 1813, the Old Testament in 1819. Along the way, he also created a six-volume Chinese dictionary. In twenty-seven years of ministry, Morrison had only ten converts—and he didn't baptize his first until seven years after his arrival!

A failure? Not at all! Morrison provides a great example for the faithful of how God can work even in the presence of a great spiritual wall. Living on Macau Island gave Morrison both the proximity and the time necessary to complete his formidable and important translation work. His efforts would pave the way for future wall-busters.

The Opium War

In the 1830s, British merchants were ignoring Chinese imperial decrees and flooding the country with opium. An effort in 1838 by Imperial Commissioner Lin Tsehsu (1785–1850) to stop this coercive drug trafficking by a foreign government resulted in the infamous Opium War (1839–1842).[263]

The conflict ended with the Treaty of Nanking that essentially bullied the Chinese into granting the British the city of Hong Kong and the right to bring their goods (read "their opium") into five Chinese ports. Some of the terms of this agreement also specified that Christian missionaries had permission to evangelize in certain areas. As noted, these missionaries often arrived on the very ships that were loaded with opium! (Sadly, the son of missionary Robert Morrison had a hand in this trade arrangement, which brought widespread drug addiction to China.)

At the risk of oversimplifying centuries of complicated history, the spiritual wall that has long thwarted Christian missionary efforts to China was built by actions like these. From the Chinese perspective, to welcome Western missionaries was tantamount to opening the door to drug traffickers.

> The fundamental goal of the Jesuits—the conversion of China to Christianity—proved to be unattainable. Many factors contributed to such an outcome; a shift from tolerance to persecution in the policies of the Ch'ing, acrimonious rivalry among the Catholic missionaries and, perhaps most significantly, the growing disrepute brought upon the Christian faith by the activities of its purported believers, the European colonizers of East Asia.[264]

The Taiping Rebellion (1850–1864)

After repeatedly failing his imperial examinations,[265] a Chinese man named Hong Xiuquan (1814–1864) suffered a breakdown of sorts. During this period he had a dream or vision in which he was caught up into heaven. Upon his recovery, Hong came across some Christian tracts (written and printed by Liang Afa, one of Robert Morrison's few converts).

Hong turned to Christianity, but soon embraced some unorthodox spiritual ideas (with serious political and social ramifications). Specifically, Hong came to believe he was the younger brother of Jesus Christ! Among the oppressed peasant class, he then began attracting followers all across China with his version of the faith known as Taiping Christianity. Hong convinced his disciples to embrace an austere lifestyle in which they even swore off relationships with women.

Taiping Christianity half-borrowed and half-recreated for Chinese purposes a full repertoire of prayers, hymns, and rituals, and preached the brotherhood and sisterhood of all mankind under the fatherhood of the one true and only God.... Taiping Christianity was a unique East-West amalgam of ideas and practices geared to militant action, the like of which was not seen again until China borrowed and sinified Marxism-Leninism a century later.[266]

Historian John Fairbank has labeled Hong "the rebel king of China" and compared his ascent to that of both Napoleon Bonaparte and Adolf Hitler, describing it as "full of drama, the mysteries of chance, and personal and social factors much debated ever since."[267]

By 1850 Hong's restless grassroots movement had become a full-fledged insurrection, known as the Taiping Rebellion. (Ironically, "Taiping" in Chinese means "great peace," yet this civil war was the most destructive in the country's history.) Even some orthodox Christians sided with Hong's insurrection. Griffith John of the London Missionary Society declared, "I fully believe that God is uprooting idolatry in this land through the insurgents, and that he will by means of them, in connection with the foreign missionary, plant Christianity in its stead."[268]

In 1851, Hong declared his Heavenly Kingdom. By 1853 he had established Nanjing as the capital for his Society for the Worship of God. When the movement began to lose traction militarily, Hong withdrew and became preoccupied with reading the new Chinese translation of *Pilgrim's Progress*.[269] The apocalyptic nature of his discombobulated Christian message continued to resonate among his followers.

His armed rebellion, undergirded with strange Christian overtones, only reinforced the prevailing suspicion that Christianity was a threat to native Chinese culture. This stoked anti-Christian sentiment and resulted in tracts with titles like "Death Blow to Corrupt Doctrines." Anti-Christian sentiments of the Chinese communist appear linked to this period, and would harass later missionaries, and institutions. Over the China Inland Mission gate a sign was posted: "What a beast is this Jesus whose venom has reached to China."[270]

Thus the wall became thicker and higher.

The Ministry of Hudson Taylor

Yet at least one Christian, arriving in China on the heels of the Taiping Rebellion, managed to find missionary success.

How did Hudson Taylor win converts during a time of great Chinese hostility toward the church? By (a) choosing—like Matteo Ricci and the early Jesuits—to immerse himself in Chinese culture (and language and dress); and (b) using the more candid approach of putting the translated Gospels directly in front of the Chinese.

In 1865, Taylor established the China Inland Mission. The name reflected Taylor's desire, distinct from other Protestant missionaries at the time, to take the Bible beyond China's port cities deep into the countryside. He called for bold believers to join him, claiming, "China is not to be won by quiet, ease-loving men and women. The stamp of men and women we need is such as will put Jesus, China [and] souls first and foremost in everything and at every time—even life itself must be secondary."[271]

The organization adopted other radical principles (at least for that time). Its missionaries were not required to have formal education, and unmarried women were not accepted for the work. All missionaries wore Chinese dress and raised personal financial support rather than depend on stipends from a denomination (an arrangement that brought both freedom of governance and financial independence). The mission was interdenominational and stated, "the mission authority would be in China, not back in London."[272] Taylor's "faith mission model was later replicated by various societies before the end of the century: The Evangelical Alliance Mission (1890), Sudan Interior Mission (1893), African Inland Mission (1895), and Liebenzell Mission (1898)."[273]

Such rules and principles may have been risky, but they proved transformative. Hundreds of churches and tens of thousands of converts resulted, in spite of occasional protest banners over the gates.

The Boxer Rebellion

It was during this period of growing resentment against foreigners that the Boxer Rebellion occurred (1899–1901).

Weary of increasing Western interference (and Christian influence within the Chinese culture), a movement calling itself the Society of the Righteous and Harmonious Fists sprang up in the summer of 1900. In Beijing (known as "Peking" at the time), mobs killed hundreds of foreigners, targeting missionaries and even Chinese Christians. This uprising prompted Western countries—including the United States—to send some sixteen thousand troops to squelch brutally the Boxers.[274] Ironically, a Chinese effort to reinforce their cultural wall resulted in precisely the kind of foreign interference the Boxers were resisting!

When the smoke cleared, China was required to make reparation payments for the loss of life and property in the rebellion. Hudson Taylor, however, rejected this offer of compensation to his China Inland Mission. He said, "Should I have a thousand pounds, China can claim them all; should I have a thousand lives, I would not spare one not to give to China."[275]

Following this violent chapter, the pendulum swung the other way, and missionaries were allowed to pour into China.[276] By 1905, some 3,445 missionaries were living there, 90 percent of them from the USA or Great Britain.

Illustrative of the complex relationship between China and the United States (even up until today), it's worth nothing that these violent events happened right on the heels of the Chinese Exclusion Act of 1882. That law forbade Chinese citizens from immigrating to the United States...and it enjoyed the enthusiastic support of the American public (and even some outspoken American missionaries—the people associated in the Chinese mind most closely with Christianity). The conclusion drawn by many Chinese? *American Christians want to save our souls...but apparently only on our soil.*

Chiang Kai-shek and Chairman Mao

In 1911 widespread unrest in China became wholesale rebellion. The emperor was forced from power. The first president of the new Republic of the United Chinese Provinces was a Christian named Sun Yat-sen. When he opened the doors wide to Protestant missionaries, there was hope that the entire country might be Christianized.

Yat-sen was succeeded by Chiang Kai-shek, a lifelong Buddhist who converted to Methodism when he married Soong Mei-ling (a descendant of Paul Hsu, who had converted to Christianity through the ministry of Matteo Ricci). In the 1920s the conservative, anti-Communist Chiang Kai-shek launched an offensive against the Communist leader Mao Tse-tung (or Zedong), whose party was growing in popularity. By the mid-thirties, Chiang had driven Mao and his forces far north. But when Japan attacked China in July of 1937, Chiang was forced to ask for Mao's help in repelling their common invader.

Following Japan's defeat in 1945, Mao renewed his attempt to turn China into a Communist state. In 1949 he succeeded, establishing the People's Republic of China.

Mao's victory led to a predictable result—Christian missionaries were expelled:

> At the time of the missionary departure in 1949, Chinese Christians were numbered at approximately 3 million Roman Catholics and three-quarters of a million Protestants.[277]

Chiang Kai-Shek and his wife Soong Mei-ling fled to Taiwan following Mao's takeover. He died there in 1975. She spent much of her energies promoting Christian missionary work, eventually moving to New York City, where she died at the age of 105.

With the Communist takeover, Western missionaries were left to wonder what would become of Chinese Christianity. Mark Tooley, president of the Institute of Religion and Democracy, notes:

> Chiang Kai-shek was Methodist, and Taiwan under the Kuomintang had relative religious freedom while Communist China under Mao tried to destroy Christianity. Yet today Taiwan is at most 5 percent Christian (with only a few dozen Methodist churches) while Mainland China, where religion still faces restriction, is at least 5 percent, and some estimate approaching 10 percent. Under current church growth rates, China in 20 years or so may have more Christians than any other country.[278]

The Three-Self Patriotic Movement (TSPM)

In an attempt to ensure a state-friendly Christianity that could be carefully regulated and controlled, Chairman Mao established The Three-Self Patriotic Movement (TSPM). The three principles of TSPM—self-leadership, self-support (i.e., no financial dependence on foreign entities), and self-propagation (i.e., indigenous missionary work)—were all aimed at removing any sort of Western influence over Chinese Christianity.

In some ways it didn't matter. A thriving, underground, house church movement had begun to spread—despite persecution. In 2002, Thomas Harvey wrote a biography of Wang Ming-Dao, the so-called dean of the house church movement in China. He described Wang's incarceration for his refusal to join the TSPM in 1955, and documented how he gained international attention for his refusal to leave prison until the government granted him true freedom. Understanding the explosive nature of the house churches, Harvey wrote: "With some thirty to seventy million souls and a growth rate of 7 percent annually, the number of Christians in China dwarfs the number of Christians in most nations of the earth. Like Christians throughout the developing world, Chinese Christians represent the vanguard of the church in the twenty-first century."[279]

Watchman Nee (1903–1972) was another prominent Chinese pastor (and prolific author with an international following) in the latter half of the twentieth century. Some historians credit him with founding the local church movement that transformed China. This movement not only survived but managed to thrive "underground" after the Communist Revolution in 1949. Like Wang, Nee was targeted by the government for his refusal to submit to the TSPM. Before dying in a labor camp, he stated, "I want nothing for myself. I want everything for the Lord."

Since the days of Mao, Chinese Christianity has been marked by constant tension between approved state churches and the underground house church movement. The Chinese government—in perpetual "wall-building mode"—now requires religious leaders to "conduct religious activities in the Chinese context, practice core socialist values, carry forward the fine traditions of the Chinese nation, and actively explore religious thought which conforms to the reality in China."[280]

Despite those heavy-handed attempts at government control, David Aikman, speaking for the Acton Institute in 2016, noted that Christians have increased from around four million when the Communists took over to around 80 million. The Pew Research Center set the number at 67 million in 2011.[281] Others estimate it may be as high as 100 million today.[282]

In response, the Communist Party of China (CPC) in 2017 "urged residents to replace personal religious displays with posters of President Xi Jinping" (under the threat of withholding government assistance).[283] In 2018, the CPC abruptly closed some mega-churches and tried to break up some key communities in the historic Underground Church movement.[284] Despite such harassment, Bob Fu, founder of the religious rights group ChinaAid, said in 2018, "I have hope for the future. These campaigns were done in Roman times, under Stalin, and under Mao, and none succeeded. It will only have the opposite effect, and if Communist party cadres studied history they would see this. Crackdowns will cause the church to grow faster, and help churches be more united."[285]

While these developments raise concerns for believers in China, they do not threaten Christianity's spread. The faith has been amazingly resilient there, just as it was in the face of fierce Roman persecution during the first three centuries of the Church's existence.

Other Heroes of the Faith in China

Chapter 11 of the New Testament book of Hebrews is a famous listing of many of the "heroes" of the Judeo-Christian faith. Perhaps a similar, abbreviated list would be appropriate here as we wrap up our brief review of the spread of Chinese Christianity:

"Lottie" Moon (1840–1912), often regarded as the "patron saint of Southern Baptist missions," gave her life and all of her resources to the Chinese people. She planted a church—a revolutionary act for a female missionary in her era—and trained one of her Chinese converts to pastor it. By the time of her death in 1912, the church had at least one thousand converts.[286] Lottie spent her final days in abject poverty due to a famine in the region of P'ing-tu. Each December Southern Baptist churches take up a special collection in her honor for foreign missionary work. Since 1888 more than $4.5 billion has been given to this "Lottie Moon Christmas Offering."

Jonathan (1859–1936) and **Rosalind Goforth** (1864–1942)—how's that for an appropriate surname for a missionary couple?—were from Canada. Their European-style home in China's Honan province became something of a tourist attraction (and thus an unlikely but highly effective tool for evangelism). Enduring great hardships (the deaths of five of their eleven children, a difficult marriage, and nearly being hacked to death in the Boxer Rebellion), the Goforths had a huge impact for Christ—Jonathan being instrumental in the famous 1908 revival in Manchuria and one of the best known evangelists in China. During one stretch of his emotional, itinerant preaching (1908–1913), some thirteen thousand Chinese reportedly professed faith in Christ.

Speaking of evangelists, we'd be remiss to leave out **John Sung** (1901–1944), often known as "the Billy Graham of China." Between

1928 and 1940, Sung crisscrossed China (and other Asian countries, including Singapore, Indonesia, and the Philippines), preaching the good news of Christ to enormous crowds. Untold numbers were converted through his ministry and people found healing through his prayers (though he did not advertise himself as a "healer").

The ministry of **Gladys Aylward** (1902–1970) was remarkable. A tiny, plucky, uneducated British maid, Gladys sensed a calling to serve God in China. Upon her arrival, she teamed up with Jeannie Lawson, an older missionary, to open an inn (at which the women attempted to "show and tell" Christ's love to travelers). During the Japanese invasion, Aylward rescued one hundred children, later establishing an orphanage.[287] Her life became the subject of the major motion picture *The Inn of the Sixth Happiness* (1958), starring Ingrid Bergman. Aylward is credited with saying:

> I wasn't God's first choice…. I don't know who it was… it must have been a man…a well-educated man. I don't know what happened. Perhaps he died. Perhaps he wasn't willing…and God looked down…and saw Gladys Aylward…and God said, "Well, she's willing…."

We can't overlook **John** (1907–1934) and **Betty Stam** (1906–1934), missionaries with the China Inland Mission. In 1934, during the Chinese Civil War, the Stams and their infant daughter were apprehended by Communist soldiers. The night of their capture, John managed to write a short message to his mission's leaders that read simply, "My wife, baby and myself are today in the hands of communist bandits. Whether we will be released or not no one knows. May God be magnified in our bodies, whether by life or by death. Philippians 1:20."[288] Though the Stams were viciously martyred (their daughter was miraculously spared), their deaths "inspired a generation of missionaries."[289]

Eric Liddell (1902–1945) was born in China to Scottish missionaries. He famously became a 1924 Olympic gold (and bronze) med-alist—a story memorialized in the Oscar-winning film *Chariots of Fire* (1981). Liddell then served as a missionary in China from 1925 until he was captured by the Japanese in 1943. He spent his final two years in a POW camp, encouraging others to "love and pray for their captors." Shortly before the camp was liberated, Liddell died of a brain tumor.

Though a wall has remained in many aspects of Chinese life up until the present, the efforts of countless believers have helped the gospel message take root among the Chinese.[290] So much so, that Christians are coming out from behind China's wall to go to other cultures. China is now a leading nation in terms of sending mission-aries to the world.

The Spread of Christianity in Mongolia

For those who have forgotten their world geography, Mongolia is that large region situated between Russia (to the north) and China (to the south). At one time, the Mongolian empire was the largest in human history, comprising parts of (modern) China, Mongolia, Korea, Iran, Kazakhstan, Russia (up to Moscow and over to the Baltic Sea), and everything in between.

Mongolian history is filled with political intrigue, stained with brutal military episodes, flavored by nomadic culture, and sprinkled with larger-than-life personalities.

Genghis Khan (ca. 1162–1227) is one of those personalities, the founder of this great and mysterious empire. While his exact reli-gious beliefs are hard to pinpoint, we know he was "a Deist supported by shamanism."[291] Of God he once said: "There is only one God, Creator of Heaven and Earth, Who alone gives life and death, riches and poverty, as pleases Him and Who has over everything an absolute power."[292]

Given such a statement, we might assume Khan was an orthodox believer. It's more likely he was introduced to monotheism via his contact with Nestorian Christians (or, more accurately, East Syriac Christians),[293] or perhaps even through his interactions with Muslims. It's entirely possible this was simply one idea from his unusual smorgasbord of religious beliefs. His grandson Kublai Khan (1215–1294) became the first non-Han to rule all of China. As emperor he established the Yuan dynasty, which survived until the Ming Dynasty in 1368.

As far as Christianity's spread to and through Mongolia, it's believed that the aforementioned Alopen (sometimes spelled Aluoben) was sent by the "Church of the East" to evangelize China *and* Mongolia in AD 635 (during the Tang dynasty). Based on statements attributed to others it's widely believed that some sort of Nestorian Christian presence remained there until at least the thirteenth century.

If Grandpa Genghis was merely intrigued by Christianity, his grandson Kublai Khan seemed genuinely interested. In fact, when the Italian Marco Polo reached Khan's court at Shangdu, the Mongolian leader allegedly requested a "hundred wise men of learning in the Christian religion."

It was not until the fifteenth and sixteenth centuries that Dominican and Jesuit missionaries came to Mongolia. They were not, however, the first Catholics. The Franciscan William of Rubruck had journeyed in 1255 to Karakorum, the capital of the Mongol Empire (a visit documented in reports given to King Louis IX of France, along with Rubruck's assessment of Nestorian Christianity in Mongolia at the time). During the latter part of the sixteenth century Jesuit missionaries Matteo Ricci and Giovanni da Montecorvino also ministered in Mongolia. From the sixteenth century until the early part of the twentieth century, the Russian Orthodox Church thrived there.

The first full Mongolian Bible translation came in the 1840s. Almost a century later, an intrepid trio of Protestant missionaries Mildred Cable (sometimes lovingly referred to as "Napoleon" by her coworkers) and sisters Eva and Francesca French helped to translate the Bible into Cyrillic script.

In the late twentieth century, the government began persecuting religious groups adhering to Buddhism, Christianity, or Mormonism. In fact, in 2000 the Mongolian government confiscated ten thousand Bibles and six hundred Christian videos that had been brought into the country. It is likely that some of these entered after the daring Bible drop (smuggling operation) in 1981 known as Project Pearl. Brothers Stupfen and Brother Andrew were instrumental in having one million Bibles (232 tons) dropped off China's coast in the Fujian Province. (For Christians, it's a heroic episode involving a specially designed tugboat, near capture, and a well-orchestrated group of two thousand Chinese Christians hauling in 232 floating crates and distributing them at night on bicycles and whatever mode worked.)[294]

Like their neighbors in China, the Mongolian people have historically embraced assorted religious beliefs. "It is clear from archaeological finds that they enjoyed wearing Christian crosses, though they might enliven these with such symbols as the Indian swastika which Buddhists had brought them."[295] However, despite centuries of Christian missionary efforts, the Communists' oppression of religion nearly wiped out Christianity in Mongolia. "In terms of Christian mission, Mongolia has been the most barren country in Asia, until the sudden demise of Communism, which happened in 1989. Before that historic year there was no reliable evidence of the existence of a single Christian in this remote country."[296]

What is happening today in this region? Though Buddhism continues to be popular, the Christian faith is spreading in Mongolia because the younger generation finds it appealing. Ulaanbaatar, the capital of Mongolia, has become the hub of Christian activity. The fastest growing groups are those being established by Korean Christian missionaries, whose work in the area has exploded.

People are once again wearing crosses in Mongolia—but without the swastikas. Some 330 Christian congregations exist, and like the Nestorians before them, they are bickering—this time over which Mongolian Bible translation is best.[297]

The Spread of Christianity on the Korean Peninsula

For the lands stretching eastward from the Arabian Sea to the Sea of Japan—including the Korean Peninsula—Christianity arrived via a combination of invaders, immigrants, and missionaries.[298] From the first centuries of the Common Era (dominated by the Roman Empire) to the thirteenth century in which the Mongol Empire stretched all the way to Baghdad, Korea had its fair share of visitors. In the end, however, Koreans were most responsible for the spread of the gospel in Korea.[299]

Documentary and archeological sources reveal that Christians were working in Sri Lanka (Ceylon) in the fifth and Indonesia in the seventh centuries, and in Korea and Japan during the seventh to ninth centuries. By the time of the High Middle Ages in the West, churches existed in the mercantile communities throughout Southeast Asia.[300]

Despite these early inroads, it took centuries for Christianity to gain a real foothold. As happened with other great missionaries to Asia, Matteo Ricci's work in China spilled over to Korea via his writings. In the early 1600s, a Korean visitor to Beijing brought back some of Ricci's Christian books, effectively introducing Christianity. In 1784, the aristocrat Yi Seung-hun was baptized in a Catholic church in Beijing. He returned to Korea and planted the first Korean church. "Today, the Korean Catholic Church is the only national Catholic church that is recognized as founded by a lay community."[301]

In 1994, Daniel M. Davies writing from the Korea Branch of the University of Maryland, noted:

> Christianity has had a profound impact upon Korean political and social life. That influence began in the 1600s and continues until the present time. Indeed, Korea has been the only East Asian nation that has incorporated Christianity in the mainstream of its political and social life.[302]

And yet the road from just a handful of Korean believers in the early 1600s to some 15 *million* South Korean Christians today (including six Christian presidents since 1948) was full of detours and U-turns.

In 1758, the Korean king called Catholicism evil and outlawed the faith. By the century's end, Chinese and French Catholic priests were welcome again.

At the beginning of the nineteenth century, Queen Jeongsun oversaw the execution of more than three hundred Catholic Christians. Witnessing this atrocity was a Christian woman by the name of Columba Kang Wan-suk. She belonged to a group called the "Unmarried Virgins," mostly affluent women who refused marriage or otherwise bucked familial societal norms by living in community and practicing celibacy.[303]

When Columba hid a priest from the authorities—so that area Catholics might be able to celebrate holy communion—she was arrested, tortured, and executed as part of what came to be known as the Sinyu Persecution (1801). Once again, Christianity was prohibited in Korea.

Back and forth the pendulum swung. After something of a reprieve for the faithful, a Korean priest was beheaded in 1846. Persecution broke out again. Before it ended in 1866, more than eight thousand Catholics in the fast-growing Korean church had sacrificed their lives for the sake of the gospel.

While studies cannot support the oft-made claim that the growth of oppressed Christian communities in Korea was directly tied to incidents of martyrdom, there is no doubt that the courage exhibited by those facing persecution (like "The Korean Martyrs") provided considerable inspiration for watching believers.

In 1885, reminiscent of Constantine's Edict of Milan, western missionaries were given permission to enter Korea legally. The first two to do so, Horace Underwood and Henry Appenzeller, were Protestants, a Presbyterian and a Methodist, respectively. (It's reported that the men came ashore together, hand-in-hand, at Inchon, to avoid any future arguments about which denomination got there first.) They entered the country to serve established Christian communities. One was in iju, near the modern-day border between North Korea and China. The other was on the west coast, at Sorae, the hometown of Suh Sang-ryun (1848–1926), one of Korea's first Protestant evangelists. That community is now regarded as the "cradle" of Protestant Christianity in Korea, a symbol of the self-supporting, self-governing, and self-propagating nature of Korean Christianity.

Many Koreans played enormous roles in the growth of the Church. The renowned "Bible woman," Kim Gang (aka Dorcas, which means "gazelle" or "deer") was beloved for preaching a 1,500-mile mountain circuit during the latter part of the nineteenth century.

In the early part of the twentieth century, Kil Sun-ju (1865–1935) burst onto the scene as one of the country's first Presbyterian ministers. (He was also one of the first two signatories of Korea's Declaration of Independence in 1919.) In the wake of a powerful prayer meeting in Wonsan in 1903,[304] Sun-ju's preaching sparked the Pyongyang Revival of 1907 (sometimes called the "Korean Pentecost). William Blair, a forty-year missionary veteran in North Korea, wrote of this spiritual awakening:

> Man after man would rise, confess his sin, break down and weep, and then throw himself on the floor and beat the floor with his fists in a perfect agony of conviction.... Sometimes, after a confession, the whole audience would break out into audible prayer, and the effect of that audience of hundreds of men praying together in audible prayer was something indescribable. Again, after another confession, they would break out into uncontrollable weeping and we would all weep together. We couldn't help it. And so the meeting went on until 2 a.m., with confession and weeping and praying.... We had prayed to God for an outpouring of His Holy Spirit upon the People and it had come.[305]

Three years later Japan conquered Korea and tried to obliterate Korean culture, demanding Koreans "to worship the gods of imperial Japan, including dead emperors and the spirits of war heroes who had helped them conquer Korea earlier in the century."[306] Despite this external pressure, Korean Christianity survived.

The Spread of Christianity in Japan

A 2014 article in the *Japan Times* summarizes well the history of Christianity in Japan. Titled "Christian Missionaries Find Japan a Tough Nut to Crack" the article says this has been true

> ...ever since the first of them, St. Francis Xavier, landed in Kyushu in 1549. His first impression, based on an initially friendly reception, was, "In my opinion no people superior to the Japanese will be found among the unbelievers." Two years later, he left disheartened, calling Japanese Buddhism "an invention of the devil....Western Judeo-Christian civilization was built on God. Japanese civilization was not. The West is absolutist, its God embodying absolute power, absolute righteousness, absolute wisdom, absolute truth. Nothing like that exists in Japan. No wonder Xavier and his Japanese hosts misunderstood each other."[307]

As noted earlier, Francis Xavier was the former roommate of Ignatius Loyola at the University of Paris and a cofounder of the Society of Jesus (i.e., the Jesuits). When he heard about "a people most desirous of knowledge" further east, Xavier departed Goa, India, for Japan.

Xavier arrived in Kagoshima in 1549. He found the Japanese people to be wonderful. "They esteem honour more than anything.... They will stand no insults nor slighting words." Despite a few language/translation issues, an estimated two thousand Japanese converted during his short time on the island.[308] The groundwork for a flourishing church was laid. However, Buddhist monks were hostile to Xavier's efforts at proselytizing and the Japanese emperor in Kyoto refused to see him. He left the country after two years.

In the mid-sixteenth century in Nagasaki, Omura Sumitada became the first Christian feudal lord.[309] The Jesuits offered him military protection from the Portuguese, but wanted, in exchange, to obliterate all pagan worship and convert the masses to Christianity. And so, in 1574 a widespread destruction of Shinto shrines and Buddhist temples ensued, along with sixty thousand baptisms (many of them forced). Despite these sorts of odious episodes, the gospel message attracted followers. In 1582 there were some 150,000 Christians and two hundred churches in Japan.

By the late 1590s, Dominicans and Franciscans had begun missions in Japan—even though the Pope had assigned the island to the Jesuits. As these factions began to quarrel, the shogun Hideyoshi began enforcing his decade-old edict against Christianity. Four Franciscan friars were permitted to stay only when they promised not to teach Christianity. "The Franciscans, having accepted this prohibition, immediately proceeded to violate it by conducting service in Nagasaki, Kyoto, and Osaka.... This open defiance of Hideyoshi's authority served to confirm his fears regarding the intentions of the Catholic Church in Japan."[310]

And so Christians came under fire, culminating in the 1597 persecutions that took the lives of the "twenty-six martyrs of Japan"— including Paulo Miki, one of Japan's patron saints. These heroes were crucified in Nagasaki and were the subject of a popular Shusaku Endo novel (1966), adapted for the screen by Martin Scorsese in the film *Silence* (2016).

In 1614 the Tokugawa shoguns (i.e., military leaders) "feared that Christianity was the opening wedge for a European takeover of Japan or that the missionaries and Japanese Christians would back some group opposed to the dynasty."[311] Consequently, the next twenty-five years saw at least four thousand Christian martyrdoms, many suffering horrific deaths:

> A typical scene was witnessed by the English trader Richard Cox in 1619: "Fifty-five persons of all ages and both sexes were burnt alive on the dry bed of the Kamo River in Kyoto, among them little children of five or six years old in their mothers' arms, crying out 'Jesus, receive their souls!'"[312]

Sadly, disagreements among believers—rather than unity—likely exacerbated this campaign, "one of the most savage persecutions in Christian history." And thus the viral spread of the faith in Japan simply did not happen. Rather than a message of new life and hope, "a wary regime saw in the sect a vanguard of foreign imperialism."[313]

And yet, even with decades of persecution, and centuries of censure, a Christian community somehow survived in Kyushu, the home territory of Xavier's translator. The Christians there "secretly passed their beliefs on to their children. Baptism was administered, and the Ten Commandments, some prayers, and basic doctrines were transmitted. The existence of this vestigial Christian community, which numbered more than fifteen thousand, was discovered after the reopening of Japan in the later nineteenth century."[314]

About the same time Hudson Taylor was evangelizing in China, missionaries began returning to Japan. One was Bernard Jean Bettelheim (1811–1870), a Hungarian Christian of Jewish descent. In Okinawa, Bettelheim quickly gained a reputation for odd, boorish behavior. (Every family—even God's—has strange and quirky members, right?) Bettelheim was argumentative. He lodged with his family *in* a Japanese temple for seven years (without permission). He reportedly engaged in what we might call "evangelistic home invasions" (i.e., bursting into homes to preach the gospel). He became so cantankerous that some Japanese officials asked US Naval Commander Perry to take the aggressive outsider off their hands, literally. After repeated requests, in 1854, the eight tempestuous years of Bettelheim's missionary service in Japan ended. One of Perry's ships escorted him away.

Fortunately most of the new wave of missionaries were not like Bettelheim. They embraced the "Indigenous Principle," an approach calling for "self-governing, self-supporting, and self-propagating" Japanese churches. This arrangement stipulated that local ownership and administration of churches and Christian ministries, including finances,[315] should belong to the locals.

And for every Bettelheim who gave the faith a black eye, there were winsome witnesses like James C. Hepburn, an Ivy League physician from Pennsylvania. Hepburn and his wife, Clara, sailed for the Far East in 1840. They spent time in Jakarta (then called Batavia), Singapore, and Macao. Delayed by the Opium War, they entered China in 1842. Illness soon forced a return to America. In 1859, the couple returned to Japan with the American Presbyterian Mission.

Japan had become more open since 1854, due in part to a Japanese-US treaty negotiated by Commander Perry. This was Japan's first commercial treaty with a Western power. It not only sped up the

Westernization of the Japan, it also aided the work of missionaries, who were arriving in droves.

> Soon there were churches in all the major cities of the nation, and native leadership emerged. It is also interesting to note that near Nagasaki Protestant missionaries found about a hundred thousand people who still retained vestiges of what their ancestors had learned centuries earlier from Francis Xavier and other Jesuit missionaries.[316]

After a rough start (mainly due to a Japanese attempt to get him to move his medical center), the Hepburns settled in 1861 at the Sokoji Temple Yokohama. There the missionary doctor trained medical students in the 1860s and 1870s, even while treating six to ten thousand patients annually. On one occasion he "amputated the gangrenous leg of a famous Kabuki actor and fitted the man with an Amercian-made prosthesis." Because the actor was able to resume his stage career, Hepburn greatly boosted the reputation of Western medicine.[317]

One of Hepburn's biggest legacies (other than his long medical practice—he died in 1911 at the tender age of ninety-six!) was his Japanese-English dictionary, published in 1867. Hepburn's extensive knowledge of Chinese helped him translate the repurposed Chinese characters of the Japanese language.

The Christian narrative in Japan is a rich one, from celebrated pioneers like St. Francis Xavier, to the Twenty Six Martyrs of the 1597 executions, to more modern "saints" like Dr. James Hepburn. Mac-Culloch summarizes this arduous journey of the Japanese church:

> The church in Japan, despite the heroism of its native faithful, was reduced to a tiny and half-instructed rem-

nant. It struggled to maintain even a secret existence for more than two centuries until Europeans used military force to secure free access to the country after the 1850s, and rediscovered it with astonishment.[318]

Today, 2 million Japanese—just 1 percent of the population—identify as Christian. The highest concentration of believers are in the western region of country—where the missionaries first landed and not far from the sites of many of the executions.

Like the apostle Thomas, most on the Asian continent were initially resistant to the news of a risen Christ. But like Thomas, a growing number have become convinced of the truth of the gospel and now want to take the good news elsewhere.

The Back to Jerusalem movement, for example, is the dream of the Chinese church to build bridges, not walls. The goal is to flood Muslim, Buddhist, and Hindu nations with missionaries, "to evangelize the unreached peoples from eastern provinces of China westwards toward Jerusalem."[319] Another example of the great missionary heart of the Chinese church was seen in 2015, at a gathering in Hong Kong, at which 850 leaders formulated a plan to send out 20,000 missionaries by the year 2030.[320] Stunning, isn't it? The country that is officially considered "atheistic" is on track to become "the world's largest exporter of the Christian faith."[321]

Imagine that...even as you read this sentence, thousands of Chinese believers (and Christians from South Korea and other Asian countries too) are learning languages like Arabic and English and undergoing missionary training so that they can fan out to places like the Middle East, Southeast Asia, the Indian subcontinent…and Africa.

That continent will be our focus in our next, and our last, chapter.

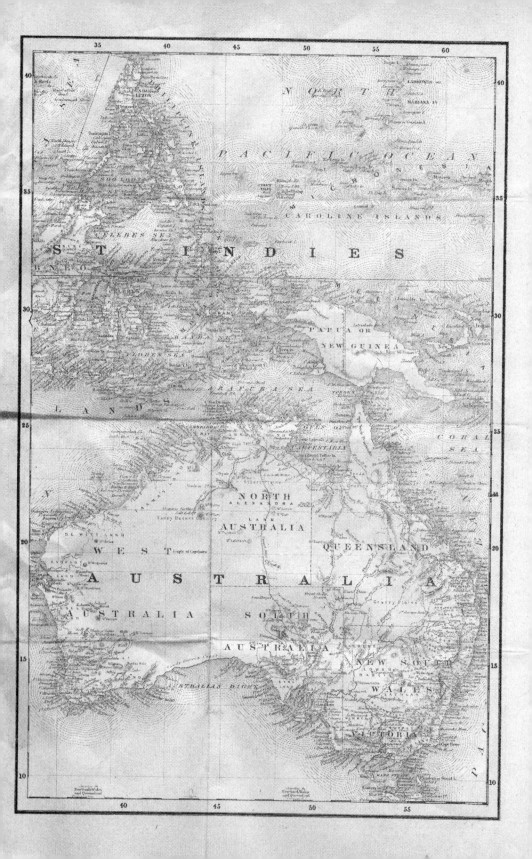

CHAPTER SIX

CONVICTS, CONVERTS, AND FULL CIRCLE

AUSTRALIA, THE ISLANDS, ANTARCTICA, AND SUB-SAHARAN AFRICA

God, send me anywhere, only go with me.
Lay any burden on me, only sustain me.
And sever any tie in my heart except the tie that binds
my heart to Yours.

David Livingstone, *missionary to Africa*[322]

On a breezy November night in far northwestern Kenya, about 120 members of the Turkana tribe[323] are clustered together in the sand, staring wide-eyed at the backside of a large diesel supply truck.

Why have they gathered in the darkness? What are they doing? They're watching the *Jesus* film,[324] and they are *mesmerized*. Few of these people have ever seen a movie. Fewer still have heard about the life, death, and resurrection of Christ.

When the images flickering on the big, makeshift screen show Jesus raise a young girl from the dead, the crowd erupts. Astonished cries of wonder mix with wild cheers and vigorous clapping. (Rest assured, no Hollywood "Applause!" sign ever elicited a quicker or more enthusiastic audience reaction.)

At the end of the night, twenty-three men, women, boys, and

girls express faith in Christ. Typically, these new believers would be baptized within a few days. However, due to drought conditions, the nearest river has been a dusty riverbed for several months. Pastor Francis, the missionary in charge of this outreach—and himself a Turkana tribesman—smiles and says, "For now we will keep teaching them God's Word. When the Lord sends rain, we will take them to the river. If the drought continues, we will go to Lake Turkana and baptize there."

Since 1997, some eighty Turkana pastors, working with Share International, have led 41,000 fellow tribe members to faith and started more than 330 new churches in villages throughout this desert region that is so remote one American described it this way: "Go until you come to nowhere...then keep going for two more days."

Turkanaland (in East Africa) is a prime example, a beautiful snapshot of what Jesus meant when he told his followers to be his witnesses "to the ends of the earth" (Acts 1:8).

☧

We've traced the astonishing spread of Christianity from a house in Jerusalem to the surrounding regions, including North Africa (chapter 1). We've explored (ever so briefly) how believers—not always with the purest motives—took the message of Jesus to and throughout Europe (chapter 2), South America (chapter 3), North America (chapter 4), and Asia (chapter 5).

In this final chapter our focus is on the gospel's arrival and subsequent influence in sub-Saharan Africa,[325] in Australia, New Zealand, Oceania, and even on the frozen continent of Antarctica. When we're done, we'll have a better feel for at least some of the ways in which "the ends of the earth have seen the salvation of our God" (Psalm 98:3).

The Explosive Growth of African Christianity

Following the New Testament era (and the flight of Christians from Jerusalem), Christianity became anchored all across the North African coast. From there, famous church fathers like Tertullian, Clement of Alexandria, Cyprian of Carthage, and Augustine of Hippo taught the faith (and fought its theological opponents). It was also there that unknown hermits and monks—and well-known martyrs like Perpetua and Felicity—lived out the faith in memorable, culture-changing ways.

Twenty centuries later Africa is once again a thriving center of Christian spirituality. Only this time it's the sub-Saharan countries—those that have either recovered from or resisted the Islamic push southward since the seventh century—that are experiencing the most growth and exerting the greatest influence. Ironically, on a continent that is nearly half Muslim (many North African countries are over 90 percent Islamic), Christianity has grown from just a few million adherents in 1910 to roughly 650 million today.[326]

Adam Taylor, the executive director of Sojourners, points to a study by the Pew Research Center as evidence that "Christianity's Future Lies in Africa."[327] If current trends hold, he suggests that by 2060, more than forty percent of the Christians on earth will call sub-Saharan Africa home, up from 26 percent in 2015.[328]

Who could have predicted, when millions of Africans were being enslaved and shipped to European colonies through West African ports like Gabon's infamous "Gate to Nowhere," that one day some of their free descendants would return with an "Africanized" gospel? Or that some of *their* descendants would willingly and eagerly take Christ's hope-filled message to other nations?

"Translating" the Gospel in Africa

Perhaps we can best explain the explosion of the gospel in sub-Saharan Africa as being the result of "translating"—i.e., interpreting and applying the Christian gospel, and the practices associated with it (e.g., frugality, piety, church attendance, gender roles, approach to wealth, healing, etc.)—through the unique grid of African culture.

Focusing mostly on the twentieth century (and echoing some of the "translation" theories expressed by the late Lamin Sanneh of Yale[329]), historian David Maxwell, the Dixie Professor of Ecclesiastical History at the University of Cambridge, has pointed out that Christianity went viral throughout southern Africa when all or part of God's Word became available in the local languages.

> Once the Bible was in the hands of Africans, they quickly seized control of its message, finding all manner of things that missionaries had omitted to tell them about and that resonated with local cultures: healing miracles, visions, exorcisms, angels and demons, food taboos, and polygamy. It was no accident that the great independent prophetic churches emerged soon after the appearance of vernacular scriptures.[330]

We'll come back to this idea shortly. For now, let's consider the "translation" of Christianity into Africa over the long term, from the first century to the present.

The Gospel Comes to Africa (AD 30–600)

How did Christianity reach Africa in the first place?

You'll recall that Luke identified a "Simon from Cyrene" (i.e., a city in Libya) as being in Jerusalem at the time of the crucifixion. In fact, this was the man forced to carry the cross of Jesus (Luke 23:26). In Luke's book of Acts (a sequel to his Gospel), he wrote about people from "Egypt and the parts of Libya near Cyrene" being present at Pentecost in Jerusalem when God poured out his Spirit on the followers of Jesus and the New Testament church was born (Acts 2:10). Acts 8 includes the additional story of a disciple named Philip sharing the good news of Christ (v. 35) with a spiritually curious but confused government official from Ethiopia.

Clearly, from the earliest moments of the Christian era, the message of Jesus was making inroads and changing the lives of Africans.

Ancient church tradition credits the expansion of the gospel further south to Mark (the author of the second Gospel and colleague of both Peter and Paul). This prompts some to argue that Christianity was essentially *indigenous* to Africa, not a later import.[331]

The problem with this theory is twofold. First, the evidence of trans-Saharan trade routes that would have carried people, much less Christianity, *to sub-Saharan Africa* during this period is relatively sketchy.[332] While *North* Africans embraced Christianity eagerly—possibly more readily than any other Roman people—this does not seem to have translated into the sub-Sahara.[333] Second, with the exception of Ethiopia, Christianity died off almost completely in North Africa following the Islamic conquests of the 640s. To reiterate a fact stated above, most North African countries are now more than 90 percent Muslim, with some closer to 100 percent. How these vital hubs of faith gave way to Islam so readily has remained a vexing problem for Christian historians.

Ethiopian and Coptic Christianity (AD 600–1500)

Following the arrival of Islam into North Africa, most of the indigenous Berbers from Morocco to Libya became Muslims and were instrumental in the conquest of Spain. Even so, scholars like Thomas Oden and his colleagues at the Center for African Christianity—and the Coptic Church worldwide—insist that the faith of early North African Christians was deep and sustained. Others like Elizabeth Isichei argue that Christianity was never really embraced in North Africa outside the Romanized cities.[334]

Such debates aside, we know that during the years *before* the Islamic conquests, an African Christian kingdom called **Aksum** (along the Red Sea) was very powerful. According to some early Islamic sources, it may even have had influence in Arabia.

Following the conquests, the only significant Christian populations left in Africa were found in Ethiopia and Egypt. "Copt" is a corruption of the old word for Egypt, and while the number of Copts continued to fall during the first three centuries of Muslim rule, Ethiopian Christians remained independent and politically strong. In the late middle ages and into the early modern period, they experienced a resurgence when, for political reasons, they made repeated attempts to reincorporate with the Catholic Church.[335]

An intriguing source for our understanding of this period of African Christianity is the *Kebra Nagast*. This fascinating Ethiopian document (with widely contested dates of origin, but possibly as late as the fourteenth century),[336] purports to tell "the true history of the origin of the Solomonic line of kings in Ethiopia."[337] The book discusses the relationship between King Solomon of Israel and the Ethiopian Queen Makeda (aka "the Queen of Sheba"). It claims the Ark of the Covenant came to Ethiopia with Makeda's son, the Ethiopian Emperor Menelik I![338] You read that right. Many Ethiopian Christians sincerely believe the gold-covered ark built during the time of Moses (see Exodus 25–26) rests today in the remote Ethiopian city of Aksum, inside the Church of St. Mary of Zion. However, before you rush to your computer to purchase plane tickets, hoping to get a glimpse of this holy relic, you should know…the only people ever allowed to see this alleged ark are its mysterious caretakers.

Catholic Missions to West and West-Central Africa (1483–1792)

In the late fifteenth century, Portuguese sailors and priests began landing on the coast of Kongo (in west central Africa). By 1491 the entire kingdom had become Christian—though the meaning of that phrase has been fiercely debated.

What's the real story here? The *Manikongo*, or ruler of Kongo, was Nzinga a Nkuwu, who personally embraced Christianity. Three years before his death in 1509, his son Nzinga Mbemba (1456–1543), who had been trained by Portuguese priests, was crowned King Afonso I.[339] Despite resisting some activities by his Portuguese visitors (especially the traders seeking slaves), Afonso wanted very much to Christianize his kingdom—making it a Catholic country. He is best remembered for his lively correspondence with the king of Portugal.

Nearby areas were also introduced to the gospel. In 1626, Ana Nzinga (1582–1663) became the *ngola* (or queen) of the African state of Ndongo, on the Central African coast (in the area known today as Angola). Historians are fascinated by Nzinga because of the sensational stories that swirl about her memory. This particular African queen was proud, refusing to let powerful men treat her as an inferior. She was fearless, sometimes dressing in male garb and leading her troops in battle against aggressors—both the Portuguese and hostile neighboring tribes. When forced to relocate her people, she was shrewd, declaring her new kingdom of Matamba a refuge for runaway slaves (and thereby building her army in the process).

We mention the enigmatic Nzinga here because she was also an avowed convert to Christianity (though some have questioned the sincerity of her commitment). In 2017, Boston University historian Linda Heywood, after spending almost a decade combing through the original records of the Dutch West East India Company, and reams of missionary correspondence, published a new and credible account of Nzinga's life.[340]

One other influential person from this period is worth noting: Doña Beatriz Kimpa Vita (1684–1706) of the Kongo. In her youth, Doña Beatriz learned the truths of Christianity and also trained as an *nganga* (one trained in traditional healing arts). At twenty-one, she claimed to have had a vision of St. Anthony in which he commissioned her to serve as a medium for his spirit, with a goal of purifying Kongolese Christianity. These events effectively launched the Antonian movement, which taught, among other things, that Jesus was actually from the Kongo! An exhibit in *The Met* summarizes Doña Beatriz's role in Kongolese history:

> Although the movement recognized papal authority, it was hostile to European missionaries, whom it consid-

ered corrupt and unsympathetic to the spiritual needs of Kongolese Catholics. Doña Beatriz and her followers briefly occupied Mbanza Kongo, from which she sent emissaries to spread her teachings and urge rulers of the divided Kongo territories to unite under one king. In 1706, however, she was captured by King Pedro II and burned as a heretic at the behest of Capuchin monks.[341]

This three-hundred-year period illustrates the dynamic kinds of "cultural translation" taking place between African notions about spirituality and the beliefs and actions of European Christians. Clearly, the Christian symbols and practices so sensible and precious to European believers, things like water baptism, made little sense to Central Africans. By necessity, priests struggled to translate the faith to this new audience.

As to the depth and/or orthodoxy of Christianity in sub-Saharan Africa during this era, scholars are divided.[342]

The Abolition of Slavery and the Rise of the Missions Society (1792–1864)

The late eighteenth century and most of the nineteenth were dominated by two world-altering movements: the tireless effort to end the slave trade and the attempt to send Christian missionaries all over the earth.

A few high points are worth noting. In 1784, Melville Horne, a chaplain in Freetown, Sierra Leone, published a *Letter on Mission*, in which he made the case for a new mission society that would transcend confessional lines between Calvinists and Arminians, liberals and conservatives. The following year the Clapham sect, a group of British social reformers, was established.

In 1787, British Quakers formed what ultimately became known as the Society for the Abolition of the Slave Trade. Because of his abolitionist views, Josiah Wedgewood, the noted pottery/china maker—and grandfather of Charles Darwin—produced the famous "Am I not a Man and a Brother" medallion for this group.[343] (You might want to check in grandma's attic for one of these medallions. In 2017, one from 1790 fetched $7,532 at a Sotheby's auction!)

A towering force in the abolition movement was the diminutive William Wilberforce. A member of the British Parliament, Wilberforce began many of his political speeches by decrying the horrors of the slave trade; however, he always did so in a humble way. For example, in 1789, he said:

> I mean not to accuse any one, but to take the shame upon myself, in common, indeed, with the whole parliament of Great Britain, for having suffered this horrid trade to be carried on under their authority.
>
> We are all guilty—we ought all to plead guilty, and not to exculpate ourselves by throwing the blame on others.[344]

With this kind of tactful, yet relentless leadership, the anti-slavery movement won incremental victories. They were aided by the 1789 publication of the widely read autobiography *The Interesting Narrative of the Life of Olaudah Equiano, Or Gustavus Vassa, The African.*

In this riveting chronicle of enslavement, Equiano wrote openly of his faith, and used Christian principles to appeal to his readers to do all within their power to end slavery once and for all. In chapter 2 of his memoir he writes, "O, ye nominal Christians! Might not an African ask you, learned you this from your God?" The combination of such passionate writings and speeches led at last to the Abolition of Slavery bill on July 26, 1833. Wilberforce, perhaps satisfied that his life's work was done at last, died three days later.

Interestingly, the goals of the anti-slavery and Christian missionary movements came together in the formation of multiple missionary societies and agencies.[345] Often, it was freed slaves who were the first converts of these mission endeavors. Samuel Ajayi Crowther (1809–1891) is a prime example. He was freed in 1822, trained in the 1830s by CMS missionaries, and consecrated to the ministry in 1843. However, simply because Crowther was African, some British missionaries wouldn't acknowledge his leadership ability and refused to serve under him.[346] In short, "the talented ex-slave collided with the roadblock of racism."[347] Even his own colleague, the English missionary Henry Townsend, trumpeted the "superiority of the white over the black man."[348] Tragically, other white missionaries in Niger agreed with Townsend.

A more uplifting story of a benevolent white missionary is the account of Robert Moffat (1795–1883), the Scottish gardener-turned-missionary, often referred to as "the father of South African missions." Serving with the London Missionary Society, Moffat's desire was to take the gospel into the African interior. He worked mostly among the Tswana—and with great effect. In the 1860s, his son, John Smith Moffat (1835–1918), led an expedition into what is now Zambia and Zimbabwe. And Moffat's daughter, Mary (1821–1862)? She married arguably the most famous African missionary of all, becoming Mary Moffat Livingstone.

David Livingstone (1813–1873) has been described as brilliant, but a "frail, temperamental human being with serious personality flaws."[349] He traversed southern Africa from 1851 until his death, befriending Africans, making important geographical discoveries, and doing what he could to end the slave trade. But his greatest achievement, at least in the eyes of historian A. J. Wills, was that he "understood the Africans in a way that no other man of his time, even Moffat, had done."[350]

When Livingstone died, his servants buried his heart in the African soil (appropriately), mummified his body, and transported it some 1,500 miles to the coast where it was shipped back to England. A state funeral for the revered missionary-explorer followed at Westminster Abbey.

Other lesser-known figures also fell in love with the African people. Charles Mackenzie (1825–1862), a Scotsman, was recruited by the Universities Mission to Central Africa (UMCA) to be the first bishop in the area that is now Mozambique, Malawi, and Tanzania. From the get-go, he endured heavy criticism for wearing vestments that identified him with the Western Christian Church and for trying to carry out his superior's order "that African Christians participate in full equality with white Christians in all church affairs."[351] Mackenzie spent a tumultuous year ministering in Manganja tribal territory[352] and his final journey is legendary for its many tribulations: mosquito attacks, a capsized canoe, loss of all medicines, and subsequently dying of a fever on Malo Island before David Livingstone and others arrived.

Colonial Christianity (1864–1918)

While colonialism wasn't *official* in most African countries until the late nineteenth century, African Christianity was colonial in its structures from the beginning. That is to say, it derived most of its momentum from outside missionaries and agencies. Historians have spent much time and effort trying to understand the roots and fruit of this complex, varied history. Defenders point to the "blessings" of colonialism—not to justify abuses, but to argue that Africa is better off now, at least educationally, medically, and spiritually, than it was before. Others see such assessments as simplistic, naïve, and grossly inaccurate.

It was a hunger for *independence* among the indigenous peoples—based on the example of Christians in Ethiopia—that resulted in the rise of the "Ethiopian Church" movement across the continent. As European colonialism spread, African believers began rejecting the paternalism of the European missionaries and mission agencies and forming their own independent churches.[353]

Assisting this drive toward autonomy was a group that some historians have labeled the *middle figures*. These gifted individuals—mission schoolteachers, midwives, and Bible translators—rendered, literally, the words and meanings of the Bible into the assorted languages and cultures of the African people. David Maxwell has called this work the "most important contribution to African history in the nineteenth century."[354] The middle figures, in short, made the Christian faith both compatible with and accessible to the African mindset.[356]

The Rise of the Independent Christianity

By 1910, most of the early colonial *resistance* movements in sub-Saharan Africa had either died down or been put down. The Germans had massacred the Herero and Nama in South West Africa (current Namibia). Rebellions had been squelched in Tanga and South Africa, and the widespread push for independence seemed to dissipate. And yet during this first half of the twentieth century, Christian institutions were where Africans began speaking truth to power.

There was a wave of conversions. In 1900, an estimated 4 million Africans claimed allegiance to the Christian faith. Between 1900 and 1950, that number increased to 34 million, through "indigenization,"[356] i.e., Africans taking hold of Christianity and making it their own. This phenomenon happened, in large part, due to powerful African church leaders.

Case in point: In 1911, Isaiah Shembe, a Zulu, founded the Nazareth Baptist Church in South Africa. The church emphasized the lost tradition of Old Testament Sabbath-worship, referred to God as Jehovah, and made pilgrimages annually to Mt. Nhlangakazi.[357] Shembe was known for telling dramatic parables and thought to have gifts of healing. His movement was the largest of its time, and has a following to the present day, even though the sect's ambiguous relationship with the person of Jesus Christ has stirred controversy.

A second factor in the growth of independent African Christianity was the rise of movements like the Aladura movement. The word *aladura* means "praying," and in 1918 a group of Yoruba (Nigerian) pastors began emphasizing the power of prayer as a very real battle between God and the devil, with divine implications on human problems like disease and poverty. As documented by J. D. Y. Peel and Birgit Meyer[358] this teaching contained the seeds of contemporary charismatic theology. One of the more prominent centers of the movement was the Church of Christ founded by the Nigerian pastor Josiah Oshitelu in 1925, which broke away from the Anglican Church Missionary Society.

In 1921 Simon Kimbangu (1887–1951), a Congolese preacher, was credited with performing healings—and even some resurrections. Word of his spiritual gifting spread, resulting in a large and loyal following that revered him as a prophet (and even called him Ngunza, which means "prophet" in the Kikongo language). Belgian authorities, nervous about his growing influence, arrested Kimbangu and imprisoned him for the final three decades of his life. Even this, however, did not diminish popular support for Kimbangu, and the Kimbanguist movement continues today. While some claim that Kimbanguism is African shamanism with a Christian overlay, others argue it resembles the early church far more than contemporary western Christianity does.

A final example of the growing autonomy of the African church came in 1928, when independent Kenyan (Gikuyu, or Kikuyu) Christian schools were created over the cliterodectomy crisis (involving the medical procedure on young women).[359] Despite the fact that Gikuyu Christians greatly valued western education via European missionaries, they resented outsiders trying to ban one of the central rituals in the Gikuyu life cycle. This is but one of the many ways in which African customs and the values of western Christian missionaries clashed.[360]

1960 to the Present

Between 1957 and 1975, many African nations were attempting to throw off colonial bonds, both political and religious. In 1963 leaders convened at the All Africa Conference of Churches to discuss what post-colonial Christianity would look like in African countries. Around that same time in South Africa, the policy of apartheid was sparking protests and outbreaks of violence were increasing. One of the loudest anti-apartheid voices was Steve Biko (1946–1977).

Raised Anglican, Biko attended St. Francis College, a Catholic boarding school, and eventually became a leader in the "Black Consciousness" movement. (He is often credited with popularizing the saying, "Black is beautiful.") In its origins, this movement was theological. In its effect, Black Consciousness was political. Biko helped organize the 1976 Soweto uprising. For that he was arrested, thrown into a van, and killed by South African police in 1977.[361]

Even as African culture was simmering, the African church was growing. From 1965 to 2000, new churches popped up all over.[362] Megachurches—mostly charismatic—dominated the 1980s and 1990s. In 1991, Frederick Chiluba, the first democratically elected president of Zambia, gave a nod to these megachurches—one of his strongest constituencies—by declaring his country a Christian nation.

It wasn't just African *churches* that multiplied in the final thirty-five years of the twentieth century. The number of individual Christians also grew exponentially, from 75 million to 351 million. By 2010, that figure was reported to be a staggering 516 million. And the growth isn't simply quantitative; surveys by the Pew Research Center suggest that these are also some of the most "committed" Christians in the world.[363]

It's always difficult for researchers to identify precise reasons for the rise (and/or fall) of any movement, but perhaps Christianity exploded in sub-Saharan Africa due to three factors:

- the long-term hardships imposed on the people;

- the gradual translation of the Christian faith into words and practices meaningful to Africans;

- the African people being given the freedom to worship in culturally appropriate ways.

Consider: The continent to which Mary and Joseph fled with their infant son Jesus for refuge (see Matthew 2) is now giving birth to countless churches and mission organizations! Christianity has come full circle, but at the center is an ancient narrative, not a new storyline.

The faith that prompted mystics to live in caves, monks to copy sacred texts, and kings to build cathedrals…now inspires Christians south of the Sahara to show the *Jesus* film in desert regions and to fill megachurches in big cities like Nairobi and Lagos.

It used to be that heads turned toward Hippo, Carthage, and Alexandria in North Africa. Now the world looks at sub-Saharan Christianity and shakes its collective head at such remarkable growth.

The Spread of Christianity to the Ends of the Earth

When we trace the spread of Christianity to the most isolated places on earth, most sources give Australia only a page or two. This isn't a statement about the continent's importance. (After all, the Aborigines of Australia are the longest surviving culture known in the world—some dating its origin seventy thousand years ago.) Rather, this is a reflection of (a) remote geography (also true with New Zealand, Oceania, and Antarctica) and (b) limited historical interaction with the rest of the world (i.e., only over the last two to three centuries).

The Gospel to Australia

John Harris, the eminent Australian church historian, insists that it's impossible to understand Australian church history without understanding how "different" Australia's history is.[364] His 1289-page tome, *One Blood: 200 Years of Aboriginal Encounter with Christianity—A Story of Hope*, is an attempt to explain that history.[365] What makes it so "different," and where does the Australian continent fit in Christianity's global spread?

We know from Paul's New Testament letters that Christianity had already spread from Jerusalem throughout the Roman Empire by the mid-first century. There is extra-biblical evidence too. Pliny the Younger, governor of Bithynia, expressly confirmed a Christian presence in Rome in at least two letters to Emperor Trajan in the late first and early second centuries. One reference mentions some Christians recanting their beliefs twenty-five years earlier, definitively placing the Roman church within the first century.[366]

In time Christians took the gospel (orally and in written codex form) to the British Isles, first to Wales and Ireland. The Benedictine monk Augustine (not the theologian Augustine of Hippo, but the man considered the "Apostle to the English") led a mission to Canterbury. There he converted King Ethelbert, the leader of the Saxons (who was married to a Christian princess from Paris). When the monk departed, he left behind a beautiful sixth-century illuminated manuscript. This illustrated copy of the gospels, known as the St. Augustine Gospels, remains in England to this day. It resides at the Parker Library, Corpus Christi College Cambridge, and it's still used in services at Westminster Abbey on special occasions.

From England, the gospel—both preached and printed—came

to Australia. How so? Here's the backstory: In the eighteenth century, crime skyrocketed in crowded British cities, overwhelming the nation's prison system. Frustrated officials finally began putting criminals on ships and sending them to the American colonies. During the 1600s many were deported to Virginia,[367] and between 1715 and 1775 some fifty thousand were sent elsewhere in the American Colonies.[368] After the Revolutionary War, the fledgling American government essentially said, "We're done being Britain's Alcatraz."

Consequently, England embarked on a new program of deporting convicts to New South Wales in eastern Australia. (Captain James Cook had claimed this land for England in 1770.) Eventually five penal colonies were established, and the number of free settlers in Australia did not surpass the number of convicts until 1830!

Accompanying these fleets of "undesirables" were some Anglican chaplains and a few Bibles. Also among the banished prisoners were several Irish Catholic priests.

Two of these "convict priests" were James Dixon and James Harold. Father Dixon had been shipped to Australia for allegedly participating in a rebellion in Ireland. However, in 1803, authorities asked him to help calm rising tensions among frustrated Irish Catholics and made him the first Catholic ecclesiastical appointment in Australia. His mediation efforts were unsuccessful, but in 1808 he was allowed to return to Ireland, eventually serving as the parish priest in Crossabeg, the very same church at which he had been serving when he was first arrested in 1798.[369]

Father Harold fared even worse. Despite claims that he was a descendant of King Harold of England, he enjoyed no royal privileges. Also accused in the Irish rebellion, he too was deported to Australia in 1800, sent to Norfolk Island, and repeatedly denied permission to carry out priestly duties until he was allowed to return to Ireland.

Only later would the Benedictine John Bede Polding (from near Liverpool) be installed as Australia's first Catholic Archbishop. He presided over a fast-growing church, weathered tremendous battles over education, and somehow managed to establish a monastery, found numerous Catholic schools, and mentor and ordain increasing numbers of Australian-born priests. Harris writes:

> Colonial New South Wales was once labelled "the most Godless place under heaven," but a Christian presence was never totally lacking. There were Christians in all sections of colonial society, among the convicts and the marines, and, increasingly, among the free settlers. While the organised churches had only a token presence, Christian people met in small groups when and where they could. Those few who owned a Bible counted it among their most treasured possessions.
>
> The Church of England was the official church, but it was a long time before clergy and resources matched the needs of New South Wales. By 1830 there were eight churches and twelve clergy, many of whom, such as Samuel Marsden and Thomas Scott, were important contributors to early Australian colonial life.[370]

Following the example of the London Bible Society (created in 1804), a group of Christians in Australia formed the *New South Wales Auxiliary of the British and Foreign Bible Society in 1817*. This was the precursor to the Bible Society in Australia, and led to the immediate production of fifty lending Bibles for St. Phillip's Church in Sydney.[371]

Other devoted Christians from various ecclesiastical backgrounds set about creating Christian communities. John Dunmore Lang was a Church of Scotland minister who established the Church of Scotland in Sydney (1826). He made multiple trips between Australia and Britain recruiting Christian immigrants and evangelical ministers to join his cause. In 1831, for example, he showed up with "fifty four adults, with their wives and families, being stonemasons and bricklayers, carpenters and joiners, blacksmiths, plasterers, etc."[372] One of his recruits was John Saunders, an English Baptist minister, who wrote in *The Baptist Magazine* (1834), "Australia affords a fine field for Christian exertion; the messenger of truth enters into a sphere where in many respects Satan's seat is."[373]

Cities began to pop up all along the Australian coastline. Brisbane was founded in 1825, Perth in 1829, Melbourne in 1834, and Adelaide in 1838. Tensions began to rise too—between Catholics and Protestants. Efforts to encourage Protestant immigration to "the land down under" paralleled events like the potato famine, which prompted waves of beleaguered Irish Catholics to look abroad for food and work. Since the Civil War in the United States made settlement there undesirable, Australia became an attractive destination. More and more Roman Catholics began boarding ships that were headed south.

Today Roman Catholicism is the largest church tradition in Australia. In 2016, there were two Catholic universities, more than 1,700 schools, and almost 5.5 million Australian Catholics, representing 23 percent of the overall population. The Catholic population continues to grow, although weekly mass attendance has declined from an estimated 74 percent in the mid-1950s to just 14 percent in 2006. Harris again notes Australia's "different" history:

> The key to our [Australian] Christian history is that we began life as a penitentiary, a jail. We are totally unlike the U.S. We have no Mayflower, no Pilgrim Fathers, no devoted Christians seeking religious freedom in a new

land.... We have instead the "First Fleet," a flotilla of eleven ships, which arrived in January 1788 and disgorged at what is now Sydney 750 convict men and women, their 250 Marine guards and one clergyman. For a generation, the only Christian clergy were the chaplains to the convicts. This has in many ways defined religion in Australia ever since. We have never been as publicly religious as the U.S. Church attendance has never been high. Australians are generally suspicious of institutions and government. (By the way, to be descended from a convict in Australia is never a matter of shame but like belonging to the Mayflower Society. People doing family research are disappointed not to find a convict!)[374]

One would assume the costs involved in shipping convicts half a world away would be prohibitive, but research suggests that from a purely economic standpoint, establishing Australia as a massive prison was tremendously positive for England.[375] In "An Acte for Punyshment of Rogues, Vagabonds and Sturdy Beggars" (1597) the crown declared that offenders "shall...be banished out of this Realm ...and shall be conveyed to such parts beyond the seas as shall be...assigned by the Privy Council." Criminals who returned to England after being exported were told to expect the gallows.[376]

Among the heroes of the Christian faith in those early colonizing days was the Anglican chaplain Richard Johnson. He and his wife, Mary, exhausted themselves trying to reach transplanted convicts—and were often opposed by corrupt officials. However, their pioneer work afforded Samuel Marsden (1765–1838) and his wife, Elizabeth, a foothold in the country. The Marsdens arrived in New South Wales in 1794, Samuel serving as an Assistant Chaplain. His regrettable, disparaging journal comments about the Aborigines aside, Marsden grounded the Australian church and engaged in many humanitarian actions over a long time. So much so that he is often referred to as the spiritual father of Australia. (As we'll see, Marsden also led the efforts to convert the Maori in New Zealand.)

Of the six colonies established in Australia, only one, South Australia, was a free settlement. George Fife Angas (1789–1879), a devout Baptist (also a wealthy ship owner, banker, and business-man) worked to draw Christian families there. Hoping that South Australia might gain "the honorable epithet of Pilgrim Land"[377] he even footed the bill for large numbers of evangelical Lutherans to immigrate under the direction of Pastor August Kavel of Prussia. The colony achieved self-government in 1856, and was progressive in its views toward women: giving them the right to vote in 1861, and the right to run for office in 1894.

On January 1, 1901, Queen Victoria became Australia's head of state when the British Parliament voted to establish the Common-wealth of Australia—a constitutional monarchy. Says Harris, "A major historical difference between Australia and the U.S. is that we became an 'independent' nation peacefully, by a vote and not by a War." He adds, "Britain knew they could not win a war on the other side of the world when they could not even win one across the At-lantic. The Australian Colonies agreed to become one nation. Britain was glad to negotiate as long as we stayed in the Empire."[378]

A key event in the growth of the Christian faith in Australia (and New Zealand) was the 1959 Billy Graham Crusade. This evangelistic effort lasted more than three *months* and drew more than 3 million people (which makes it the largest gathering in Australian history). More than 143,000 people packed the Melbourne Cricket Ground for the final meeting of the crusade, a record that stood for decades. All told, some 150,000 people at these meetings "went forward" to express faith to Christ. This made the "Southern Cross Crusade" the largest and most successful evangelist campaign in human history."[379] There had never before been anything like it, in Australia, or anywhere else.

And it wasn't just a soon-forgotten event. Church attendance soared, as did enrollments in Bible colleges and seminaries. Three future archbishops of Sydney were converted during the crusade, a fact that might explain the conservative, evangelistic bent of the Anglican Church in that city a generation later.

We can't discuss the gospel's spread to Australia without mentioning the horrific treatment of the Aborigines. Though some early missionaries gave their lives to reach the Aborigines with the gospel, the majority of Australia's first settlers—including many self-proclaimed Christians—didn't even consider these indigenous peoples to be human beings.

Some settlers in Australia went so far as to liken themselves to the ancient Israelites and the Aborigines to the biblical Canaanites. They then twisted biblical texts like Numbers 33:52–53 to justify genocide. "In less than thirty years, the white Europeans killed 90 percent of the four thousand Aborigines around Hobart Town."[380] "Many were cruelly tortured, maimed, blinded, burnt, and castrated. The evidence in official documents is horrifying enough without guessing at that which was never divulged."[381] The grim bottom line? By the end of the so-called great missionary century, though not all aboriginal peoples in Australia had been killed, the full-blooded Tasmanian Aborigines *were* extinct.[383]

When John Harris served as president of the Zadok Institute for Christianity and Society, he wrote candidly about the plight of the Aborigines. Noting the errant theology that applied the Hamite curse (see Genesis 9:25 and 10:6) to African (black) peoples, he pointed out that even though the Christian church never endorsed or sanctioned violence against the Aboriginal people, it "failed miserably for a century or more to stand publicly against the oppression of the original inhabitants of the land."[383] To paraphrase Edmund Burke, evil triumphed because far too many good men and women did and said *nothing*.

Or they said shameful things. The otherwise praiseworthy Marsden suggested that the Aborigines were the "most degraded of the human race," not capable of being civilized, not ready "to receive the knowledge of Christianity."[384] It was actions, attitudes, and statements like these that prompted Christian historian James Bonwick to say in 1870: "We cover our faces while the deep and solemn voice of our common Father echoes through the soul, 'where is thy brother?'"[385]

Lancelot Threlkeld, who produced the first translation of the Bible in an Aboriginal language (the Gospel of Luke in Awabakal), was one who did speak up, loudly. He bravely exposed and vigorously condemned such godless attitudes and inhumane actions. He and other right-thinking, right-acting Christians eventually won the day, and the sad chapter of these atrocities came to an end.

Since that time many Aborigines have graciously accepted apologies for the past sins of Australia's early settlers. Perhaps chief among these attempts at reconciliation was Archbishop Grindrod seeking forgiveness on behalf of the Anglican Church from Aboriginal Bishop Arthur Malcolm. Because of such efforts, the last few decades have seen a revitalized partnership and mutual respect between Aborigines and Christian missionaries. Revivals have even occurred—like the "Black Crusade" of Echo Island in 1979 and the "Miracle Days at Mt. Margaret" in 1982.[386] Stunningly, by the grace and mercy of God, many Aborigines are now believers in Christ and part of a vibrant Christian church in Australia. Whereas 61 percent of Australians claim to be Christians, 73 percent of Aborigines (and Torres Strait Islander peoples) self-report as Christians.[387]

Australia's religious development has been further shaped by massive population growth—quadrupling since World War I— mostly from immigration. From World War II until 2000, almost 5.9 million new immigrants arrived. In the 2016 census, the population's most commonly claimed ancestries were English (36.1%), Australian (33.5%), Irish (11.0%), Scottish (9.3%), Chinese (5.6%), Italian (4.6%), German (4.5%), Indian (2.8%), Greek (1.8%), and Dutch (1.6%). All told, more than a quarter (26%) of the population had been born elsewhere.

Harris says this surge of immigrants "brought an influx of Catholics—Italian, Polish, Serbian, etc., which actually revived the flagging Catholic Church which had been Anglo-Irish."[388] It also spawned ethnic Catholic churches and Greek Orthodox, Coptic, and other Christian branches.

Though Australia is marked by numerous strong religious communities, at least two Christian entities wield significant influence that extends far beyond the land of koala bears and kangaroos. The conservative Sydney Anglicans—via the biblical theology movement—continue to hold sway over a worldwide network of Anglican theologians, and they consistently advocate for "conservative" evangelical views on social issues.

A second international influence is Hillsong Church, specifically Hillsong Music Australia. The church's music is distributed in more than ninety countries and is sung most weekends in churches across North America and Europe—and even in many African churches.[389]

Two other megachurches of note, both based in Melbourne, are CityLife Church (founded in 1967), with multiple campuses, and Planetshakers City Church (begun in 2004). Planetshakers has more than ten thousand members and oversees Youth Alive. This is a high-profile ministry to Australian teens that evangelizes youth via large gatherings, training them in spiritual leadership through the church's Youth Alive Academy.

The Message of Christ to New Zealand

The late arrival of Christianity to New Zealand (as is the case with Australia) is due in large part to the country's remoteness. (It may also be due to widespread reports that the island's indigenous people, the Maori, were known to eat visitors.)

The *Boyd* incident is the best-known example. Under the command of Captain John Thompson, the *Boyd* anchored in Whangaroa Harbour in 1809 to load valuable kauri timbers. Two factors were working against the ship's crew of seventy. First, only a year before, another European ship had introduced disease to the area, resulting in the deaths of a large number of locals. Because of this, the Maori were, understandably, on high alert. Second, one of the ship's crew members, Te Ara, happened to be the son of a local Maori chief—and he had been flogged brutally during the ship's voyage. When he reported his mistreatment to his fellow tribesmen, they promptly exacted *utu* (i.e., revenge) on the sailors, killing and eating almost all of them when they ventured ashore.

Around this same time, the aforementioned Samuel Marsden, Anglican chaplain from Australia, providentially met and befriended a Maori named Duaterra (aka Ruatara). With his help, Marsden began to learn the Maori language. Ultimately, it was Duaterra who vouched for Marsden when he came to New Zealand in 1814.

> In one of history's most remarkable plot twists—just five years removed from the *Boyd* massacre—some 400 Maori sat on overturned canoes and listened to Marsden preach the gospel of Christ (part of which he delivered in their native tongue). In a show of great faith, Marsden then slept unprotected on the beach instead of in the relative safety of his ship. In the light of the violent cannibal attack five years before, this was a tremendous gesture of goodwill.

Over time Marsden won the Maoris' trust. Many converted, turning away from a god they believed to be "a vindictive Being"...to "a God of mercy and love, willing to do them good."[390]

The message of Christ had spread from the early church in Jerusalem to Rome to England, and to Australia on a fleet full of convicts in 1788. By 1814 Marsden was leading the first Christian service in northern New Zealand. By mid-century, the Methodists and Catholics would join the Anglicans in establishing missions in New Zealand.

Not all of these ventures succeeded; frustrated missionaries in 1830 concluded, "The perverse levity and awful depravity of these savages appear to be unequalled in the history of man."[391] But eventually, the Bible's message of forgiveness and grace penetrated and transformed hearts. Large numbers of Maori exchanged the consumption of foreign blood[392] for salvation through the shed blood of Jesus. In 1842, Anglican bishop G. A. Selwyn declared that the tribe's "conversion was complete."[393] In 1988, Max Mariu became the first Maori Catholic bishop—affirming that whether the transition from "mission outpost to indigenous church" had taken place during Selwyn's time, it certainly had since.

Through the establishment of more churches, seminaries, and Christian colleges (especially around Auckland), and complemented by massive revivals like the Billy Graham Crusade of 1959,[394] more than 40 percent of New Zealanders today profess to be Christian.

Approximately 1 million of them (or about a quarter of the population) are evenly divided between Catholics and Anglicans. The number of Catholics of Irish descent has dropped sharply. By the 2010s Catholic congregations in New Zealand contained many more Korean, Indian, Filipino, Iranian, and Burundian faces.

In 1989, the Anglican Church named its first woman bishop— Penelope Jamieson, then serving in Dunedin, New Zealand. (Although she was born and educated in England and Scotland, her husband was a native New Zealander.) With their tremendous socio-economic diversity, New Zealand Anglicans are marked by great political and theological diversity and sharp disagreement on moral and social issues.[395] And whereas the church once was in a position to speak to society from a central position of authority and influence, it now finds itself pushed to the margins by an increasingly pluralistic, secular culture.

As in Australia, New Zealand has an assortment of houses of worship, including megachurches like City Impact Church and Destiny Church in Auckland.

City Impact Church was founded in 1982 by Peter and Bev Mortlock. It's a nondenominational, multi-campus church with Pentecostal beliefs, and it has spawned a network of City Impact Churches in Tonga, the Philippines, Mexico, India, and Canada.

Bishop Brian Tamaki and Pastor Hannah Tamaki are the leaders of the controversial Destiny Church, a Pentecostal church they established in 1998. Aligned with Bishop Eddie Long, a megachurch pastor in Atlanta, Georgia, Destiny Church advocates prosperity theology and strict adherence to fundamentalist biblical morality. The church is notable for its patriarchal views, and for its calls for a national return to biblical conservative family values and morals. Criticisms over the Tamakis' use of church funds and the bishop's linking of the Christchurch earthquakes to God's judgment took a toll on attendance in the early 2000s.[396] However, by June of 2012 the church still had eleven remaining campuses, and about three thousand regular attendees.

The world's largest Polynesian church is in New Zealand—the Newton Pacific Island Church. Reflecting specifically on Samoan culture within New Zealand, Rev. Lapan Faletolu says, "To be Samoan means that you want to know your culture...to know your language, you want to know your roots, you want to know your church, your Christianity, your faith. That's being Samoan."[397] Reflecting the diversity within its community, the church holds services in English, Cook Island Maori, Niuean, and Samoan languages.

Despite New Zealand's rich and interesting spiritual history, the overall commitment to Christianity and religion in general has waned in recent years. It is now one of the few countries globally (along with the Netherlands and France) "where the nonreligious are expected to outnumber the religious"[398] by 2050.

The Spread of the Gospel to the Pacific Islands

Where was the world's largest Protestant congregation in 1840? Given the First Great Awakening of the mid-1700s and the Second Great Awakening of the early 1800s, perhaps you'd be inclined to guess a city like New York, Chicago, or London. If so, you'd be wrong, by thousands of miles.

Actually, the world's largest single Protestant congregation in 1840 was in the South Pacific of all places, on the island of Honolulu. Between 1838 and 1840 the pastors of Hilo Church baptized and took into communion more than eight thousand new converts!

However, years before this Hawaiian megachurch came into existence, Christian missionary efforts were taking place all across the vast South Pacific. Lest you've forgotten all that world geography you learned back in grade school, here's a quick recap: geographers divide the islands of the Pacific, or Oceania, into three groups: Polynesia (those scattered between Hawaii and New Zealand), Micronesia (those located between Hawaii and the Philippines), and Melanesia (those found between Micronesia and Australia).

We're talking a *lot* of islands. For example, the Federated States of Micronesia includes more than six hundred. The archipelago of Fiji is comprised of more than three hundred. Tonga has 169 islands, but only thirty-six with permanent residents. Samoa, on the other hand, has only two large and eight small islands. The Solomon Islands include six large islands and over nine hundred smaller ones. You get the idea.

Time and space don't permit a thorough review here of the diligent missionary efforts to reach all the peoples of these varied island cultures, but at least a handful of stories and historical figures are worth mentioning.

British Protestants, enthralled by the stories of Captain Cook, formed the London Missionary Society in 1795, with the hope of taking the gospel to native peoples scattered across the remote islands in the South Sea. In August of 1796, a group of thirty missionaries (a few with wives and children) set sail on the *Duff*. Following an almost seven-month journey, most of the group disembarked in Tahiti. Others went on to Tonga, and the final two men continued on to the Marquesas, where two very attractive, very friendly, very unclad native women greeted them as they came ashore. One of the shocked missionaries departed the island the next day. The other stayed but didn't last a year.

The missionaries in Tonga faced similar temptations—and a civil war that cost three of them their lives. Back in Tahiti, a missionary named Henry Nott persevered in the face of departing colleagues and the island's promiscuous culture, eventually seeing King Pomare II confess Christ and forsake his idols.

In 1819, Hawaii—which is where Captain Cook was killed in 1779—became a focal point of the American Board of Commissioners for Foreign Missions (ABCFM). Hiram Bingham and his wife (of two weeks!), Sybil, were among the first to bring the gospel to this island paradise. In fact, it was one of Sybil's converts, a queen named Kapiolani, who caused a stir by (a) publicly mocking the goddess Pele (thought to live in the Kilauea volcano) and (b) openly sharing her Christian faith with her astonished audience. This holy eruption rocked the Hawaiian islands as much as any volcano ever did.

The most famous missionary to the Pacific was, arguably, John Williams. He was born in England in 1796, the same year the *Duff* set sail for Tahiti. At age twenty, with little formal training, he and his brand-new wife headed for Oceania. There, against the wishes of his superiors, Williams first tried to purchase, then finally built a ship (called the *Messenger of Peace*) so he could travel from island to island, sharing the gospel.

He introduced numerous Polynesian islands to the gospel, beginning with the Cook Islands (not long after they were discovered). Within a year after landing on Tahiti in 1817, Williams had learned the Tahitian language and was beginning to see converts. He founded the Tahitian Missionary Society, and enjoyed great support from the London Missionary Society. In fact, during a furlough to London, this group helped him print the Bible into one of the island languages.

Williams, recognizing the value of indigenous leaders, trained a highly effective group of Polynesian preachers. By having them take the gospel to islands like Rurutu and Samoa, Williams showed the weakness of the old missionary model that relied solely on European leadership. Following one mission to Ruruto, he reported, "After an absence of little more than a month, we had the pleasure of seeing the boat return laden with the trophies of victory, the gods of the heathen taken in this bloodless war, and won by the Prince of Peace." It's said that by 1834, Williams had visited every island within two thousand miles of Tahiti. No wonder he was given the title "Apostle of the South Seas."

While the gospel was enthusiastically embraced by many native peoples, others proved more challenging. In 1839, Williams and fellow missionary James Harris engaged the residents of the island of Erromango (part of the New Hebrides, i.e., the modern-day Republic of Vanuatu) only to be killed and eaten! What the good-hearted missionaries didn't know was that only days before, European sandalwood traders had killed some of the islanders. In fear and anger, the islanders assumed the worst of the missionaries, clubbed both of them, Harris to death, and then shot Williams with arrows while he was running into the sea.

In 2009, a reconciliation, covered by the BBC, took place between the descendants of the missionaries and the island people. Iolo Johson Abbil, the president of Vanuatu at the time, called this "a very important event for the country as a whole." President Abbil explained that many citizens believed Erromango was under a curse for having killed these missionaries. "Since we claim to be a Christian country it is very important that we have a reconciliation like this." Vanuatu even changed the name of the bay where the massacre occurred from Dillons Bay to Williams Bay.

The American evangelist/pastor Titus Coan (1801–1882) decided to concentrate on Hawaii. He was a seasoned pro at open air preaching (due to his relationship with Charles Finney and his experiences in the Second Great Awakening), but an untested rookie at foreign missions. No matter. He partnered in 1833 with David and Sarah Lyman and their Hawaiian congregation of just 23 members, becoming the church's itinerant evangelist. Coan then crisscrossed the main island on foot, often over treacherous terrain since the island had few roads. He befriended the locals, took every opportunity to proclaim the message of Christ, and by many accounts appeared to enjoy divine favor. In droves the Hawaiian people eagerly embraced his message. Even some of the island's witch doctors—who had previously killed anyone who rejected the local pagan volcano gods—converted.

By 1840, Kamehameha III (Kauikeaouli) was declaring his Hawaiian kingdom a Christian nation. The Hawaiian Constitution of 1840 began: "God hath made of one blood all nations of men to dwell on the earth, in unity and blessedness. God has also bestowed certain rights alike on all men and all chiefs, and all people of all lands."

We need to mention one more influential missionary in the South Pacific: John G. Paton.

Paton (1824–1906) was from a poor Scottish Presbyterian family. He came to Christ in his youth and worked for a time in the inner city of Glasgow, but it was the missionary exploits of John Williams and his stories of the South Seas that made Paton's heart race.

In 1858, those stories prompted him to board a ship with his new wife, Mary Anne, for the tiny (just 212 square miles) island of Tanna in the New Hebrides. Life there was beyond difficult; the natives were violent, and the new missionary couple battled illness and culture shock constantly. When Mary Anne (and the couple's infant son) died in 1859, Paton nearly went mad from grief.

But he persisted. Converted natives from nearby islands joined him in the work. On a much-needed furlough, Paton raised money and remarried. He then went to the island of Aniwa, where he built schools, orphanages, and established a growing church. In his later years he translated the Bible into the vernacular of the Aniwa people. Thanks to his efforts, by 1900 most of the islands in the New Hebrides had heard the message of Christ crucified, buried, and resurrected.

Making Disciples in Antarctica

When most people think of Antarctica, they think—rightly so—of penguins, endless expanses of ice, and research stations staffed by shivering, slightly nutty scientists (who, apparently, must be drinking antifreeze rather than coffee, most mornings).

Most of what we know about this mysterious, vast continent (twice the size of Australia!), we've learned in the last two hundred years. Who can forget the harrowing story of Captain Robert Scott (1868–1912)? The last five members of his expedition froze to death while returning from their unsuccessful attempt to be the first to reach the South Pole (the Norwegian team led by Roald Amundsen beat Scott's team by five weeks).[399] The stories—explorers floating away on icebergs and falling through thin ice—are chilling (no pun intended). The novel *Antarctica* references this disastrous trip with an adaptation of an old whalers' adage, "Below the 40th latitude south there is no law.... Below the 50th, no God, and below the 60th no common sense. And, below the 70th...no intelligence whatsoever."[400]

While beach lovers and sunbirds might be inclined to nod at that last statement about there being "no intelligence" in a place so cold and remote, the idea of God being absent below the fiftieth latitude simply isn't true. Turns out God is alive and well at the bottom of the world.

From the sixteenth century on, explorers like Ferdinand Magellan, Francis Drake, and John Davis began spotting Antarctica's islands and plotting how they might investigate the frigid continent beyond those islands. As we've seen, many of history's explorers were motivated, at least in part, by a desire to propagate the Christian faith. In fact, when he discovered what are now referred to as the "Magellan Straits," the Portuguese explorer Magellan gave the passageway the title of "Canal de Todos los Santos (All Saints' Channel)."

It was Edward Bransfield, from a prominent Irish Catholic family, who made the first attested landing on the actual continent of Antarctica, around 1820. He named the area "Trinity Peninsula." It was almost a century later, with at least a mile-thick layer of ice beneath him and in temperatures more than 100 degrees below zero, that Captain Scott wrote his last correspondence. In this heralded "Message to the Public," he noted that he would "now bow to the will of Providence."[401] The following day he did. In 1916, the Ross Sea Party planted a cross at Wind Vane Hill at Cape Evans. No God below the fiftieth parallel? Au contraire! There are all sorts of divine hints and reminders of God at the South Pole.

Unlike everywhere else on earth, it has been exploration, not evangelism, that has prompted nations and organizations to send ships to Antarctica. This is because earth's southernmost continent has no indigenous people to convert.

The first documented church service in Antarctica took place in 1947. It was led by William Menster, a Catholic priest from Iowa and a chaplain in the United States Navy. On the continent for a large military operation called "Operation High Jump,"[402] Menster consecrated Antarctica to God before an audience of scientists and military personnel.

Missionary Brett Baddorf says that during the winters at Amundsen-Scott South Pole station, only five to eight of the fifty individuals on site typically meet in a conference room for ecumenical worship services. During summer (or peak season), when the station's population swells, as many 150 may attend. All told, the entire population of Antarctica (at all research stations) varies between about 1,100 people (scientists and staff) in winter, and around 4,400 in peak season. At least 95 percent of this constantly changing population is between fifteen and fifty-nine years of age.[403] Oftentimes, as many people can be found on the ships in the waters surrounding Antarctica as can be found living on the continent![404]

Some eight hundred miles from the South Pole at the Argentine Belgrano II Base, there's an actual church building—carved out of ice. Located underground, this Catholic chapel, called Our Lady of the Chapel of the Snows, is the world's southernmost church. A different Chapel of the Snows—an actual building (not made of ice)—is located at the American McMurdo station on Ross Island. It seats just over sixty people, and its altar is supposedly from Captain

Robert Scott's home church in New Zealand. This chapel is interdenominational, offering both Catholic and Protestant services. It also hosts services and meetings for other faith groups such as Latter-day Saints, Baha'i, and Buddhism…and even nonreligious groups such as Alcoholics Anonymous.

With a few dozen science stations and thirty countries represented, it's not surprising that Antarctica's eight churches (all built since 1956) represent diverse Christian traditions.

Obviously, the Christianity that's seen and celebrated in Antarctica is mostly an extension of the faiths and cultures of the explorers and scientists. But regardless of the "flavor," the presence and practice of the Christian faith there—and on the other six continents of earth—is a reminder of an ancient prophecy by Isaiah.

"Sing to the LORD a new song, his praise from the ends of the earth, you who go down to the sea, and all that is in it, you islands, and all who live in them" (Isaiah 42:10).

CONCLUSION

The story, if you can get your head around it, is enough to take your breath away. Beginning with a roomful of believers in Jerusalem, the message of Christ's life and love has spread in less than two thousand years to every continent on the face of the earth.

What a parade of mystics and martyrs, monks and missionaries! Such a history of mistakes and mysteries, missteps and miracles! Mostly, the story is a testimony to God's incomparable goodness, power, and grace—that he could and would choose to work in and through such flawed people to bring others to new life in Christ.

Believe it or not, there are *still* places on earth where people have not yet heard the name of Jesus, much less had the chance to embrace his good news of forgiveness and love. Some ethnic groups still do not yet have God's Word in their native language.

Thankfully, however, even as you read this sentence, Bible translators are working, missionaries are building relationships, and other believers are giving generously and praying fervently. The spread of Christianity isn't over, not yet.[405]

Revelation, the final book of the Christian Bible, is a record of the apostle John's strange vision of heaven, his brief peek at the world to come. In one place he describes seeing a Lamb—universally believed to represent the resurrected Christ—sitting on a throne. Before him creatures bow and sing. John quotes these worshippers as saying the following, "With your blood you purchased for God persons from every tribe and language and people and nation" (Revelation 5:9).

"Persons from *every* tribe and language and people and nation."

In other words, people from every continent on earth.

ENDNOTES

1   There is alternative use of "Christian history" and "history of Christianity" and they are used here interchangeably. Various organizations provide an array of helpful information on topics related to our discussion. An easily accessible popular source is *Christian History Magazine*, associated with Christianity Today. A few of the scholarly resources include the *Anchor Bible Dictionary; Church History: Studies in Christianity and Culture; Journal of Early Christianity; Reformation; Journal of World Christianity; Evangelical Quarterly; Greek Orthodox Theological Review; History of Religions; Vigiliae Christianae; Studies in World Christianity; Bulletin for Biblical Research, The Catholic Historical Review, Catholic Biblical Quarterly; The Oxford Dictionary of the Christian Church*, and; *Fides et Historia*, a publication of the Conference on Faith and History (see https://www.faithandhistory. org/). Three helpful, engaging, and much longer treatments of the history of Christianity than this present book are: Justo L. Gonzalez, *The Story of Christianity: The Early Church to the Dawn of the Reformation*, vol. 1, and *The Reformation to the Present Day*, vol. 2 (Harper Collins, 2010, revised edition); Diarmaid MacCulloch, *Christianity: The First Three Thousand Years* (Viking Penguin: 2009), and; Robert G. Clouse, Richard V. Pierard, and Edwin M. Yamauchi, *Two Kingdoms: The Church and Culture through the Ages* (Chicago: Moody Press, 1993). For a high-tech Bible curriculum that shows the history, story, and impact of the Bible, see Jerry A. Pattengale, Editor-in-Chief, and co-author with Gil Ilutowitch and Tim Dalrymple, The Book: *The Narrative, History and Impact of the Bible*. Vols. 1-4. (Ramat Gan, Israel: Compedia and Washington, DC: Museum of the Bible, . 2017), and at the App Store.

2   *Inexplicable: How Christianity Spread to the Ends of the Earth* (six episodes), Norman C. Mintle, executive producer, Amy Hollingsworth, script editor, Jerry Pattengale, historian and background writer (Tustin, CA: Trinity Broadcast Network, 2020).

3   For more on this topic see Jerry Pattengale, Nick DeNeff, and Daniel Freemyer, *Is the Bible at Fault? How the Bible Has Been Misused to Justify Evil, Suffering, and Bizarre Behavior* (Franklin, TN: Worthy/Hachette, 2018).

4   Acts 28:19-20 (ESV); this is part of "The Great Commission," Acts 28:16-20.

5   Christopher De Hamel, *Meetings with Remarkable Manuscripts* (Allen Lane: 2016), p. 327.

6   Michael Green, *Evangelism in the Early Church*, (Grand Rapids: William B. Eerdmans Publishing Company, 2003), 173.

7   They had been prevented from completing this task on Friday evening due to the arrival of Sabbath.

8   The night before his crucifixion, Jesus had gathered his disciples in an upstairs room in Jerusalem to celebrate Passover and give them final instructions (see John 13–17). During that last meal with his followers, he had discussed the fact that he was going away. Because of that, he pledged to send them "another advocate to help you and be with you forever" (14:16).

9   This is a more detailed account than what we find in Luke 24, which seems to come on the heels of the Resurrection instead of 40 days later. Also, the short reference in Mark 16:19 is widely considered by scholars to be part at the appended verses (after v. 8) to Mark since it is absence from earliest manuscripts.

10   Peter Larson, Prism (January/February, 2001). Larson's statement is a common quote and appears in a wide array of sources, including Richard A. Kaufman, "Christmas: Quotations to Stir Heart and Mind," Christianity Today (December 9, 2005); accessed at https://www.christianitytoday.com/ct/2005/december/22.62.html.

11   Max Fisher, "Our Christian Earth: The Astounding Reach of the World's Largest Religion, in Charts and Maps," *The Washington Post* (December 18, 2012); Accesses at https://www.washingtonpost.com/news/worldviews/wp/2012/12/18/our-christian-earth-the-astounding-reach-of-the-worlds-largest-religion-in-charts-and-maps/?utm_term=.6f1f2a6f2af3 . This is based on "The Global Religious Landscape" by the Pew Research Center (2012); accessed at http://www.pewforum.org/2012/12/18/global-religious-landscape-exec/

12   This section on persecution relies heavily on the author's much longer treatment in *The New Book of Christian Martyrs* (Tyndale House Publishing, forthcoming in 2020), a major update of John Foxe's *Actes and Monuments* (or more commonly called, *Foxe's Book of Martyrs*).

Used here with the author's permission, and that of the co-author, Johnnie Moore.

13 Peter Kirby, "Historical Jesus Theories," *Early Christian Writings* website, accessed February 1, 2019, http://www.earlychristianwritings.com/theories.html. For Ignatius's letter to Polycarp, see online at http://www.earlychristianwritings.com/srawley/polycarp.html.

14 Kenneth Berding, "John or Paul: Who Was Polycarp's Mentor?" *Tyndale Bulletin* 58, no.2 (2007): 135–143; accessed February 19, 2019, https://legacy.tyndalehouse.com/Bulletin/59=2008/8%20Berding.pdf.

15 See "The Letter of Ignatius to Polycarp" in *Apostolic Fathers*, 3rd, ed. Michael W. Holmes (Grand Rapids, MI: Baker Academic, 2007), 262–271.

16 "Martyrdom of Polycarp [9.3]," in *Apostolic Fathers*, 3rd, ed. Michael W. Holmes (Grand Rapids, MI: Baker Academic, 2007), 316 Greek/317 English.

17 A hagiographic trope found in various stories.

18 Perpetua, *The Passion of Perpetua and Felicity*, trans. W.H. Shewring (London: 1931), accessed February 19, 2019, https://sourcebooks.fordham.edu/source/perpetua.asp.

19 Cited from "Perpetua: High Society Believer," *Christian History* website, accessed February 19, 2019, https://www.christianitytoday.com/history/people/martyrs/perpetua.html.

20 Perpetua, *The Passion of Perpetua and Felicity*, https://sourcebooks.fordham.edu/source/perpetua.asp.

21 *The Passion of the Holy Martyrs Perpetua and Felicitas*, accessed February 19, 2019, http://www.tertullian.org/anf/anf03/anf03-54.htm#P12104_3374882 .

22 In addition to biblical accounts of some of the Christian martyrs on this list, and the context behind religious-political tensions, we have a wealth of tradition passed down to the present. For a short introduction to persecution, see Everett Ferguson, "Persecution in the Early Church: Did You Know?" *Christian History* 27 (1990), http://www.christianitytoday.com/history/issues/issue-27/persecution-in-early-church-did-you-know.html. A suggested chronology of the early martyrdoms also appears in the same *Christian History* issue, https://www.christianitytoday.com/history/issues/issue-27/persecution-in-early-church-christian-history-timeline.html. It dates Stephen's death to approximately AD 35, and those of Peter and Paul to AD 65. From robust Roman Catholic sources chronicling Christian saints, familiar in liturgy through the "Roman Martyrology," to the various versions of *Acts and Monuments* (or, *Foxe's Book of Martyrs*, with mixed levels of reliability), many names are in common on the lists. One of these sources perhaps ranks next to the Bible in importance for the Men-

nonites and the Amish, i.e., *The Martyrs' Mirror*, or more formally by its full title, *The Bloody Theater or Martyrs Mirror of the Defenseless Christians who baptized only upon confession of faith, and who suffered and died for the testimony of Jesus, their Saviour, from the time of Christ to the year A.D. 1660,* Thieleman J. van Braght (Holland: 1660). Like the work of John Foxe, Braght's work surfaced posthumously in other editions by other editors. He died in 1664 and the noble second edition appeared in 1685. A searchable index is available online at: http://www.homecomers.org/mirror/index-general.htm. See Nanne van der Zijpp, Harold S. Bender, and Richard D. Thiessen. "Martyrs' Mirror," *Global Anabaptist Mennonite Encyclopedia Online,* last updated February 21, 2019, https://gameo.org/index.php?title=Martyrs%27_Mirror . This section on persecution is adapted from the author's *The New Book of Christian Martyrs,* forthcoming. Used with permission by the author.

23   Tacitus, Annals, XV.44.2–8; cited from The New *Eusebius*, 2–3.

24   Cited from Stephen Tomkins, "Pliny's Letter to Trajan," Christian History Institute; accessed at https://christianhistoryinstitute.org/study/module/pliny.

25   Robert G. Clouse, Richard V. Pierard, and Edwin M. Yamauchi, *Two Kingdoms: The Church and Culture through the Ages* (Chicago, IL: Moody Press, 1993), 46.

26   John Foxe, *Foxe's Book of Martyrs,* edited by William Byron Forbush (Peabody, MA: Hendrickson Publishers, 2004), 30.

27   Frend, *Rise of Christianity,* 604.

28   Julian, *Letter* XXII. Cited from Frend, *Rise of Christianity, 601.*

29   This is a common hagiographic trope—when later editors add touches that appear in various accounts such as beast refusing to attack them.

30   Eusebius, *History of the Church,* 147.

31   Ibid.

32   "Jews," Pew-Templeton Religious Futures Project, 2010 statistics; accessed at http://www.globalreligiousfutures.org/religions/jews .

33   See Yosef Porath, Mindi Epstein, Zaraza Friedman, and Talila Michaeli, *Caesarea Maritima I: Herod's Circus and Related Buildings Part 1: Architecture and Stratigraphy,* Jerusalem: Israel Antiquities Authority, 2013, and; Yosef Porath, Gabriela Bijovsky, Hannah M. Cotton, Werner Eck, Gerald Finkielsztejn, Peter Gendelman, Rivka Gersht, Yael Gorin-Rosen, Karmit Gur, Natalya Katsnelson, and Omri Lernau. *Caesarea Maritima I: Herod's Circus and Related Buildings Part 2: The Finds.* Jerusalem: Israel Antiquities Authority, 2015.

34   This metropolis was called Palaestina Prima during the third through early fifth centuries.

35   These were excavated in 2017. See Nir Hasson, "Archaeologists Uncover Ancient Entrance to Caesarea in Israel," *Haaretz* (April 19, 2017); accessed at https://www.haaretz.com/israel-news/MAGA-ZINE-archaeologists-uncover-entrance-to-caesarea-1.5465507.

36   Josephus, *BJ*, I, 21: 5-7.

37   Acts 23:35; see John D. Currid and David W. Chapman, editors, *Archaeology Study Bible,* Wheaton, IL: Crossway, 2017, pp. 1654-55 (note and picture to this verse).

38   Pausanias, *Description of Greece,* Book 5, chapter 11 (2nd century BC). See Mark Cartwright, "Statue of Zeus at Olympia," *Ancient History Encyclopedia* (July 24, 2018); accessed at https://www.ancient.eu/Statue_of_Zeus_at_Olympia/

39   Robert G. Clouse, Richard V. Pierard, and Edwin M. Yamauchi, *Two Kingdoms: The Church and Culture through the Ages* (Chicago: Moody Press, 1993), p. 54.

40   W. H. C. Frend, *The Rise of Christianity* (Philadelphia: Fortress Press, 1984), p. 310.

41   Lucian Turcescu, "Prosōpon and Hypostasis in Basil of Caesarea's 'Against Eunomius' and the Epistles," *Vigiliae Christianae* 51, no. 4 (1997): 374-95. Also see Stephen M. Hildebrand, "A Reconsideration of the Development of Basil's Trinitarian Theology: The Dating of Ep. 9 and 'Contra Eunomium'," *Vigiliae Christianae* 58, no. 4 (2004): 393-406. For Origien's connection to some of these same debates, see Ilaria L.E. Ramelli, "Origen's Anti-Subordinationism and Its Heritage in the Nicene and Cappadocian Line," *Vigiliae Christianae* 65, no. 1 (2011): 21-49.

42   Conrad Henry Moehlman. "The Origin of the Apostles' Creed." *The Journal of Religion* 13, no. 3 (1933): 304.

43   Eusebius, *HE* II.15.1.

44   Jerry Pattengale, "Thomas C. Oden, Author of the African Memory of Mark," Intervarsity Press (June 6, 2014) https://www.youtube.com/watch?v=W3znjZYVF6Y

45   Justo L. Gonzalez, *The Story of Christianity: The Early Church to the Dawn of the Reformation,* vol 1 (Harper Collins, 2010), p. 37.

46   "Alexandria," Sv., *Encyclopedia of Ancient Christianity,* p. 78.

47   "Clergy" is from *kleros,* meaning "lot."

48   "Christianity: Christianity in North Africa." *Encyclopedia of Religion.* Accessed at Encyclopedia.com: https://www.encyclopedia.com/environment/encyclopedias-almanacs-transcripts-and-maps/christiani-ty-christianity-north-africa

49   W. H. C. Frend, *The Rise of Christianity* (Philadelphia: Fortress Press, 1984), p. 293.

50 Frend, *The Rise of Christianity*, p. 422. Arsinoë was the capital of this province (nome), and a place where thousands of wealthy gathered near the lake (See Strabo 17.1.38). P. J. Sijpesteijn, "A List of Villages in the Arsinoite Nome," *The Bulletin of the American Society of Papyrologists* 10 (1973): 27-30.

51 Livius, *Acts of the Scillitan Martyrs,* Livius.org, 2018, accessed at https://www.livius.org/sources/content/acts-of-the-scillitan-martyrs/translation/

52 Clouse, Pierard, and Yamauchi, *Two Kingdoms,* p. 50.

53 Ibid., p. 56.

54 Another important early church text is the *Didache,* discovered in a monastery in Constantinople that dates to the late first or early second century. It includes our earliest look at instructions in many aspects of Christian living and polity. See http://www.earlychristianwritings.com/didache.html.

55 "John Chrysostom: Early Church's Greatest Preacher," *Christian History,* Christianity Today, Accessed at https://www.christianitytoday.com/history/people/pastorsandpreachers/john-chrysostom.html . See also Robert L. Wilken, "John Chrysostom: Recommended Resources," *Christian History,* Christianity Today (1994). Accessed at https://www.christianitytoday.com/history/issues/issue-44/john-chrysostom-recommended-resources.html.

56 Ignatius of Antioch, *Letter to the Romans,* (section iv) in *The Early Christian Fathers: A Selection from the Writings of the Fathers from St. Clement of Rome to St. Athanasius,* edited and translated by Henry Bettenson (London: Oxford University Press, 1956). See Ignatius *Rom.* 1.2. His martyrdom quest is discussed in detail in the Appendix.

57 Daniel Hoffman, "Ignatius of Antioch" in Jerry Pattengale, *History of World Civilizations: A Christian Perspective* (Marion, Indiana: up). Ignatius quotations from Cyril C. Richardson, *Early Christian Fathers* (New York: Macmillian, 1970).

58 Clouse, Pierard, and Yamauchi, *Two Kingdoms,* p. 54.

59 For a list of helpful general sources on this, see Dan Graves, "In Hoc Signo Vinces [In this sign conquer]," Christian History Institute, Accessed December 1, 2018 https://christianhistoryinstitute.org/incontext/article/constantines-cross.

60 Salzman, "The Evidence for the Conversion of the Roman Empire to Christianity," 362–78. See also Mark A. Noll, *The New Shape of World Christianity* (Downers Grove: InterVarsity Press, 2009), 191.

61 *Code of Theodosius* 16.1.1-2. The second sentence emphasizes belief in "the equal majesty" of the three persons of "the Holy Trinity."

62 "The Global Catholic Population," Pew Research Center, posted February 13, 2013, accessed December 1, 2018, http://www.pewforum.

org/2013/02/13/the-global-catholic-population/.

63 A fuller discussion of this development is found at the beginning of the section on Australia: "We know from the book of Romans, likely written by Paul from Corinth, that a body of Christians was present in Rome by the mid-first century. And, the congregation was predominantly Gentile with a strong Jewish minority. We also know through the letter of Pliny the Younger to Emperor Trajan of a substantial presence of Christians in Rome. Pliny was governor of Bithynia (AD 111–113, where in AD 325 its prominent city of Nicaea would host the important Council of Nicaea, and the resulting Nicene Creed). Among his over 200 extant letters, two to and from Trajan expressly mention the Christians—that is, how to punish those so charged. One reference mentions that some Christians had recanted their beliefs twenty-five years earlier, easily placing this movement within the first century. (See: Pliny the Younger, *Letters* 10.96-97, accessed December 1, 2018, http://faculty.georgetown.edu/jod/texts/pliny.html.) St. Peter had labored among the Romans (likely writing 1 Peter from there, the "Babylon," he notes in 1 Peter 5:13), and we have strong church tradition that he was martyred and buried in Rome (likely in AD 64 under Nero)—and thus the site and reverence for St. Peter's basilica (the current 16th-century basilica was built on the site of the earlier fifth-century one). Numerous early Christian writers refer to his martyrdom in Rome, and some to Mark's work there as well, e.g., Bishop Papias of Hierapolis, Clement of Alexandria, Eusebius, Irenaeus, Ignatius of Antioch, and Tertullian.

64 David C. Parker, *An Introduction to the Early New Testament Manuscripts and Their Texts* (Cambridge: Cambridge University Press, 2008); Luke Timothy Johnson, *The Acts of the Apostles*, Sacra Pagina (Collegeville: Liturgical Press, 1992); Ben Witherington III, *The Acts of the Apostles: A Socio-Rhetorical Commentary* (Grand Rapids: William B. Eerdmans, 1998), and Eckhard J. Schnabel, *Early Christian Mission*, 2 vols. (Downers Grove: InterVarsity Press, 2004).

65 Justo González, *The Story of Christianity*, (New York: HarperOne, 1984), Volume I, pp. 165-166.

66 The actual date was 8/24 in AD 410.

67 Bruce L. Shelley, *Church History in Plain Language*, (Waco: TX: Word Books, 1982), p. 141.

68 Augustine, *The City of God*, cited in C. Warren Hollister, Joe W. Leedom, Marc A. Meyer, and David S. Spear, *Medieval Europe: A Short Sourcebook* (New York: McGraw-Hill, 1992), p. 16.

69 Evan Andrews, "Six Infamous Sacks of Rome," *History*. Accessed at https://www.history.com/news/6-infamous-sacks-of-rome .

70 David C. Parker, *An Introduction to the Early New Testament Manuscripts and Their Texts* (Cambridge: Cambridge University Press,

2008); Luke Timothy Johnson, *The Acts of the Apostles*, Sacra Pagina (Collegeville: Liturgical Press, 1992); Ben Witherington III, *The Acts of the Apostles: A Socio-Rhetorical Commentary* (Grand Rapids: William B. Eerdmans, 1998), and Eckhard J. Schnabel, *Early Christian Mission*, 2 vols. (Downers Grove: InterVarsity Press, 2004).

71 Jerry Pattengale, "Berea," S.v., *Anchor Bible Dictionary*, Vols 1-2, also "Achaia"; "Crete"; and "Delos."

72 See 1 Corinthians 16:1–4, 2 Corinthians 8:1–9:15, and Romans 15:14–32.

73 John P. Meier, *A Marginal Jew: Rethinking the Historical Jesus, Volume One: The Roots of the Problem and the Person* (New York: Doubleday, 1991), 91–92, 102 n. 16.

74 Suetonius, *The Deified Claudius* 25.4, Book V of *Lives of the Caesars*, in *Suetonius*, with an English Translation by J. C. Rolfe, Loeb Classical Library 38 (Cambridge, MA: Harvard University Press, 1914), 2:52–53. Emperor Claudius reigned from AD 41-54.

75 Rodney Stark, *The Rise of Christianity: A Sociologist Reconsiders History* (Princeton: Princeton University Press, 1996), 13.

76 Salzman, "The Evidence for the Conversion of the Roman Empire to Christianity," 362–78. See also Mark A. Noll, *The New Shape of World Christianity* (Downers Grove: InterVarsity Press, 2009), 191.

77 *Code of Theodosius* 16.1.1-2. The second sentence emphasizes belief in "the equal majesty" of the three persons of "the Holy Trinity."

78 The claims range for the passionate, like Charles Augustus Briggs, "The Real and the Ideal in the Papacy," *The North American Review* 184 (1907): 347, to the more ecclesiastical, like Cardinal Joseph Ratzinger, "The Primacy of the Successor of Peter in the Mystery of the Church," *Congregation for the Doctrine of Faith*, accessed December 1, 2018, http://www.vatican.va/roman_curia/congregations/cfaith/documents/rc_con_cfaith_doc_19981031_primato-successore-pietro_en.html

79 Charles B. McClendon, "The History of the Site of St. Peter's Basilica, Rome," *Perspecta* 25 (1989): 32–65. Historic sketches of the excavations of St. Peter's tomb are found in figures 62, 63, and 65 (pages 59–60).

80 L. E. Hudec, "Recent Excavations under St. Peter's Basilica in Rome." *Journal of Bible and Religion* 20 (1952): 16.

81 Diarmaid MacCulloch, *Christianity: The First Three Thousand Years* (Viking Penguin: 2009), p. 294.

82 *Encyclopedia Britannica*, s.v. "Edward Gibbon: British Historian," by David Morrice Low, last modified May 6, 2018, accessed December 1, 2018, https://www.britannica.com/biography/Edward-Gibbon.

83 Edward Gibbon, *The History of the Decline and Fall of the Roman*

Empire, Vol. 1, (London: Strahan and Cadell, 1776), 15.1, "Progress of the Christian Religion," online at sacred-texts.com, accessed December 1, 2018, http://www.sacred-texts.com/cla/gibbon/01/daf01047.htm.

84   Ibid., pp. 39—42.

85   Ibid., 43.

86   This is a legend with many variations. See: https://mtncatholic.com/2014/12/23/thor-stboniface-and-the-origin-of-the-christmas-tree/

87   While Martin Luther is commonly praised in most Protestant accounts, readers should temper this assessment in the light of anti-Semitic writings.

88   Fulcher de Chartres, Chronicles of the First Crusade, trans. M. E. McGinty (Philadelphia: University of Pennsylvania Press, 1941), pp. 15-17.

89   Andrew Knighton, "Twelve Battles that Defined the Crusades," (February 11, 2016), accessed https://www.warhistoryonline.com/medieval/12-battles-definedcrusades.html

90   Hollister, *Medieval Europe*, p. 189.

91   Much of the Crusades' section is adapted from Pattengale, *History of World Civilizations*, u.p.

92   Ibid., p. 130. Bernard cites Romans 13:4 as his proof text.

93   Adapted from John Carey, editor, *Eyewitness to History* (Harvard University Press, 1988), pp. 36-37. Some of the Ottoman and later sources use "Mussulman" while referring to a Muslim.

94   Pattengale, "When the Crusades Became the Killing Fields: The Ramifications of Misplaced Doctrinal Beliefs," Chapter 11, *Is the Bible at Fault?*, pp. 159-176.

95   Kate Connolly, "Pope Says Sorry for Crusaders' Rampage in 1204," *The Telegraph*, June 30, 2004, https://www.telegraph.co.uk/news/worldnews/europe/italy/1465857/Pope-says-sorry-for-crusaders-rampage-in-1204.html.

96   Clouse, Pierard, and Yamauchi, *Two Kingdoms*, p. 138.

97   *Carolingian* means "related to the Frankish dynasty established by Charlemagne's father Pepin III."

98   *Two Lives of Charlemagne*, by Einhard and the Monk of St. Gall, ed. by Prof. A. J. Grant, A Lui Finit La Dissolutions de L'Ancien; Monde, A Lui Commence L'Editfication Du Monde Moderne, A Digreads.com Book, Digireads.com Publishing, 2012, p. 14.

99   Though it's unclear how well he could read, since he struggled late in life to write. However, for the influence of Augustine on Charlemagne, see Sidey, Thomas K. "The Government of Charlemagne as Influenced by Augustine's *City of God*." *The Classical Journal*14, no. 2 (1918): 119-27. http://www.jstor.org/stable/3288069.

100   Alessandro Barbero, *Charlemagne: Father of a Continent*. (University of California Press, 2004): 46-47.

101   Five of these are included in Brian Tierney, Donald Kagan and L. Pearce Williams, *Charlemagne—The Maker of Europe?* (New York: Random House, 1967). Also included are excerpts from his biographer, Einhard, and his advisor, Alcuin of York.

102   Mayr-Harting, Henry. "Charlemagne, the Saxons, and the Imperial Coronation of 800." The English Historical Review 111, no. 444 (1996): 1113-133. http://www.jstor.org/stable/575852. The quotes is from Christopher Dawson, "Charlemagne and Christian Culture," in Tierney, Kagan and Williams, *Charlemagne—The Maker of Europe?* P. 6.

103   Tierney, Kagan and Williams, *Charlemagne—The Maker of Europe?* P. 4.

104   Einhard, *The Life of Charlemagne*, section 21.

105   Ibid., section 27.

106   Einhard, *The Life of Charlemagne*, section 27.

107   Bill Austin, *Austin's Topical History of Christianity* (Wheaton: Tyndale, 1983), 146.

108   Trompf, G. W. "The Concept of the Carolingian Renaissance." *Journal of the History of Ideas* 34, no. 1 (1973): 3-25. doi:10.2307/2708941.

109   Clouse, Pierard, and Yamauchi, *Two Kingdoms*, p. 157.

110   Roland K. Harrison and Edwin M. Yamauchi, "Calendars," in Edwin M. Yamauchi and Marvin R. Wilson, editors, *Dictionary of Daily Life: In Biblical and Post-Biblical Antiquity* (Hendrickson Publishers, 2017), pp. 243-244.

111   Pope Boniface VIII, *Unam Sanctam* (One God, One Faith, One Spiritual Authority), November 18, 1302. Papal Encyclicals Online, accessed at http://www.papalencyclicals.net/bon08/b8unam.htm.

112   Justo L. Gonzalez, *The Story of Christianity: The Early Church to the Dawn of the Reformation*, vol 1 (Harper Collins, 2010), p. 455.

113   Ibid, p. 148.

114   Confessionals would become private after the Council of Trent.

115   Thomas Kempis wrote this between 1417 and 1428, and it is among the most-translated books in history. It actually emphasizes the contemplative life, and not the outward actions like the Friars.

116   H. G. Koenigsberger, George L. Mosse, G. Q. Bowler, *Europe in the Sixteenth Century*, (New York: Longman, 1968), pp. 209-210.

117   Ibid., p. 208.

118   Justo L. Gonzalez, *The Story of Christianity: The Early Church to the Dawn of the Reformation*, vol 1 (Harper Collins, 2010), p. 454.

119 Ibid., p. 459.

120 Ibid., 455.

121 Ibid., pp. 212-213.

122 For an image of this saint—St. Oliver Plunkett—see Marea Harris, "The Severed Head of a Martyr now Displayed in an Irish Church," *The Vintage News* (Aug 13, 2018); accessed at https://www.thevinta-genews.com/2018/08/13/st-peters-roman-catholic-church/.

123 The Caribbean island where de Montesinos preached is located between Puerto Rico on the east and Cuba on the west. Columbus called it Hispaniola (which means "little Spain"). Today that island is comprised of Haiti on the west, and the Dominican Republic on the east. Santo Domingo is on the southern coast of the Dominican Republic.

124 Justo L. Gonzalez, "Lights in the Darkness: As sincere believers marched to subjugate a continent, other Christians had to oppose them," *Christian History,* Christianity Today, Issue 35 (1992). Accessed at https://www.christianitytoday.com/history/issues/issue-35/lights-in-darkness.html

125 Justo Gonzales, "Lights in the Darkness," *Christian History*, issue 35.

126 Scholars don't agree over the identity of this island. San Salvador, Grand Turk Island, Samana Cay, and Plana Cays have all been mentioned as possibilities.

127 Christopher Columbus, "A Letter Concerning Recently Discovered Lands," sent to King Ferdinand II of Aragon and Queen Isabella I of Castille (sometime after January 1493, written en route back to Spain).

128 Alfred J. Andrea and James H. Overfield, *The Human Record: Sources of Global History Vol. I* (New York: Houghton Mifflin Co., 1998), p. 17.

129 Or "La Navidad," see James MaClellan, "The Lost Fort of Columbus," *Smithsonian Magazine* (January). Accessed at https://www.smithsonianmag.com/history/the-lost-fort-of-columbus-8026921/. The contents are rich with additional information.

130 "Christopher Columbus's Santa Maria wreck 'found.'" BBC News (March 13, 2014). Accessed at https://www.bbc.com/news/world-us-canada-27397579

131 See footnote 8.

132 Russell Schimmer, "Hispaniola," Genocide Studies Program, Yale University. Accessed at https://gsp.yale.edu/case-studies/colonial-genocides-project/hispaniola.

133 Alvaro Enrigue, "The Curse of Cortes," *New York Review of Books* (May 24, 2018). Accessed at https://www.nybooks.com/arti-

cles/2018/05/24/mexico-curse-of-/

134 36, Gonzalez.

135 Clouse, Pierard, and Yamauchi, *Two Kingdoms*, pp. 295-296.

136 Rebecca Moore, *Voices of Christianity: A Global Introduction* (New York: McGraw-Hill, 2006), p. 316.

137 Joel Morales Cruz and Alisha Lofgren. *The Histories of the Latin American Church: A Brief Introduction.* (Minneapolis: Fortress Press, 2014), p. 419.

138 Jacques Mercier, *The Temptation of Chocolate* (Lannoo Uitgeverij, 2008),

139 Clouse, Pierard, and Yamauchi, *Two Kingdoms*, pp. 293-294.

140 For a simple comparative chart see https://www.granburyisd.org/cms/lib/tx01000552/centricity/domain/287/fact_sheet_u1_comparison_of_eng_fr_sp_col.pdf.

141 James A. Michener, *Iberia: Spanish Travels and Reflections*, pp. 30-31.

142 Gonzalez and Gonzalez, *Christianity in Latin America: A History*, p. 3.

143 Ibid., pp. 28-29.

144 Ibid., p. 29.

145 There are alternate spellings depending on the Portuguese or Spanish usage.

146 Gonzalez and Gonzalez, *Christianity in Latin America: A History*, p. 28.

147 Ibid.

148 MacCulloch, *Christianity*, p. 690.

149 Ibid., p. 691.

150 González and González. *Christianity in Latin America: A History*, p. 29.

151 Of the eleven million slaves transported to the New World, some 42% ended up in North America, 49% in South America, and the rest were taken to the Caribbean.

152 González and González. *Christianity in Latin America: A History*, p. 47.

153 Ibid., p. 30.

154 Ibid., pp. 29-30.

155 Rodney Stark, cited in Mangalwadi, p. 101.

156 Smith, "The History of the Catholic Church in Latin America and Liberation Theology." Also see Rollie E. Poppino, *Brazil: The Land and People* (New York: Oxford University Press, 1968), p. 81.

157 Robert Ricard, *The Spiritual Conquest of Mexico: An Essay on the Apostolate and the Evangelizing Methods of the Mendicant Orders*

in New Spain, 1523-1572, translated by Lesley Byrd Simpson. Berkeley: University of California Press 1966.

158   Ramon Hernandez O.P., "The Internationalization of Francisco de Vitoria and Domingo de Soto," translated by Jay J. Aragones, *Fordham International Law Journal*, Vol. 15, Issue 4, 1991, p. 1045. Accessed at https://ir.lawnet.fordham.edu/cgi/viewcontent.cgi?referer=https://en.wikipedia.org/&httpsredir=1&article=1325&context=ilj.

159   Ibid, pp. 1046-47.

160   Victor M. Salas, Jr., "Francisco de Vitoria on the *Ius Gentium and the American Indios*", Ave Maria Law Review, 2012 Archived 2014-09-11 at the Wayback Machine

161   Edward Markham, *The Real America in Romance: An Authentic History of America from the Discovery to the Present Day*, Vol. 13 (William H. Wise & Company, 1914), p. 388

162   John Maust, "Bartolomé de Las Casas (1474–1566)" S.v. in "Columbus and Christianity in the Americas: A Gallery of Champions for the Oppressed," *Christian History*, Christianity Today, Accessed at https://www.christianitytoday.com/history/issues/issue-35/columbus-and-christianity-in-americas-gallery-of-champions.html.

163   Las Casas, Bartolome de, *A Brief Account of the Destruction of the Indies*, Casas. "A Brief Account of the Destruction of the Indies Or, a Faithful NARRATIVE OF THE Horrid and Unexampled Massacres, Butcheries, and All Manner of Cruelties, That Hell and Malice Could Invent, Committed by the Popish Spanish Party on the Inhabitants of West-India, TOGETHER With the Devastations of Several Kingdoms in America by Fire and Sword, for the Space of Forty and Two Years, from the Time of Its First Discovery by Them." Gutenberg. October 10, 2018. Accessed April 19, 2019. http://www.gutenberg.org/cache/epub/20321/pg20321-images.html.

164   Maust, "Bartolomé de Las Casas (1474–1566)."

165   Ondina E. Gonzalez and Justo J. Gonzalez, *Christianity in Latin America: A History* (Cambridge: Cambridge University Press, 2007), p. 46. The two debaters included Juan Gines de Sepulvada, who called for a militant evangelism, and Bartolome de Las Casas, who defended the "Indians" and noted that they were the only ones fighting a just war, defending their families and territories. This was one of the first major moral debates in Europe on the colonists' rights (or, the enslaved).

166   González and González. *Christianity in Latin America: A History*, p. 91.

167   We see these numbers for his mentor as well. However, the UNESCO project reports among its five basic facts about Cartagena is "Between 1595 and 1640, the Portuguese brought to Cartagena about 125,000 enslaved Africans." See *Donde Cartagena*, accessed at https://donde.co/cartagena/articles/slavery-route-cartagena-de-in-

dias-27287. This site is especially helpful as it gives the details of the historic site associated with "The Slave Route" (see A-Q).

168　John Slattery, *The Life of Saint Peter Claver, S.J.: The Apostle of the Negroes* (1893). This was a fundraising book. Slattery, like Alonso Salvador and the prevailing European view earlier during Claver's time, was advocating European paternalism along with the notion that it is better to be a slave in South America than free and going to Hell in Africa as a pagan.

169　Ibid, p. 92. See the earlier versions in the opening section.

170　The actual event is recorded, and the following site plays it with actual pictures of the event: https://www.youtube.com/watch?v=tC-62Grvn2vM and his canonization ceremonies: https://www.youtube.com/watch?v=EGROjsTwsaA and https://www.facebook.com/CatholicNewsAgency/videos/mass-of-canonization-of-st-paul-vi-and-st-oscar-romero/703369746701759/.

171　Jon Lee Anderson, "Archbishop Óscar Romero Becomes a Saint, But His Death Still Haunts El Salvador," *New Yorker* (October 22, 2018); accessed at: https://www.newyorker.com/news/daily-comment/archbishop-oscar-romero-becomes-a-saint-but-his-death-still-haunts-el-salvador .

172　Oscar Romero, "Voice of the Voiceless: The Four Pastoral Letters and Other Statements," (Maryknoll, NY: Orbis Books, 1985), pp. 177-187.

173　Ondina E. Gonzalez and Justo J. Gonzalez, *Christianity in Latin America: A History* (Cambridge: Cambridge University Press, 2007), p. 4.

174　Ibid, cf. pp. 272-277.

175　Ibid., p. 283.

176　Ibid, p. 284.

177　402, Cruz, 2014.

178　The Greek word translated *fish* in the New Testament is *ichthys* (transliterated *icthus*), the letters of which happen to be an acrostic for the phrase "Jesus Christ, God's Son, Savior." Probably, the fish was adopted because of Christ's call to his first disciples, *"Come, follow me," Jesus said, "and I will send you out to fish for people"* (Matthew 4:19, NIV).

179　"The First Charter of Virginia, April 10, 1606," The Avalon Project (Yale Law School); accessed at https://avalon.law.yale.edu/17th_century/va01.asp#b1.

180　The 102 passengers on the *Mayflower* consisted of 50 men, 19 women and 33 young adults and children. https://www.history.com/topics/colonial-america/mayflower-compact

181　Edwin S. Gaustad, "Quest for Pure Christianity," *Christian History*, Christianity Today (Issue 41). Accessed at https://www.christianitytoday.com/history/issues/issue-41/american-puritans-did-you-know.html

182   For an outline of the Puritans that provides the wider context for their trip to North America, and development within it, see Francis J. Bremer, "The American Puritans: Christian History Timeline" *Christian History,* Christianity Today, accessed at https://www.christianitytoday.com/history/issues/issue-41/american-puritans-christian-history-time-line.html

183   William J. Bennett, *America: The Last Great Hope.*

184   John Winthrop, "A Modell of Christian Charity," 1630. Hanover Historical Texts Project, Hanover College https://history.hanover.edu/texts/winthmod.html .

185   Harry S. Stout, "Puritanism," S.v. *The Jonathan Edwards Encyclopedia,* Harry Stout, gen. ed., Kenneth P. Minkema and Adriaan C. Neele, associate editors (Grand Rapids, MI: William B. Eerdmans Publishing Company, 2017), p. 479. See Harry S. Stout, *The New England Soul: Preaching and Religious Culture in Colonial New England* (Oxford: Oxford University Press, 1986).

186   Alexis de Tocqueville, *Democracy in America,* trans. Harvey C. Mansfield and Delba Winthrop (Chicago: University of Chicago Press, 2002), pp. 38-39. He goes on to state that in spite of these mistakes the benefits of their decisions would prove instrumental in founding a successful democratic self-governance.

187   Rabbi Daniel Lapin, *America's Real War* (Sisters, Oregon: Multnomah Publishers, Inc., 1999), p. 99.

188   MacCulloch, *Christianity,* p. 716, 719.

189   Morison, *Concise History,* p. 28.

190   Mathew Spalding, *We Still Hold These Truths: Rediscovering Our Principles, Reclaiming Our Future* (Delaware: Intercollegiate Studies Institute, 2009): 13-14. Part of the debate noted below this excerpt between David Barton and the Baylor Professors represents sources like this one, since Spalding is from the Heritage Foundation. Their main concern is true of vetted academic works elsewhere—just making sure they reflect a responsible use of sources.

191   The Appendix "America's Christian Beginnings" outlines these views.

192   Justin Taylor, "Christian History: How David Barton Is Doing It Wrong," *The Gospel Coalition* (May 12, 2017); accessed at https://www.thegospelcoalition.org/blogs/evangelical-history/christian-history-why-david-barton-is-doing-it-wrong/.

193   Thomas S. Kidd, "The DNA of a Nation," in Steve Green, *The Bible in America: What We Believe about the Most Important Book in Our History* (Oklahoma City, OK: DustJacket Press, 2013), p. 109.

194   Ibid, p. 110.

195 This Bible was also called The Breeches Bible because it translated the passage of Adam and Eve covering themselves with "breeches" instead of leaves or a cloth (Genesis 3:7).

196 There is debate about which version of the Bible was most prevalent among the Pilgrims and earliest Puritan immigrants to North America. See Gordon Campbell, *Bible: The Story of the King James Version, 1611-2011* (Oxford: Oxford University Press), p. 194.

197 The Geneva Bible would later be utilized heavily by the scholars commissioned to create the King James Bible

198 English Bibles at this time consisted of the Tyndale Bible, the Coverdale Bible, the Matthew's Bible, and the Great Bible.

199 Schiffman and Pattengale, *The World's Greatest Book*, p. 203.

200 Dr. John Reynolds, a Puritan, was president of Corpus Christ College, Oxford.

201 Gordon Campbell, *Bible: The Story of the King James Version, 1611-2011* (Oxford: Oxford University Press), p. 194. The Bible was ipso facto authorized by King James, but not officially authorized until later.

202 "Mohawk Scriptures" (the sales catalogue for the 1818 version, which sold for $3,500 at Sotheby's in 2016). Accessed at http://bibles.wiki-dot.com/mohawk.

203 *The Gospel According to Saint John* (In the Mohawk Language), (New York: American Bible Society; D. Fanshaw, Printer) 1818.

204 See Jeff Wallenfeldt, "The Six Nations of the Iroquois Confederacy," S.v., *Encyclopedia Britannica*; accessed at

205 Due to the war, the $10,000 promised to Aitken was never paid.

206 Anthony Schmidt, Senior Curator and Amy Van Dyke, Lead Curator of Exhibitions, "The Slave Bible: Let the Story Be Told," The Museum of the Bible (Washington, DC: 11/28/18 - 09/01/19).

207 Only 11 copies of this book are known to be in existence. In 2013, a copy owned by the Old South Church in Boston was auctioned at Sotheby's in New York for a record $14.165 million.

208 Smith, "The New-England Primer."

209 James Samuel Smith, "The New-England Primer," S.v., *Encyclopedia Brittanica*, accessed at https://www.britannica.com/topic/The-New-England-Primer. This site shows some of the woodcut images.

210 Numerous sites recount some of his biblical teachings; see Bill Federer, "McGuffey's Readers—A Million Copies a Year for 100 years!" Accessed at https://newsmaven.io/americanminute/american-history/mcguffey-s-readers-a-million-copies-a-year-for-100-years-WXm9RNy-8qEyifAcDACYfLg/.

211 The numbers vary, but the steady message is that the readers were

commonplace in American society; "McGuffey's Readers," Ohio History Central, http://www.ohiohistorycentral.org/w/McGuffey's_Reader?rec=1469.

212   A number of other educational institutions (or foundations) were founded during the colonial era, and appear on lists of colleges— such as Moravian College. It began as Bethlehem Female Seminary in 1742 (Pennsylvania).

213   The College of William and Mary wavered between public and private support and status, but became permanently public in 1906. It began as a school to the Indians long before Harvard was founded, but stopped operations after Indian raids. "On February I, 1693, King William III and Queen Mary II of England signed the charter for a 'perpetual College of Divinity, Philosophy, Languages, and other good Arts and Sciences' to be founded in the Virginia Colony. And William & Mary was born." William and Mary website, accessed at https://web.archive.org/web/20120430074128/http://www.wm.edu/about/history/index.php .

214   The engraving is in all caps, no punctuations, and the letter "U" is the common "V" from engravers.

215   "Nine Colonial Colleges," Going Colonial, accessed at https://www.goingcolonial.com/colonial-colleges/. For an engaging account of these proceedings, including insights into the magnetic leadership of its president, the Scottish John Witherspoon, and various quotes from letters of participants about the cramped quarters, see Constance Escher, "When Princeton was the Nation's Capital," *Princeton Alumni Weekly* (October 5, 1983); accessed at https://paw.princeton.edu/article/continental-congress-nassau-hall. Escher writes, "Princeton was a war-ravaged village of only 50 to 60 houses and not more than 300 people."

216   "Dartmouth: History and Traditions," accessed at https://home.dartmouth.edu/life-community/explore-green/history-traditions.

217   http://www.newenglandhistoricalsociety.com/dwight-l-moody-yankee-preacher-meets-abe-lincoln-in-little-hell/

218   See Gregg L. Quiggle, "D. L. Moody," in *A Legacy of Preaching, Volume Two—Enlightenment to the Present Day: The Life, Theology, and Method of History's Great Preachers*, Benjamin K. Forrest, Kevin King Sr., William J. Curtis, Dwayne Milioni, John D. Woodbridge, editors (Grand Rapids, MI: Zondervan, 2018).

219   Ibid.

220   "The Sunday School Movement," Gale Library of Daily Life: American Civil War, *Encyclopedia.com.* (May 29, 2019). https://www.encyclopedia.com/history/applied-and-social-sciences-magazines/sunday-school-movement

221   Timothy Larsen, "When Did Sunday Schools Start?" *Christian History,*

Christianity Today. Accessed at https://www.christianitytoday.com/history/2008/august/when-did-sunday-schools-start.html.

222   Thomas S. Kidd, "Great Awakening," in Stout, *The Jonathan Edwards Encyclopedia*, p. 265. Whitefield's life was a stream of actions to help the disenfranchised.

223   Thomas S. Kidd, "Great Awakening," in Stout, *The Jonathan Edwards Encyclopedia*, p. 266.

224   Fabio Augusto Darius, "Charles Finney (1792-1875)," in Stout, *The Jonathan Edwards Encyclopedia*, p. 230.

225   Alexis de Tocqueville, *Democracy in America* (New York: Schocken, 1961), 1:359-60; cited in Clouse, Pierard and Yamauchi, *The Story of the Church*, p. 462. For a contrary view, see Thomas G. West, "Misunderstanding the American Founding," in *Interpreting Tocqueville's Democracy in America*, Ken Masugi, editor (Lanham, MD: Rowman and Littlefield, 1991), pp. 155–177.

226   Allan G. Hedberg, "Slavery," S.v. *The Jonathan Edwards Encyclopedia*, pp. 535-536.

227   Mark Galli, "Slaveholding Evangelist" Whitefield's Troubling Mix of Views," *Christian History* (Christianity Today, 1993); accessed at https://www.christianitytoday.com/history/issues/issue-38/slaveholding-evangelist.html.

228   The discussions are far from over in North America on reparations. Besides responses from Christians individually and corporately, this is playing out anew in the secular space. As this book goes to press the discussions of reparations to descendants of enslaved peoples have resurfaced in the national press, especially among political factions. See "Here's What Ta-Nehisi Coates Told Congress about Reparations," *New York Times* (June 19, 2019); accessed at https://www.nytimes.com/2019/06/19/us/ta-nehisi-coates-reparations.html. See also Ana Lucia Araujo, *Reparations for Slavery and the Slave Trade: A Transnational and Comparative History* (New York: Bloomsbury, 2017). The author reminds us of the tragic toll of lives lost in and around the Middle Passage, around 4 million in addition to the 10.7 million enslaved Africans who actually survived the journey. Then she adds: "The past three decades witnessed an increasing number of ventures memorializing slavery in the Americas, Europe, and Africa. Many of these initiatives were eventually transformed into official projects. Yet, the construction of monuments and memorials neither healed the slave past, nor mitigated the legacies of slavery. Instead, it made more visible the scars of racial violence and racial equalities of which black populations, most of whom are descendants of slaves, are still the main victims in former slave societies. In this new context, in which public memory of slavery is increasingly institutionalized, the means of financial and material reparations for slavery in the Atlantic

slave trade are again resurfacing, against the odds of many scholars and activists who by the end of the twentieth century declared the case for financial material reparations dead" (pp. 1-2).

229   Mark A. Noll, *From Jonathan Edwards to Abraham Lincoln* (Oxford: Oxford University Press, 2002).

230   MacCulloch, *Christianity,* p. 760.

231   MacCulloch, *Christianity,* p. 761.

232   Mark Sidwell, "The First Heroes of African American Christian History," *Christian History* (Issue 62, 1999); accessed at https://www.christianitytoday.com/history/issues/issue-62/black-christianity-before-civil-war-gallery--fruit-of.html

233   Dana L. Robert, "Stewart, John," in *Biographical Dictionary of Christian Missions,* ed. Gerald H. Anderson (New York: Macmillan Reference USA, 1998), 641-642.

234   Thelma Marsh, "John Stewart, Indian Missionary," from *Moccasin Trails to the Cross,* accessed at http://www.wyandot.org/stew1.htm

235   Richard Snoddy, "Lemuel Haynes (1753-1833)," S.v., *The Jonathan Edwards Encyclopedia,* p. 279.

236   Sidwell, "The First Heroes of African American Christian History."

237   Eric Washington, "Jarena Lee," *Christian History* (Christianity Today, May 23, 2017), accessed at https://www.christianitytoday.com/history/people/pastorsandpreachers/jarena-lee.html.

238   Accessed at https://www.episcopalchurch.org/library/sermon/absalom-jones.

239   David A. Hollinger and Charles Capper, *The American Intellectual Tradition, Volume 1, 1630-1865* (Oxford University Press, 2016), pp. 532-545.

240   Sojourner Truth, "Ain't I a Woman?" Fordham University, accessed at https://sourcebooks.fordham.edu/mod/sojtruth-woman.asp (the full text is posted). The text various slightly in different sources.

241   Gaustad, "Quest for Pure Christianity," (Issue 41).

242   Grace, "Under the Shadows of Death," p. 61.

243   Bennett, *America,* pp. 47-48.

244   Sister Pat Davis, "The Life of St. Isaac Jogues," in *Our Saints, Our Story,* St. Issac Jogues North American Martyrs (u.p.); accessed at St. Isaac Jogues Catholic Church (Wayne, PA), https://stisaac.org/life-of-st-isaac-jogues/.

245   "America's Changing Religious Landscape," Pew Research Center: Religion and Public Life (May 15, 2015); accessed at https://www.pewforum.org/2015/05/12/americas-changing-religious-landscape/.

246   Where Jesus had been speared (after dying) by a Roman soldier (John 19:34).

247 "Christianity 2015: Religious Diversity and Personal Contact" (PDF). Gordonconwell.edu. January 2015. Archived from the original (PDF) on 2017-05-25. Retrieved 2019-07-17 (https://web.archive.org/web/20170525141543/http://www.gordonconwell.edu/resources/documents/1IBMR2015.pdf)

248 "The Surprising Early History of Christianity in India," *Smithsonian Journal Travels Quarterly*; accessed at https://www.smithsonianmag.com/travel/how-christianity-came-to-india-kerala-180958117/ . There remains much debate about St. Thomas, and many challenges about some of the legends, e.g., converting groups of Brahmins (seems anachronistic, and as one commenter on this site points out, likely would not have talked with him—though William Carey was successful with converting members of the higher caste).

249 "The Surprising Early History of Christianity in India," *Smithsonian Journal Travels Quarterly*; accessed at https://www.smithsonianmag.com/travel/how-christianity-came-to-india-kerala-180958117/ . There remains much debate about St. Thomas, and many challenges about some of the legends, e.g., converting groups of Brahmins (seems anachronistic, and as one commenter on this site points out, likely would not have talked with him—though William Carey was successful with converting members of the higher caste).

250 "William Carey: The Father of Modern Protestant Missions," *Church History,* Christianity Today (1992); accessed at https://www.christianitytoday.com/history/people/missionaries/william-carey.html.

251 Ibid.

252 Witold Rodzinski, *The Walled Kingdom: A History of China from Antiquity to the Present* (New York: Free Press, 1984), p. 43.

253 See chapter six of Earl H. Pritchard, *Anglo-Chinese Relations during the Seventeenth and Eighteenth Centuries* (Octagon Books, 1931, 1970).

254 Diarmaid MacCulloch, *Christianity: The First Three Thousand Years* (Viking Penguin: 2009), p. 896.

255 Arthur Cotterell, *China: A Cultural History* (New York: Meridian, 1988), p. 152.

256 Cotterell, *China*, p. 153.

257 Rodzinski, *The Walled Kingdom*, p. 154.

258 Robert G. Clouse, Richard V. Pierard, and Edwin M. Yamauchi, *Two Kingdoms: The Church and Culture through the Ages* (Chicago: Moody Press, 1993), p. 309.

259 Mungello, "Reinterpreting the History of Christianity in China," p. 536. The world order, placing Confucian first places respects the less-domineering colonial approach of the pre-1800 Jesuits. And, synthesis versus syncretism implies a more intellectual application and

less an assimilation in the Chinese culture.

260 Gernet, *China and the Christian Impact,* pp. 15-47, 64-72.

261 Aikman, *Jesus in Beijing,* p. 36.

262 Peter W. Fay, "The Protestant Mission and the Opium War." *Pacific Historical Review* 40, no. 2 (1971): 145-61.

263 Rodzinski, *The Walled Kingdom,* p. 180.

264 Ibid., p. 171.

265 Passing these civil service tests was a prerequisite for landing a job in the Chinese government.

266 Fairbank, *China,* p. 208.

267 Fairbank, *China,* pp. 207-208.

268 Aikman, *Jesus in Beijing,* p. 39.

269 MacCulloch, *Christianity,* p. 897.

270 *China's Millions,* pp. 116-117.

271 Aikman, *Jesus in Beijing,* p. 40.

272 David Aikman, *Jesus in Beijing: How Christianity is Transforming China and Changing the Balance of Global Power* (Washington, DC: Regnery Publishing, Inc., 2003), p. 40.

273 Robert G. Clouse, Richard V. Pierard, and Edwin M. Yamauchi, *Two Kingdoms: The Church and Culture through the Ages* (Chicago: Moody Press, 1993), p. 500.

274 *The Church in China,* p. 62.

275 Aikman, *Jesus in Beijing,* p. 42.

276 *The Church in China,* p. 144.

277 Aikman, *Jesus in Beijing,* p. 44.

278 Mark D. Tooley, "What *The Washington Post* Doesn't Understand About Taiwan Christians and Gay Marriage," *The Christian Post* (April 27, 2017); accessed at https://www.christianpost.com/news/what-the-washington-post-doesnt-understand-about-taiwan-christians-and-gay-marriage.html

279 Thomas Alan Harvey, *Acquainted With Grief: Wang Mingdao's Stand for the Persecuted Church in China* (Grand Rapids, MI: Brazos Press, 2002), p. 159 (also cited in an extended quote in Aikman, *Jesus in Beijing,* p. 191.)

280 Mark Galli, "What to Do about Persecution in China," *Christianity Today* (November 3, 2018); accessed at http://blackchristiannews.com/2018/11/mark-galli-what-to-do-about-persecution-in-china/

281 See "10 Countries with the Largest Number of Christians," *Global Christianity* (Pew Research Center Forum's on Religion and Public Life, December, 2011). This chart is included near the end of this docu-

ment; it also lists the numbers of Christians in China in 2011 at 5% of its total population.

282   91-92, *The Oxford Handbook of Christianity in Asia*, Felix Wilfred, 2014

283   Kate Shellnutt, "China Tells Christians to Replace Images of Jesus with Communist President" *Christianity Today* (November 17, 2017); accessed at https://www.christianitytoday.com/news/2017/november/china-christians-jesus-communist-president-xi-jinping-yugan.html

284   Kate Shellnutt, "China Closes Megachurches Before Christmas," *Christianity Today* (December 18, 2018); accessed at https://www.christianitytoday.com/news/2018/december/china-churches-early-rain-rongguili-wang-yi-samuel-lamb.html.

285   Benjamin Haas, "'We are scared, but we have Jesus': China and its war on Christianity," *The Guardian* (September 28, 2018); accessed at https://www.theguardian.com/world/2018/sep/28/we-are-scared-but-we-have-jesus-china-and-its-war-on-christianity

286   Ibid. Note that not all of these heroic efforts had happy endings—that is, venerated by the church historians as saints or martyrs. The man indirectly responsible for Hudson Taylor going to China, whom he called "the grandfather of the China Inland Mission," Karl F.A. Gützlaff, died in shame in 1953 having been bamboozled by Chinese helpers (reporting grossly inflated numbers, and reselling distributed Bibles for profits).

287   "We're Sorry Gladys...But God Can't Use You in China," *Christianity Today/Christian History*, 1988; accessed at https://www.christianitytoday.com/history/issues/issue-19/were-sorry-gladysbut-god-cant-use-you-in-china.html.

288   https://omf.org/us/the-martyrdom-of-john-and-betty-stam/

289   Gordon Dunn, "The Martyrdom of John and Betty Stam," OMF; accessed at https://omf.org/us/the-martyrdom-of-john-and-betty-stam/. Some of the Stams' original letters are in the Museum of the Bible's collections, Washington, DC.

290   Whether legal or illegal, the Christians maintained a presence and place in China's development. The large numbers of new Christians claimed, however, need put in the context of the significant growth among Buddhists as well; Rodney Stark and Eric Y. Liu, "The Religious Awakening in China," *Review of Religious Research* 52, no. 3 (2011): 282-89. See also Nancy Bernkopf Tucker, "An Unlikely Peace: American Missionaries and the Chinese Communists, 1948-1950." *Pacific Historical Review* 45, no. 1 (1976): 97-116.

291   Earthy, E. Dora. "The Religion of Genghis Khan (A.D. 1162-1227)." *Numen* 2, no. 3 (1955): 228-232, see p. 229.

292   Ibid., p. 229.

293 Nicolini-Zani, Matteo. *China Review International* 18, no. 3 (2011): 354-58.

294 This is recounted with some flair and many details in Aikman's *Jesus in Beijing*, pp. 268-270. And, a full account is in Brother David with Paul Hattaway, *Project Pearl: The 100 Million Smuggled Bibles That Changed China* (Monarch Books, 2007). Several people are still alive who were involved in this project, including Sealy Yates, of Yates and Yates.

295 Ibid., this entire section is an engaging read (P. 269, the end of the chapter, through p. 275).

296 Kyo Seong Ahn, Christian Mission and Mongolian Identity: The Religious, Cultural, and Political Context. *Studies in World Christianity* (2003 9:1), 103-124; p. 103. In 2019, David Hamilton (an executive leader at Youth with a Mission) informed the author that his team has interviewed residents from the area that attest to a handful of Christians who survived this season of oppression.

297 Mark Galli, interview of Mark Noll, "The Freedom and Chaos of Sola Scriptura," *Christianity Today* (May 26, 2017); accessed at https://www.christianitytoday.com/ct/2017/june/freedom-and-chaos-of-sola-scriptura.html. John Gibbons ("and his Mongolian wife") are credited with producing an early Mongolian translation, begun in 1972.

298 For the sake of most of our discussion here, it was still one Korea; it was divided at the 38th Parallel following the end of World War II (1945).

299 Kirsteen Kim and Hoon Ko, "Who Brought the Gospel to Korea? Koreans Did," *Church History*, Christianity Today (February 9, 2018).

300 Robert G. Clouse, Richard V. Pierard, and Edwin M. Yamauchi, *Two Kingdoms: The Church and Culture through the Ages* (Chicago: Moody Press, 1993), p. 212.

301 Kim and Ko, "Who Brought the Gospel to Korea?"

302 Daniel M. Davies, "The Impact of Christianity upon Korea, 1884-1910: Six Key American and Korean Figures." *Journal of Church and State* 36, no. 4 (1994): 795. His footnote 2 provides of litany of helpful source on this general overview of Christianity in Korea.

303 Kim and Ko, "Who Brought the Gospel to Korea?"

304 Young-Hoon Lee, "Korean Pentecost: The Great Revival of 1907," *AJPS*, 4/1 (2001), p. 73. Accessed at http://www.apts.edu/aeimages/File/AJPS_PDF/01-1-yhlee.pdf.

305 Lee, "Korean Pentecost," p. 77. Also see "The North Korean Revival of 1907," The Gospel Coalition; accessed at https://www.thegospelcoalition.org/blogs/evangelical-history/the-north-korean-revival-of-1907/.

306 Erin Blakemore, "How Japan Took Control of Korea," *History* (Febru-

ary 27, 2018); accessed at https://www.history.com/news/japan-col-onization-korea. This quotation is taken from Donald N. Clark, cited below, p. 49.

307   Michael Hoffman, "Christian missionaries find Japan a tough nut to crack.," *The Japan Times* (December 20, 2014). Accessed at https://www.japantimes.co.jp/news/2014/12/20/national/history/christian-missionaries-find-japan-tough-nut-crack/#.XR6cQuhKhPY

308   Richard Cavendesh, "St. Francis Xavier Departs from Japan," *History Today*, Volume 51 Issue 11 (November 2001). Accessed at https://www.historytoday.com/archive/st-francis-xavier-departs-japan.

309   Ibid.

310   Ibid., p. 64.

311   Ibid., p. 308.

312   Michael Hoffman, "Christian missionaries find Japan a tough nut to crack," *The Japan Times* (December 20, 2014). Accessed at https://www.japantimes.co.jp/news/2014/12/20/national/history/christian-missionaries-find-japan-tough-nut-crack/#.XR6cQuhKhPY

313   Michael Hoffman, "Japan's historical resistance to Christianity," *The Japan Times* (December 16, 2017). Accessed at https://www.japan-times.co.jp/news/2017/12/16/national/history/japans-historical-resis-tance-christianity/#.XR6K6ehKhPY.

314   Clouse, Pierard, and Yamauchi, *Two Kingdoms*, p. 308.

315   MacCulloch, *Christianity*, p. 898; Kim and Ko, "Who Brought the Gospel to Korea?"

316   Gonzalez, *The Story of Christianity*, II, p. 429.

317   Bruce G. Dunning, "James Hepburn 32's Influence Lives on in Japan," *The Paw* (July 18, 2007); Accessed at https://www.princeton.edu/~paw/web_exclusives/plus/plus_071807hepburn.html.

318   MacCulloch, *Christianity*, pp. 708-709.

319   https://backtojerusalem.com/about/

320   https://www.christianitytoday.com/ct/2016/january-february/made-in-china-next-mass-missionary-movement.html

321   https://www.scmp.com/news/china/society/article/2099968/se-cret-lives-chinese-missionaries-northern-iraq

322   Cited in *Walking from East to West: God in the Shadows*, by Ravi Zacharias, Zondervan, 2009.

323   A semi-nomadic, religiously animistic tribe numbering more than 850,000 (according to the 2009 Kenyan census).

324   This movie version of the Gospel of Luke was made in the late 1970s by Campus Crusade for Christ (now known as Cru). The film has been translated into more than a thousand languages and has been seen

by perhaps as many as three billion people. Cru claims this film has resulted in more than 400 million professions of faith in Christ.

325 Sub-Saharan Africa refers to the bulk of the continent which lies south of the Saharan desert.

326 Although there is a range of estimates for 1910, the number is most likely lower than five million.

327 Adam R. Taylor, "Christianity's Future Lies in Africa," *Sojourners* (April 12, 2019), accessed at https://sojo.net/articles/christianitys-future-lies-africa

328 Pew Research Center, cited in Taylor, "Christianity's Future Lies in Africa."

329 Lamin Sanneh (1942-2019), born in Gambia, was Professor of History at Yale University and D. Willis James Professor of Missions and World Christianity at Yale Divinity School.

330 David Maxwell, p. .See John Parker and Richard Reid, editors, *Handbook of Modern African History* (Oxford: Oxford University Press, 2016), chapter 14, fn. 47.

331 See, for example, Thomas Oden's recent *How Africa Shaped the Christian Mind* (Intervarsity, 2007) and *The African Memory of Mark* (Intervarsity, 2011) which claim that Africa was the "seedbed" for Christianity. The wider argument about the role of African thought in the classical world was best *expressed* (though long pretty much repudiated) by Martin Bernal in his classic *Black Athena* (Rutgers, 1987), in which he suggests that ALL classical civilization had its roots in North Africa and Asia, rather than in Greece as the Enlightenment has taught us. Recent scholars have suggested that Ethiopia may even have had an Enlightenment of its own in the 17th and 18th centuries. See also François Decret, *Early Christianity in North Africa* (Cambridge, 2011).

332 There's debate about this. Some scholars claim that the Romans traded wine for salt across the desert (see Js. McDougall and Judith Scheele, *Saharan Frontiers* [Indiana, 2012], 58-70) Others, like Ralph Austin, date the trade to the 5th century CE, when Christianity was alive, but not for very much longer, in the Maghrib. Ralph Austin, *Trans Saharan Africa in World History* (NY: Oxford, 2010), ch. 1.

333 Maxwell, p. 263.

334 Elizabeth Isichei, *A History of African Christianity* (Africa World Press, 1995), pp. 42ff.

335 There is a growing literature on Ethiopia. One book that's been around for a while is Taddesse Tamrat's *Church and state 1270-1527* (Oxford, 1972).

336 The dates for its composition vary widely. See Sir E. A. Wallis Budge, translator, *The Queen of Sheba and Her only Son Menyelek (Kebra*

Nagast), (Cambridge, Ontario: In Parentheses Publications Ethiopian Series, 2000), p. iii, ". . . it seems to me that we should not be far wrong if we assign the earliest form of Kebra Nagast to the sixth century AD. Its compiler was probably a Coptic priest, for the writings he used were accepted by the Coptic Church." Accessed at http://www.yorku.ca/inpar/kebra_budge.pdf. However, Arabic origins for parts of the text, and lack of earlier external references, prompt others to date it centuries later; see David Allan Hubbard, *The Literary Sources of the Kebra Nagast* (University of St. Andrews, 1956), p. 352.

337 http://www.sacred-texts.com/chr/kn/kn000-5.htm

338 There is a copy of part of this document in the sourcebook referred to in the works cited.

339 See John K. Thornton, *Africa and Africans in the Making of the Atlantic World* (Cambridge, 1992).

340 Linda M. Heywood, *Njinga of Angola: Africa's Warrior Queen* (Harvard: Harvard University Press, 2017).

341 Alexander Ives, Bortolot, "Women Leaders in African History: Dona Beatriz, Kongo Prophet," in *Heilbrunn Timeline of Art History*. New York: The Metropolitan Museum of Art, 2000. Accessed at https://www.metmuseum.org/toah/hd/pwmn_4/hd_pwmn_4.htm.

342 Isichei, *A History of African Christianity,* p. 46.

343 See Anne Forschler-Tarrasch, "Am I Not a Man and a Brother," Birmingham Museum of Art (March 27, 2018); accessed at https://artsbma.org/am-i-not-a-man-and-a-brother-medallion/.

344 William Wilberforce, Speech to the House of Commons, May 2, 1789, p. 1 (one of two recorded accounts); accessed at: http://abolition.e2bn.org/people_24.html

345 Chief among them, the Baptist Missionary Society (1792), London Missionary Society (1795), Church Missionary Society (1801), British and Foreign Bible Society (1804), the American Board of Commissioners for Foreign Missions (1810), the Basel Mission (1815), and the Wesleyan Methodist Missionary Society (late 1810s)

346 Adrian Hastings, *The Church in Africa, 1450-1950* (Clarendon, 1994); and African Christianity (Seabury Press, 1976), pp. 2-3.

347 Ted Olsen, "Bishop Before His Time," accessed at https://www.christianitytoday.com/history/issues/issue-79/bishop-before-his-time.html

348 Ibid.

349 Ruth Tucker, *From Jerusalem to Irian Jaya,* p. 128 digital edition.

350 A. J. Wills, *Introduction to the History of Central Africa* (Oxford, 1976), 96

351 The Editors of Encyclopaedia Britannica, "Charles Frederick Mackenzie," *Encyclopædia Britannica* (April 6, 2016); accessed at https://

www.britannica.com/biography/Charles-Frederick-Mackenzie

352 Ibid.

353 Ibid.

354 Maxwell, "Christianity," p. 268.

355 This is the great contribution of Nancy Rose Hunt's *A Colonial Lexicon of Birth Ritual Medicalization and Mobility in the Congo* (Duke, 1999)

356 Maxwell, "Christianity," 277.

357 Benjamin Ray, *African Religions* (Prentice Hall), 199-206; Koschkorke, *History of Christianity*, 220-22.

358 Ray, *African Religions*, 206-215; J. D. Y. Peel, *Religious Encounter and the Making of the Yoruba* (Indiana, 2000); and Birgit Meyer, *Translating the Devil* (Edinburgh, 1999).

359 Also known as female genital mutilation, this cultural ritual is an elective surgical procedure that removes the clitoris in girls ranging from one week to 14 years old.

360 This is an intensely complicated history, but an incredible example of the movements we're talking about. See especially John Lonsdale, *Histories of the Hanged: The Dirty War in Kenya and the End of Empire* (Norton, 2005) for a great introduction to this history.

361 Daniel R. Magaziner has written an entire book on the connection between Black Consciousness and theology. *The Law and the Prophets: Black Consciousness in South Africa, 1968-1977* (Ohio University Press, 2010).

362 Isichei, *History of Christianity*, 334-335.

363 Joey Marshall, *Pew Research Center, Fact Tank*, "The World's most committed Christians live in Africa, Latin America—and the US," (August, 22 2018), pewresearch.org.

364 John Harris to Jerry Pattengale, email interview, 9.28.2019, 11:04 PM.

365 John Harris, *One Blood: 200 Years of Aboriginal Encounter with Christianity—A Story of Hope* (Claremont, CA: Albatross Books, 1990, second edition, Australians Together, 2013).

366 Pliny the Younger, *Letters* 10.96-97. Accessed at http://faculty.georgetown.edu/jod/texts/pliny.html.

367 James Davie Butler, "British Convicts Shipped to American Colonies," *American Historical Review*, Vol. 2, No. 1 (Oct. 1, 1896): 12-33.

368 A. R. Ekirch, "Bound for America: A Profile of British Convicts Transported to the Colonies, 1715-1775," *William & Mary Quarterly*, 3rd ser., XLII, (1985): 184-200.

369 Vivienne Parsons, "Dixon, James (1758–1840)," *Australian Dictionary of Biography*, National Centre of Biography, Australian National University, http://adb.anu.edu.au/biography/dixon-james-1980/text2401,

published first in hardcopy 1966.

370   John Harris, "A New Story for an Old Land: 200 Years of the Bible Society in Australia," *ABC Religion and Ethics* (March 7, 2017). Accessed
at https://www.abc.net.au/religion/a-new-story-for-an-old-land-200-
years-of-the-bible-society-in-au/10095998.

371   For a closer look at Evangelicals, especially tied to English history
and the British Bible Society's history and related developments, see
the works of Andrew Atherstone (Wycliffe Hall, Oxford University),
e.g., Andrew Atherstone and David Ceri Jones, editors, *The Routledge Research Companion to the History of Evangelicalism,* London:
Routledge, 2018, and; Andrew Atherstone and John Maiden, editors,
Evangelicalism and the Church of England in the Twentieth Century,
UK: Boydell Press, 2014.

372   Murray, *Australian Christian Life*, p. 112.

373   A. C. Prior, *Some Fell on Good Ground, A History of the Beginnings
and Development of the Baptist Church in New South Wales, 1831-
1965* (Sydney: Baptist Union of New South Wales, 1966), p. 29.

374   Harris, email.

375   Frank Lewis, "The Cost of Convict Transportation from Britain to
Australia, 1796-1810," *Economic History Review,* Vol. 41, No. 4 (Nov.,
1988): 507-524.

376   Robert Hughes, *The Fatal Shore* (New York: Alfred A. Knopf, 1987),
25.

377   Sanneth and McClymond, *Wiley Blackwell Companion*, p. 577.

378   Ibid.

379   Piggin and Lineham, "Christianity in Australia and Oceania," p. 584.

380   Ibid., pp. 180-181.

381   Harris, *One Blood*, p. 89.

382   Jerry Pattengale, Nick DeNeff, Daniel Freemyer, *Is the Bible at Fault?
How the Bible Has Been Misused to Justify Evil, Suffering, and Bizarre
Behavior* (Franklin, TN: Worthy/Hachette, 2018): pp. 179. With per-
mission of the authors and publisher, this book's final chapter, "The
Degradation of the Australia's Aborigines: Why Misreading a Passage
Might Displace a People," is used liberally for our current project.

383   Harris, "Justice," (1987), p. 8. The final quote is taken from Dove,
"Aborigines of Tasmania," p. 249. Cited in Pattengale, DeNeff, Freemyer, *Is the Bible at Fault?*, p. 182.

384   Dove, cited in Harris, *One Blood*, 24.

385   James Bonwick, *The Last of the Tasmanians* (London: Sampson Low,
Son and Marston, 1870, p. 400; from Harris, *One Blood*, p. 86.

386   Pattengale, DeNeff, Freemyer, *Is the Bible at Fault?*, p. 182. For the
discussion of the revivals, see J. E. Stanton, "Mt. Margaret: Mission-

aries and the Aftermath," in T. Swain and D. Rose, eds., *Aboriginal Australians and Christian Missions* (1988): pp. 292–307 (see 303), cited in Harris, *One Blood*, p. 849.

387 Riches, "Redeeming Australia Day."

388 Ibid.

389 See https://hillsong.com/ and https://hillsong.com/music/

390 Samuel Marsden, recorded in his journal, 1820; cited from Timothy Yates, *The Conversion of the Maori: Years of Religious and Social Change, 1814-1842.* Grand Rapids, MI: Wm. B. Eerdmans Publishing Co., 2013, p. 19.

391 *Annual Report of the Wesleyan-Methodist Missionary Society*, Year Ending December 1830, p. 39; recorded in resourceful article, J. M. R. Owens, "Christianity and the Maoris to 1840," *New Zealand Journal of History*, p. 18, accessed at http://www.nzjh.auckland.ac.nz/docs/1968/NZJH_02_1_03.pdf.

392 Perhaps consumed in what Professor Paul Moon calls "post-battle rage," see https://www.nzherald.co.nz/cultures/news/article.cfm?c_id=105&objectid=10462390.

393 Yates, *The Conversion of the Maori*, p. xii.

394 See *New Zealand History*, "Evangelist Billy Graham Arrives for 11-Day Crusade," (March 29, 1959); accessed at https://nzhistory.govt.nz/page/evangelist-billy-graham-arrives-11-day-crusade. This article claims: "The 1956 census found that just 0.5% of adult New Zealanders claimed to have no religious belief. By contrast, nearly 42% of those who responded to the 2013 census professed no religious belief."

395 "Anglican Church," Te Ara: Encylopedia of New Zealand, last updated April 20, 2018, https://teara.govt.nz/en/anglican-church.

396 Te Papa, the National Museum of New Zealand, has included one of Tamaki's suits in its display entitled *Uniformity: Cracking the Dress Code, An Exhibition Designed to Investigate the Meaning of Clothing or Uniforms.*

397 A. K. Davidson and Peter J. Lineham, eds., *Transplanted Christianity: Documents Illustrating Aspects of New Zealand Church History*, 5th ed., (Auckland: Kereru Press, 2005) 241–83.

398 Patrice Dougan, "Religious Affiliation Fades as New Zealand Bucks Trends," *New Zealand Herald* (April 10, 2015), accessed at https://www.nzherald.co.nz/nz/news/article.cfm?c_id=1&objectid=11430295 See the "New Zealand 2016 International Religious Freedom Report," accessed at https://www.state.gov/documents/organization/268998.pdf.

399 Apsley Cherry-Garrard, *The Worst Journey in the World* (1922). There are numerous editions, and a 2007 BBC docudrama. Also, it informs

the 1948 film, *Scott of the Antarctic*. The "worst journey" actually refers to a thirty-six-day excursion to collect eggs from the emperor penguins' rookery. Captain Scott's journals were also published (1913) in the two-volume set referenced below.

400   Kim Stanley Robinson, *Antarctica: A Novel* (Bantam, 1999), p. 23.

401   Robert F. Scott, edited by Leonard Huxley, "Scott's Message to the Public," *Scott's Last Expedition,* Vol. 1, Dodd, Mead, and Company, 1913, pp. 605-607.

402   This was the fourth of five initiatives to establish U.S. bases in Antarctica. It took place 1946-47, and the five efforts spanned from 1929 to 1958.

403   "Antarctica: General Data on the Continent," Populstat, last updated December 20, 2004, http://www.populstat.info/Oceania/antarctg.htm.

405   Central Intelligence Agency, "Antarctica," *The World Fact Book.* Accessed at https://www.cia.gov/library/publications/the-world-fact-book/fields/2119.html

405   The *illumiNations* exhibit (room) at the Museum of theBible in Washington, DC, chronicles this work well. Nearly all languages are represented in bound volumes, with varying colors determining if all, part, or none of the Bible is in a language. This display is augmented by digital displays (https://www.museumofthebible.org/illumina-tions-donation). Its website says: "The illumiNations exhibit celebrates the almost universal accessibility of the Bible, showcasing Bibles in over 2,000 different languages. Visitors are able to touch, read and explore these Bibles. Through our collaborations with Every Tribe Every Nation, Wycliffe Bible Translators, Biblica, SIL International, and many other gracious organizations, we have already collected 1,000 Bibles for this exhibit. But we still need your help to find Bibles in over 800 languages."

ATTRIBUTIONS

In a book covering two thousand years of history across the continents many people deserve thanks for assisting with its conception, research, and writing. These include scholars present and past. Let me begin by thanking those most directly involved in this book's final form.

Meet Amy Hollingsworth, the type of dynamic personality that reflects the best of the intense heroes of this very book on Christianity's spread. Imagine working for over a year with a bestselling author who is as passionate about capturing a comment as she is a culture. About both authenticity and accuracy. About both the historical character and his or her context. Many know her through her books, like *The Simple Faith of Mr. Rogers*. Her tenacious attention to sources and storyline flow helped shape this book. She first helped with the much longer text behind a TV series.

That series carries the same name as this book, *Inexplicable: How Christianity Spread to the Ends of the Earth* sponsored by TBN, and airing twice during 2020. Its six one-hour episodes align directly with these book chapters. Amy gave careful attention to my first 750-page script, along with a careful read of its numerous sources. I will miss the many long phone calls with her and our team, conversations ranging from the person of Bartolomé de las Casas to the correct wording and context of William Bradford's diary. I wish the world could have listened in to her representation of martyrs Felicitas and Perpetua—a research meeting that was as spiritually uplifting as it was professionally enhancing.

Our colleagues at TBN, especially Ashley Andrews and Dr. Norman C. Mintle, were sounding boards during this daily journey. Ashley has that quiet presence with a sharp yet fluid pen, and the persona of talent clothed in humility's hue. Norm, executive producer of the series, assisted with numerous scholars' interviews that informed this text as well, including trips to Cambridge and Oxford, and a memorable day filming at the Gonzálezes' home in Decatur, Georgia. He has that type of Niagara Falls whisper that rattles a restaurant, and a deep laugh that would interrupt even Jim Gaffigan. Any writer would benefit from a veteran producer like Norm, my biggest champion in getting this to press. And an aside that most wouldn't know—thirty years before the #metoo movement, he defended women colleagues when it was unpopular to do so. He's their hero all these decades later, and a good friend I hope to hear laugh until the Rapture. And maybe on the other side we can chat in Spanish without me confusing Iberian and American accents.

Thanks to Bob Fopma and Tom Newman at TBN for believing in this book, and for their freedom for this unorthodox author in bringing it to fruition. Their publishing colleagues at Trilogy are wonderful, especially Shane Harwell and Bryan Norris. Their enthusiasm after reading it was a boost during the busiest of seasons. Diane Whisner in design can make a mud fence look like Parian marble—and she's joyful in the process. She reminds me a bit of Jeana Ledbetter at Hachette, an outstanding editor who deserves credit for recommending me for the film project—and indirectly this book.

Now I climb atop my car and salute toward the great state of Louisiana, thanking one of the best voice editors available—Len Woods. He helped me take 750 pages and distill them into this book a third their length, and maintain a flow. His stylistic fingerprints are clearly visible many places as you find yourself turning pages. This is our second book together. The last one, co-authored with the eminent scholar Dr. Lawrence Schiffman at NYU, was well received (*The World's Greatest Book*, with Jeana Ledbetter its editor). I'm writing this page at Marion's Country Café about an hour after recommending him to yet another author—something I do often.*

On the research side, Nicholas DeNeff, Dr. Daniel Freemyer, Dr. Stephen Pierce, Dr. David Riggs, and Dr. Mark Smith contributed to various topics within the larger 750-page manuscript that helped frame this book. Nicholas is executive assistant to the president of Christianity Today and has hyper-charged dendrites. The others are history faculty members at Indiana Wesleyan University (IWU), and Dr. Riggs the dean of the John Wesley Honors College. Also, a shout out to my writing partners who are a consistent motivation in staying on task—the prolific Dr. Todd Ream (Taylor University) and

---

* See Len's website at www.lenwoods.com. Various editors or writers have their unique strengths. Some are brilliant but cantankerous. Some are pleasant but slower than *Jiffy Pop* on a candle. Many are great technically, especially with grammar. But Len is not only self-effacing while gifted, but excellent, gracious, and lightning fast. We first met at NYU's Skirball Department of Hebrew and Judaic Studies working on the Worthy/Hachette book. The publisher had highly recommended him—and when his chapter drafts began arriving, we understood why.

Dr. Christopher Devers (Johns Hopkins University). All writers need this constant presence for both accountability and motivation. And, to share the journey. The same with Drs. Kiersten Priest and Sarah Farmer for their insights on aspects of African American history.

Drs. Skip Stout and Ken Minkema at the Jonathan Edwards Center (Yale Divinity School) were invaluable in their responses and published resources on early American religious history. The same with Justo Gonzalez, Mark Noll, Wilfred McClay, Robin Lane Fox, W. H. C. Frend, and Diarmaid MacCulloch for their foundational books on key aspects of Christianity's development.

The support of Dr. David Wright and Dr. Stacy Hammons, president and provost at IWU, is an amazing commitment to scholarship and important discussions. It is one thing to be honored with the university's first "University Professor" title, it's quite another to be supported at such a level to pursue a litany of projects, including one of the magnitude of this book and TV series. With every attempt to remain humble, and I assume I fail often enough, I hope my work honors well my faculty and administrative colleagues. A special thanks to Lynn Munday and Jeanette Wisehart, executive assistants to Drs. Wright and Hammons, for their assistance with many of my logistical requests.

In many ways, this book began in 1975 in IWU classrooms— then a fledgling little worn-brick campus, not the large attractive campus of today. Nonetheless, some rather engaging professors parted my 70's shag haircut. Their lectures proved formative to my understanding and interest in Christianity's rise and spread. I was a new Christian—less than a month, made a very late decision to attend a Christian university, and was homeless. A full scholarship guaranteed a place to stay dry with access to endless food. Their lectures and mentoring fueled intrinsic motivation and deepened my interest in religious instruction and history. Their provocative lectures prompted a lifetime of historical research. And frankly, some *inexplicable* changes in my own heart.

From the Holy Spirit to the Trinity, so much didn't make sense in those early days (and still require ongoing faith). However, on the history side, they helped me wrap my mind around the Church's rise. During that era many writers still used "The Triumph of Christianity," but some of my professors prompted us to look more deeply at what was actually happening in history. That various religions were still persisting alongside Christianity. That numbers of adherents to a religion or view didn't of itself mean correctness—after all, in many eras in Russia, Asia, and Japan, Christian populations were decimated. They were far from "triumphant" by any reasonable metric. I also learned that one's rejection of the Truth (which I held and still hold the Bible to represent) doesn't nullify that same Truth.

Drs. Bud Bence and the late Dr. Lee Haines introduced me to heroes of the faith—along with various wayward self-seeking souls. Their faith in the Christ of the New Testament was evident and very much alive in their lives, but they also taught that history shows the fallen nature of humankind. The late Dr. Glenn Martin challenged all of his students to process all of history around life's ultimate question—one of theology. That is, *"Is God who he is because of who I am, or am I who I am because of who he is?"* And our answer to that question forms how we answer the huge philosophical questions (of ontology, axiology, epistemology, and axiology). It's little wonder that his funeral was packed, and that over two hundred students from numerous countries had come to study with him, mainly finding him via his annual lectures for Youth with a Mission (or YWAM). My one regret was that while he gave his life passionately and unabashedly to teaching, he never published his views. It challenged me to pursue publishing.

Various professors at Wheaton Graduate School prompted me to pursue balanced research while remaining true to orthodox beliefs, showing me these two weren't in conflict but were actually complementary. Though we joked that the *New Testament Survey* textbook was actually "The world according to Merrill C. Tenney," we respected an outline from such a philologist—something on which to hang our thoughts. Dr. Edwin Yamauchi, my PhD advisor at Miami University (OH), was and remains a wonderful mentor on most things historical. His *Two Kingdoms* book is one of many of his resources that helped frame thoughts for this work, along with his most recent book (in which he included me and other former students), *Dictionary of Daily Life in Biblical and Post-Biblical Antiquity.*

Many historians helped inform this book for general readership through their popular pieces, and I pause especially to thank Mark Galli at *Christianity Today (CT)* for capturing many of these. *Christian History*, long under *CT's* auspices, is perhaps the most easily accessible collection of these scholars.

A word of appreciation to the owners of JAX, McConn, The Bridge, Arbor Trace, The Branch, Abbey Coffee, Midwest Coffee, Country Café, Starbucks and other local places where I sat many days reading and editing pages.

Last but not least, a thanks to Cindy, my wife of three decades, for helping me lug bags of books around the world, coopt additional non-office space in our home, establish a mobile office with my laptop in the passenger's seat, and forego many weekends to help bring this book and the movie series to fruition.